Factors Affecting Customers‘ Decisions to Buy Retail Banking Services

# Schriften zur Unternehmensplanung

Herausgegeben von Franz Xaver Bea, Alfred Kötzle und Erich Zahn

Band 79

PETER LANG

Frankfurt am Main · Berlin · Bern · Bruxelles · New York · Oxford · Wien

Hadia H. Abdel Aziz

# Factors Affecting Customers' Decisions to Buy New Retail Banking Services

## Their Implications on the New Service Development Process

Empirical Study on the Egyptian Market

PETER LANG
Internationaler Verlag der Wissenschaften

**Bibliographic Information published by the Deutsche Nationalbibliothek**
The Deutsche Nationalbibliothek lists this publication in the Deutsche Nationalbibliografie; detailed bibliographic data is available in the internet at <http://www.d-nb.de>.

Zugl.: Stuttgart, Univ., Diss., 2007

Cover illustration:
Erich Zahn

D 93
ISSN 0175-8985
ISBN 978-3-631-57783-7



www.peterlang.de

## Acknowledgments

First I would like to thank the two great universities, Stuttgart University and the German University in Cairo (GUC), for giving me the opportunity to carry out this thesis study through their fruitful noble aimed cooperation. I would specially like to thank Prof. Ashraf Mansour, the Chairman of the BOT of the GUC, and Prof. Fritsch, the former president of Stuttgart University for facilitating all procedures to enable me to accomplish this task.

Words of thanks would never be enough to express my feelings of gratitude towards my life teacher and thesis advisor, Prof. Erich Zahn. Prof. Zahn taught me a lot, not only on the academic, but also on the personal level. He demonstrated a life example of how great and knowledgeable, yet modest, tender, and giving a professor should be. No matter how busy he was, he always had the time to open up new streams of knowledge in front of me, inspire me with new ideas, guide my career progress with his sound professional advice, and help me through even the most tedious tasks. Prof. Zahn, thank you for all what you have done for me. I will never stop applying what I have learned from you and will never waste a chance to continue learning from your unlimited knowledge and wisdom.

I would like also to thank Prof. Burr, Prof. Amin, and Prof. Englmann for accepting to be members of my examination committee and for their valuable discussion and comments.

My gratefulness is also extended to the GUC president, Prof. Mahmoud Abdel Kader, and the Management Faculty Dean, Prof. Ralf Klischewski, for supporting me with all the facilities I needed to finish my thesis. I also appreciate so much the encouragement and backing that all the GUC family members have always fueled me with. Thanks to my colleagues in the Faculty of Management for always being a great source of energy.

Special thanks are owed to Dr. Tarek El Badawy for his support and assistance during times of uncertainty and questioning throughout my thesis preparation time. He has always been a source of valuable feedback and assurance in my work.

My deep heart thanks are extended to my family, husband and kids, for their patience and support. I know that there were so many times when I failed to be with them and so many happy or sad moments that I did not share. Yet, they have never failed to share my dream, and have always been the greatest motivator for me to continue.

Last but not least, I would like to thank my parents and role models; my mother who taught me how to be both a caring mother and a successful career woman; and my father who taught me how to appreciate the value of knowledge. I will never forget Prophet Mohamed's saying that he adapted as a life approach and always recited in front of me "the best people among you are those who acquire knowledge and transfer it"

Cairo, August 2007 Hadia Hamdy Abdel Aziz

## Zusammenfassung

Seit Beginn der 80er Jahre erfährt das Privatkundengeschäft im ägyptischen Bankenmarkt signifikante Veränderungen. Banken, die diesem Geschäftsbereich bislang wenig Aufmerksamkeit gewidmet haben, sehen hier mittlerweile beachtliche Wachstumspotentiale bei relativ geringen Risiken. Zur Realisierung dieser Potenziale haben die Banken inzwischen erhebliche Anstrengungen unternommen–durch Einführung neuer Informationstech- nologien, adäquater Marketinginstrumente und vor allem innovativer Produkte. Der Wettbewerb ist dadurch insgesamt dynamischer geworden. Um hier zu bestehen, müssen die Anbieter neuer Services nicht nur ihre Konkurrenten im Auge behalten. Sie müssen insbesondere lernen, die Bedürfnisse ihrer Kunden besser zu verstehen und ihre Fähigkeiten zur Einführung neuer Bankprodukte zielbewußt weiter zu entwickeln. Dabei erweisen sich das Bildungsniveau der Kunden, deren mangelhafte Erfahrungen aus Bankenbeziehungen und nicht zuletzt die Stellung der Banken im Islam als Erschwernisse. Das Privatkundengeschäft in Ägypten ist noch unterentwickelt. Professionelle Entwicklung und Vermarktung von Serviceinnovationen nach Kundenbedürfnissen sind die Ausnahme.

Die Arbeit präsentiert deshalb einen Gestaltungsrahmen zur Entwicklung und Einführung von Serviceinnovationen im Privatkundengeschäft, der Banken in ihren Bemühungen zur Erringung von Wettbewerbsvorteilen unterstützen kann.

Zu diesem Zweck werden im Rahmen einer empirischen Untersuchung zunächst Faktoren erhoben, die Kunden bei ihren Entscheidungen zum Kauf von neuen Bankenservices beeinflussen. Diese Faktoren werden dann in einem systematischen und umfassenden Prozess zur Entwicklung und Vermarktung neuer Services integriert. Die Ergebnisse der empirischen Studie zeigen, dass Kunden bei ihren Kaufentscheidungen neben banken- und servicebezogenen Faktoren auch Umweltbedingungen und demographische Größen berücksichtigen. Während Kunden bei neuen Spar-Services Risiko und Convenience der anbietenden Bank die höchste Bedeutung beimessen, legen sie bei neuen Kredit-Services den größten Wert auf Dienstleistungsbedingungen und –merkmale.

Im Interesse des Erfolgs neuer Services sollten die identifizierten und möglichst nach Kundentypen geclusterten Faktoren bereits ihren Niederschlag in Aktivitäten der Vorentwicklung finden. Diese mündet im Service-Konzept, und sie determiniert den generischen Rahmen für Aktivitäten im Prozess der kundenspezifischen Entwicklung und Vermarktung von neuen Finanzdienstleistungen. Der nachhaltige Erfolg laufender Innovationsbemühungen hängt nicht zuletzt von deren Integration in die Geschäftsstrategien einer Bank ab. Banken, die ihre Kunden verstehen, die in ihren Leistungsangeboten kaufentscheidende

Faktoren konsequent berücksichtigen und diese damit als Differenzierungshebel nutzen, haben bessere Chancen auf Wettbewerbsvorteile.

# Contents

## List of Tables

## List of Figures

## List of graphs

## Abstract

This research presents a framework for introducing new customer oriented retail financial services that would help banks to achieve market leadership and win the innovation race. This is attained through first, identifying the factors affecting customers' decisions to buy new retail banking loan and saving services through an empirical study in the Egyptian market. Second, incorporating those factors into a systematic comprehensive new service development process as deduced from the literature. Results reveal that when buying new retail financial services, customers consider the political, legal, and economic environmental conditions; the offering bank's risk and relationship convenience, which are attributed the highest importance for new saving services; and finally the service conditions and features which are attributed the highest importance for new loan services. The study also reveals that customers' interest in new retail banking service as well as the level of importance they attribute to different factors is affected by their demographic variables of gender, age, education, marital status, number of children, employment status, and level of income. Those identified factors should be directly incorporated into the predevelopment activities of the New Service Development (NSD) process which establish the service concept and set the stage for the development and launch activities. In addition, banks that would like to have a solid base on which they can build up a stream of continuously successful innovations must also incorporate those factors that customers look for in any bank offering a new service into the bank's corporate strategy.

# Chapter 1 – Introduction

## 1.1 Background

The 1980s have been a decade of rapid changes in the financial service sector allover the world. The most prominent of these changes was the tremendous growth and development of retail financial services. This growth was mainly driven by the banks' wish to spread risk and diversify sources of revenue. It was also forced by the removal of many barriers to competition, the advancing technology, and more sophisticated customers. It was since the 1980s that banks started to regard the retail business as a major profit generator not just as a cheap source of funds to finance corporate loans growth (Johanssen, 1992). It was also since then that banks started to be regarded as financial supermarkets and their services as product ranges.

The retail business proved to be very rewarding but also very dynamic throughout the last two decades. While the main functions that make up the industry of retail financial services (offering instruments for investment of savings, extension of credit, and risk management) did not change, the structure of the industry has changed dramatically (Frei, Harker, & Hunter, 1998). The traditional retail banking market with its oligopolistic nature, high barriers to entry and little attention given to the personal sector has become a highly competitive and sophisticated market with almost no barriers to entry and with special emphasis on the personal sector (Gardner, Howcroft & Williams, 1999). In terms of delivery systems, the traditional branch network with limited sales force has emerged into key branch networks offering 24 hours service. Banks no longer open their doors at 9:00 and close at 3:00 just waiting for customers to come in. They no longer depend on mass market, are product oriented, or price their products based on cost. They now segment their market, position themselves, base their price on perceived benefits, and have become much more customer oriented (Gardner, Howcroft & Williams, 1999). They have now to respond with great flexibility to the more demanding customers, intensified international competition, rapid change in information technology, innovation in new financial instruments, and ease of imitation in financial services. They already started since the mid nineties to offer new core services supported by an attractive range of other services that include extended operating hours, on line services, internet banking, 24, hours banking, off-site banking, and trained staff who would go to customers in order to get more business and build relationships with technology oriented customers who no longer go to branches (Lian, 1995). They started to realize that in the future, "triple A" banks will be the trend. This means banks that can deliver their products anytime, anywhere, anyhow in order to satisfy their customers who became increasingly individualistic in their relationships with banks. Therefore, they started to act strategically in order to balance market and customer orientation with the bank's internal resources and cost base (Gardner, Howcroft & Williams, 1999).

Within these changes, banks are coming to realize that the most powerful source of competitive advantage and growth is innovation (Hedley, White, Petit dit de la Roche, & Banerjea, 2005). There is a growing pressure on the retail banking industry to change and innovate in services and delivery channels in order to survive, and even to run in an endless race for innovation if they want to lead. "The need to develop new products in the short term in order to ensure longer term survival is a fact of life" (Pete Naude & Dengler, 1998, P.54). However, given the ease of imitation and absence of patents in retail financial services, retail banks must have a consistent trend of innovative activities in order to have the opportunity to develop a system of strategic attributes. Those attributes evolve over time into a unique competitive advantage that leads to an attractive market position and superior financial performance (Roberts & Amit, 2003).

As customers are the final targets for any service or process innovation and are the ultimate judges of the success or failure of this innovation, any new service development (NSD) effort must be customer oriented in order to be valued and desired by them. This means that customers' voice must be incorporated in every step of the NSD process and that their needs, logic, and assessment criteria must be carefully studied. Based on those studies, ideas for new services should be selected, and the whole innovation process should be directed in order to ensure the market success of the new service.

If this need to study customers' logic and adoption criteria in terms of pricing, quality, etc... is generally important when designing any new product or service, it is crucially important in the development of new retail financial services. This is due to the special characteristics of financial services that include sophistication, involvement of risk, and usually a substantial amount of investment. Those characteristics make the purchasing decision of new retail banking services for non- financially educated people, whom retail banking usually target, a major one that is usually based on a complicated set of factors.

This research is going to examine the factors that affect customers' decisions to buy new retail banking loan and saving services. It will discuss how those factors could be incorporated into a customer oriented NSD process. Such a process would result in a retail banking service that customers regard as valuable and desirable. The study will be conducted in Egypt as one of the developing markets that has a huge potential for growth; however, it will result in a process that, with the variability of inputs corresponding to different cultural and market conditions, could be adopted in any other country.

The retail banking industry in Egypt started to grow since the late 1990's. This growth was recently fueled by the severe problems faced by the Corporate Banking business that mostly resulted from the current economic recession. These problems forced most banks to shift their focus to the less risky retail banking business which they previously regarded as a hopelessly low margin endeavor. They started an aggressive competition to capture more share of the existing market as well as to expand target market to include other potential segments that are estimated to be three times as large as the current 8 million accounts market (Oteify, 2003).

Unfortunately, most of the services offered in the Egyptian market are not differentiated and are not designed to satisfy customer needs or to suit their requirements. Most banks are product driven rather than market driven. They introduce products that they think will be successful without any evidence that they will be and without conducting any research (El Ganady, 2000). Therefore, banks sometimes are surprised with the market success or failure of a newly introduced service for which they expected a completely different outcome.

This situation was faced by American Express Bank Egypt when it decided to launch a new equity mutual fund in April 1997. Staff and analysts expectations of success were low as the stock market index in Egypt was at a very high point and the fund was the 15th in the market with another one launched at the same period. The fund was originally advertised as a $30 million fund (then equivalent to LE 100 Million) with an LE 100 issued value for each certificate.

Surprisingly, the market success of the fund was phenomenal. People have been lining up every day starting from 7:00 am for a month to invest in the fund. The amount of the fund had been increased to LE 300 million and still it closed at 8 times the amount with 55,000 investors. The operational performance of the fund however was very poor. The par value per certificate decreased from LE 100 to LE 94.36 by the end of 1997, it then continued fluctuating below par until it reached its lowest point of LE 66 by the end of 2001 (EFG Hermis Report, 2002).

Two years later in 1999, the same bank decided to launch its second mutual fund. This time, the fund was a daily income fund investing in fixed income low risk instruments such as treasury bonds, inter-bank deposits and so on. The idea was new to the market and bank staff and management had very high expectations of success as the fund was offering the same advantages of current and call accounts with much higher expected return that would be added daily to the principal. The amount of the fund was LE 300MM with LE 1000 issued value per certificate.

Contrary to expectations, the fund only realized moderate market success. However, its operational performance exceeded expectations. The interest rate of the fund fluctuated between 9% and 11% calculated and added daily which was almost 5% higher than market average.

In order to be able to lead the still immature retail banking market in Egypt, and to avoid the high image, effort, time and money costs associated with failures, banks need to introduce differentiated new services with new features and unique functionality other than the currently offered services that became more or less "commodities offered on price". Those services must be designed to suit customer needs. They must take into consideration the factors that affect customers' selection of new services rather than the bank's capacity or other products offered in the market.

## 1.2 Research Problem

Financial services in general have special characteristics that distinguish them from any other services offered in the market. These characteristics include involvement of risk, substantial price, and close relation to economic performance. For a financial specialist or a management graduate, it is easy to make an educated decision to buy a new financial service. However, for ordinary people whom retail banking usually target, trying a new retail banking service may be regarded as risky, and the decision to buy an innovative service would depend on many factors such as education, age, bank reputation, bank service quality, previous experience with new products, etc… As those customers are the target of any new retail banking service, identifying those factors that affect their purchasing decision and incorporating them into a systematic new service development process is crucial to avoid the high rate of new service failure that is mainly attributed to the lack of a well prepared, systematic, and customer oriented NSD process (Alam & Berry, 2002; Andrew, 1986; Demoranville, Kaminski, Ridnour & Young, 1999; and Storey & Easigwood, 1996)

This research is going to look into the interest of Egyptian customers in new retail banking loan and saving services and the demographic characteristics that affect this interest. The key factors affecting interested customers' decision to buy new retail banking loan and saving services will be examined and how those factors could be incorporated into the NSD process will be explained. New retail banking services in the context of this study refer to new services that are offered by a bank for the first time whether they are new to the market or were previously offered by other financial institutions. Examples of the first type include internet cards, daily income mutual funds, and speedy loans, while examples of the later include credit cards or car financing programs offered by some banks for the first time.

Based on the above, the research will be mainly divided into two parts:

First, using empirical data, customers' interest in new retail financial loan and saving services will be examined, compared, and related to their demographic variables such as age, gender, education, marital status, number of children, employment status, and income. Interested customers will be asked to rate the below listed three sets of factors according to their importance in making purchasing decisions for loan or saving services.
An analysis of which factors are more dominant in making the decision for both saving and loan services will be conducted. The effect of demographic variables on the importance attributed to different factors will also be examined.

The three set of factors that will be tested are:

**A - New service related factors**

- Service uniqueness (in terms of a unique advantage of service offering or fulfillment of an unsatisfied need)
- Service sophistication (in terms of familiarity of service type and understanding of features and operating mechanisms)
- Pricing (in terms of competitiveness and stability of interest and commission rates)
- Tenor (in terms of flexibility of deciding on service duration)
- Liquidity (in terms of ability to decide on service amount without restrictions)
- Service risk (in terms of expected consequences of new service failure and level of guarantees provided from the bank)
- Documentation required (in terms of amount and legal responsibility of signed documentation)
- Availability of information (in terms of availability of informative advertising through different media)
- Previous positive experience with new retail banking services either directly or through trusted acquaintances

**B- Bank related factors**

- Bank performance (as measured by market share, strength of financial position and profitability growth)
- Service quality (as measured by staff friendliness, efficiency and accuracy of transactions and speedy services)
- Convenience (in terms of coverage and location convenience of branches and ATMs)
- Availability of a wide range of other services
- Availability of technologically advanced services

- Performance of previous new services
- Bank's reputation (in terms of brand name and continuity in the market)
- Previous positive experience with the bank (either directly or through trusted acquaintances)
- Ownership/ nationality of bank

**C- Environment related factors**

- Level of competition (in terms of availability of competitive and substitute services)
- Overall performance of the banking sector (in terms of sector investments and profitability growth)
- Country Economic performance (in terms of overall economic conditions, economic forecasts, and stability of interest and exchange rates)
- Legal stability (in terms of stability of economic legislations and banking policies)
- Political stability (in terms of absence of internal and external political turmoil)

Second, previous literature on NSD will be used to discuss how banks can use the findings to come up with a customer oriented NSD process that to introduce new successful retail banking services that customers regard as valuable and desirable.

## 1.3 Major definitions

This section contains the definitions and discussions of our major constructs.

### 1.3.1 Financial services

Defining and distinguishing between different financial services has always been one of researchers' most difficult tasks and one of the strong burdens exerted on financial service research (McGoldrick & Greenland, 1994, p.199). As for the basic function and description of financial services, there seems to be no disagreement that financial services are means to an end not an end by themselves. The end can be security, return, deferred payments, etc….; and that financial services are "A service or package of services that is typically provided for any one consumer by one type of financial firm and is aimed at a particular market" (Meidan, 1996, p.84). However, the difficulty in defining financial services stems from the difficulty of describing the components of this "service or package of services". This is mainly because financial services are usually diversified, complex, and involve both tangible and intangible features.

The term financial services and financial service products are usually used inter-changeably to denote offerings of financial institutions that incorporate the expected benefits, service features and other supporting services, both tangible and intangible. McGoldrick & Greenland (1994, p.199) differentiated between three levels of financial service products as follows:

- The core product: a product that introduces a core benefit like saving, loan, money transmission etc.
- The actual product: a particular type of the core product that has a brand name and provides specific features such as certificates of deposits, credit cards,---.
- The augmented product: additional features and benefits such as grace period.

They explained that this distinction is not rigid and should be applied with great flexibility as what represents an augmented product for one customer might be a core product for another.

Along the same line, Meala (1994) considered banking services from three different prospects as follows (Abdel Naby, 1999):

- Core Service: which represents the main reason or the expected benefits from the service, for example, customers may ask for loans to solve a financial problem or buy a deposit service to get interest. Charfas (1999) sorted the core financial requirements for retail consumers in terms of importance as follows: save and borrow, invest and trade, make quick payments, and keep dependable accounts without being bothered by details.

- Real service: which represents the characteristics of the service itself and that make customers prefer some services to others for example, customers may search for better pricing, services, or guarantees for loans.

- Supporting services: this refers to the whole service package, the core service, the real service, and all other related features and benefits that satisfy customers' needs.

Lasheen (1992) distinguished between two sides of financial services as follows:

- The marketing side of the service as one or group of benefits that customers need and that must meet their objectives (e.g. return, safety, saving, ---).
- The description of the service using its basic components that differ from one bank to another (e.g. interest rate, fees, ATMs, ---).

Easingwood & Storey (1993) explained that the basic product that the customers seek, such as loans or savings, can not be separated from the delivery process, the communication strategy, and other features that affect customers' perception of the service itself. They defined financial products as an augmented service offering that "consists of the intangible service core, plus a number of other factors such as the accessibility of the service, the quality of communication between contact staff and consumers" (p. 42)

Other researchers tried to differentiate between financial services along different angles. For example, along the sophistication and degree of risk angle, McGoldrick & Greenland (1994) classified financial services into the following four categories:

- Basic services: Personal banking and personal credit that provide the basic cash, cheque, credit and debit services.
- House ownership and protection: Mortgages and property insurance
- Financial provisions for the future: Life insurance, pensions and annuities.
- Financial investments: unit trusts, shares

Along the same angle of sophistication and degree of risk, Devlin (1998) differentiated between two types of financial services:

- Simple financial services which are those services whose features and associated benefits are reasonably understood by the customer so that he can make a satisfactory pre purchase evaluation. These are usually regarded as low risk services.
- Complex financial services which are those services that customers find confusing and complicated with regard to features and benefits. Those services are usually regarded as medium to high risk with difficult pre purchase evaluation.

In the context of this research, Easingwood & Storey's point of view that the core services can not be separated from the other features is adopted. As customers can not choose their desired supporting service features, they regard the core service with all of its related features as one package. As such, the financial service is defined in the context of this research as "a core intangible service introducing a major benefit, such as saving or loan, and supported by other services and features that provide it with its unique differentiating identity such as ease of access, quality of service, etc..".

### 1.3.2 Retail banking services

Retail banking services are one type of financial services that basically targets individuals and small businesses and is mainly offered by commercial banks. Besides the traditional loan and saving services, banks today provide retail insurance services, brokerage services, and consultancy services. These were recently introduced as the market is getting more competitive and deregulated, and less specialized and classified. Charofas (1999) also adds to these other ancillary retail banking services that include real estate, travel agencies tasks and safe custody.

Retail banking is defined by researchers as:

- "Small quantity activities" as opposed to the large volume corporate business (McGoldrick & Greenland, 1994, p. 1).
- "Typical mass market banking where individual customers use local branches of larger commercial banks. Services offered include: savings and checking accounts, mortgages, personal loans, debit cards, credit cards, and so forth." www.investopedia.com
- "A financial service or group of services offered through an institution to personal customers" (Howcroft & Lavis, 1986, p. 9)
- "Retail banking generally encompasses the provision of banking and financial products to consumers and small businesses by commercial banks and many other kinds of financial services firm" (Gardener, Howcroft, & Williams, 1999, p.83 )

Abdel Naby (1999) divides available retail banking services in Egypt into two major types:

- Financial intermediary services: such as loans, and deposits, mainly interest based
- Fee generating services: such as transfers, treasury, and foreign exchange which are mainly commission based.

In this research we will concentrate on the traditional core retail banking loan and saving services. Loans in the context of this research are those services that banks launch for solving customers' financial problems through lending them money against interest, and savings are those services that retail banks launch for protection, security and return including investment services with minimal risk such as mutual funds. Other retail banking services are new to most emerging markets like Egypt and they are still not widely adopted by customers.

### 1.3.3 Service innovation

Some Researchers equate innovation with creativity in introducing new ideas for new services, products, or processes. For example Avlonitis & Papastathopoulou (2001, p. 709) define innovation as "The creation of a product, service, or process". Others assert that innovation is not only creating but also making use of new ideas. In this view, Sciulli (1998, p.2) defines innovation as "an idea, product, service, or technology perceived as new and in the early stage of acceptance or use by the organization". Tidd, Bessant, and Pavitt (2001, p.38) define innovation as "the process of turning opportunity into new ideas and of putting these into widely used practice"

In financial services, financial innovation was defined by Frame & White (2002 p.3), as "something new that reduces costs, reduces risks, or provides an improved product/ service/ instrument that better satisfies participants' demands".

In general, innovation is usually interpreted as the creation, implementation, and commercialization of new ideas related to products, services, processes, distribution channels, promotional strategies, organizational structure, or measurement systems. In our research, retail banking innovation will be interpreted as the creation, development, and commercialization of a new retail banking service package, incorporating an existing core service, such as loan and saving services, in addition to other supporting features such as interest rate, accessibility, etc...

### 1.3.4 New services and new service development (NSD)

The word "new services" was interpreted by researchers along many dimensions, among which were newness to the company, newness to the market, or whether the introduction is for a new service or a new process. Some of these interpretations are:

- "The degree of familiarity with the new product, and/or the related technology and/ or target markets (Song & Montoya-Weiss, 1998, p.124).
- New services are "Offerings not previously available to customers resulting from the addition of new service items or changes in the service delivery process that allow for new services to be offered" (Menor, 2000, p.9)
- A new service is "One which was new to the organization concerned " (Drew, 1995, p.6)

NSD involves developing offerings such as financial services, telecommunication services, health care services, information services, travel services, educational services, consultancy services, and so on. These services can be sold to other businesses, to consumers, or both. According to Johne & Storey (1998, p. 185), new service development can be defined as "The development of service products which are new to the supplier". As such, they could be new to the market or were previously available.

This research deals with new retail banking services as services offered for the first time by the bank whether they are new to the market or not. Linking the retail financial service to the offering bank is necessary in light of the special characteristics of financial services that will be discussed later and that result in considering customers' evaluation of the offering bank as part of their evaluation of the new service itself.

In conclusion, the definition of new retail banking services as presented in the context of this research is "small quantity service packages that target personal customers and incorporate an existing core service, such as loan and saving, in addition to other supporting features such as accessibility, service quality, etc...; and that are created, developed, and commercialized by the bank for the first time whether they are already available in the market or not"

## 1.4 Conceptual Research Model

The areas of NSD, customer oriented new services, and consumer behaviors with regard to financial services are all given considerable attention by researchers. However, there is a lack of studies aiming to link them together in terms of identifying the factors that affect customers' decisions to buy new retail banking services and incorporating them into the NSD process to come up with successful customer oriented new services. Identifying and making use of those factors became especially important after the decline of bank loyalty and changing customers' behavior that made them buy different retail banking services from different banks. However, given the special characteristics and the risky nature of new financial services, the set of factors involved in the decision are much more comprehensive and sophisticated than in any other new product or service.

To identify and investigate the factors that are considered important to customers in making their decisions to buy new retail banking loan and saving services, the researcher employed multiple exploratory methods. These include:

- Literature reviews of the available published academic literature related to the factors affecting customers' choice of a bank, customers' demand for retail banking services, and market success of new services.

- Reviews of articles and features addressing new financial services and their market and technical performance in financial service and business magazines.
- Reviews of marketing material for new services (such as leaflets, newspapers ads, internet ads, and direct marketing material) which reflect bank's points of view of what are the most important factors that customers care about.
- A series of semi structured interviews with retail banking managers to probe around the factors that they see the most important in making customers' decisions.
- A series of semi structured in depth interviews with a limited sample of the population to probe around their interest in new retail financial services and which factors may affect their decisions to buy those services.
- The researchers previous work experience in the banking sector.

To develop the conceptual model, frequently mentioned factors and concepts from the exploratory research were identified. The importance of those factors was further investigated through pilot testing. Factors that are considered important by customers in making their decisions to buy new retail banking services should be incorporated into the different stages of a new service development process. Several researchers such as Cowell (1988), Bowers (1989), Scheuing & Johnson (1989), Hope & Muhlemann (1997) and Allam & Perry (2002), introduced several models of new service development processes. The model used in the study incorporates the most important and comprehensive stages that have to be systematically, completely, and proficiently carried out in order to ensure the success of any new service effort. A visual representation of the research under study is presented in figure 1 below.

The research answers the following central questions:

- Do demographic variables affect customers' interest in new retail banking loan and saving services?
- What environment, bank, and service related factors affect customers' decisions to buy new retail banking loan and saving services?
- Which factors are considered the most important in taking the decision to buy new retail baking loan and saving services?
- Do the most important factors affecting customers' decisions to buy new retail banking loan services differ from those affecting their decisions to buy new retail banking saving services?
- How do demographic variables affect the importance that customers attribute to different factors for both new retail banking loan and saving services?
- How can we integrate the most important factors affecting customers' decisions to buy new retail banking loan and saving services into the new

service development process in order to ensure the market success of the new service?

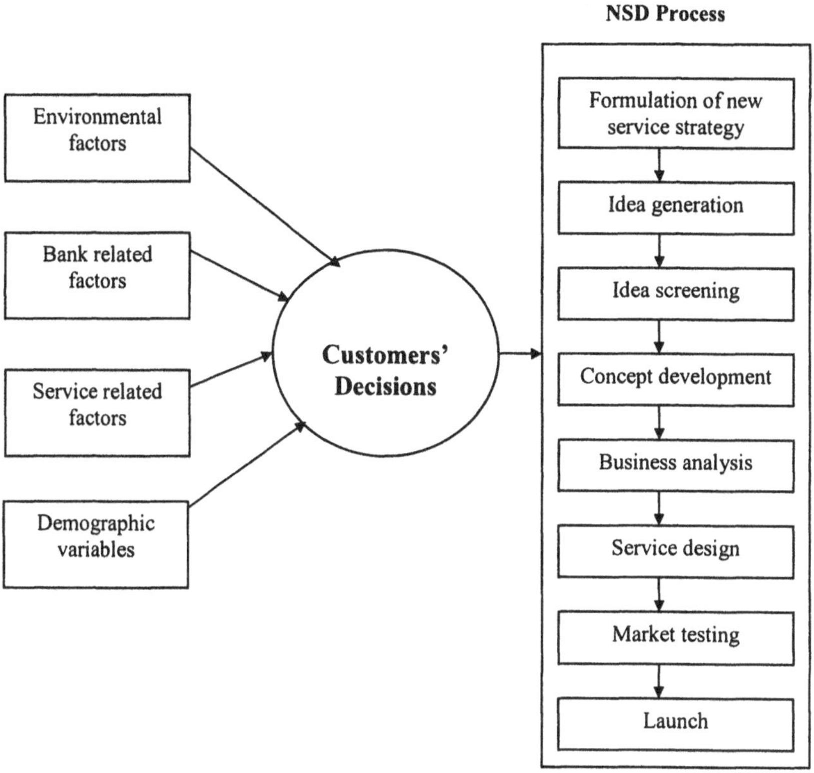


**Figure 1: Conceptual Research Model**

To answer these research questions, the following generic hypotheses are formulated:

### 1.5 Generic research hypotheses

Hypothesis 1: The demographic variables of (a) gender, (b) age, (c) level of education (d) marital status, (e) number of children, (f) employment status, and (g) level of income affect customers' interest in buying new retail banking loan and saving services.

Hypothesis 2: The following sets of factors are important for customers when taking the decision to buy new retail banking loan and saving services.

a. **Service related factors:** (1) service uniqueness (2) service sophistication, (3) pricing, (4) tenor, (5) liquidity, (6) service risk, (7) documentation required, (8) availability of information and (9) previous positive experience with new retail banking services.

b. **Bank related factors:** (1) bank performance, (2) service quality, (3) convenience, (4) availability of a wide range of other services, (5) availability of technologically advanced services, (6) performance of previous new services, (7) bank reputation, (8) previous positive experience with the bank, and (9) ownership/ nationality of bank.

c. **Environment related factors:** (1) level of competition, (2) overall performance of the banking sector, (3) country's economic performance, (4) legal stability, and (5) political stability.

Hypothesis 3: Some factors are considered more important for customers when taking the decision to buy new retail banking loan and saving services than others.

Hypothesis 4: Most important factors affecting customers' decisions to buy new retail banking loan services are different from those affecting their decision to buy new retail banking saving services.

Hypothesis 5: The demographic variables of (a) gender, (b) age, (c) level of education, (d) marital status, (e) number of children, (f) employment status, and (g) income affect the importance that customers attribute to different factors when taking their decision to buy new retail banking loan and saving services

## 1.6 Importance of Study

On the academic level, the study introduces a relatively new conceptual model dealing with the choice of new retail financial services on a stand alone basis not as part of the choice of the bank. This becomes important in light of the new market and customers' behavior changes that enabled customers to buy different services from different banks. The study identifies some of the factors that affect customers' interest in new retail financial services in general. It also captures some of the most important factors affecting customers' decisions to buy new retail banking services as they emerge from factors identified in previous research as well as some new factors identified through the exploratory research. In doing so, the study highlights the difference between the factors affecting customers' decision to buy new saving vs. loan services. It then presents a framework for incorporating those factors into a customer oriented NSD process. This process, with different inputs reflecting different cultures and market conditions, could be used in all countries of the world.

On the empirical level, the most important factors affecting customers' decisions to buy new loan and saving retail banking services will be identified and methods to incorporate them into the different stages of a new service development process will be discussed. This would help retail banks to:

- Establish strategic directions to build the competencies that would enable them to introduce new valuable services that are demanded by customers.
- Gain competitive advantage through developing focused business strategies for new services that emphasize those attributes that are considered important for customers for both loan and saving services.
- Increase customer satisfaction, improve customers' retention rates, invade new markets, and increase their market share.
- Ensure that the elements of the marketing mix of new services reflect what the customers view as important for different services.
- Have more insight about the effect of demographic variables when segmenting new retail banking services.
- Implement a structured NSD process in which the voice of the customer is incorporated. Thus, offering customer oriented new services and repositioning themselves as customer- centric institutions.
- Carry out a focused and efficient NSD process with no major changes during development. This would lead to shorter development time and, consequently, will decrease competitors' chance to copy the new service.
- Allocate their resources between development activities in an optimum way which will reduce development costs and increase profitability margins.

Given the young age of the retail banking market in Egypt, this study will help both academics and practitioners to have a deeper understanding of the Egyptian retail financial customers. This is specifically important at the current stage in which the market is tremendously growing and witnessing major structural changes. Finally, the profitability and growth of the retail banking sector will positively reflect on the competitiveness of the Egyptian economy.

## 1.7 Organization of the dissertation

In order to answer the central research questions, this thesis is organized into six chapters as follows:

**Chapter 1: Introduction**

This present chapter addresses the research background, research problem, major definitions, conceptual research model, and generic research hypotheses. It also addresses the importance of this research on both the academic and the empirical levels.

↓

**Chapter 2: Theoretical foundations**

This chapter reviews all available academic literature related to the problem under study. This includes previous research conducted on customers' behavior with regard to retail financial services and which factors affect this behavior, as well as, on financial service innovation and the new financial service development process. It also discusses the importance of customer orientation and the available literature on customer oriented new services. Finally, it presents an overview of the retail banking market in Egypt.

↓

**Chapter 3: Methodology**

This chapter discusses the methodology used to answer the central research questions. This includes research design, population, sample design, instrument development, testing for instrument validity and reliability, data collection, and finally data analysis techniques.

↓

**Chapter 4: Results**

This chapter introduces the results of the statistical analysis of the data. It examines the demographic characteristics of the sample, customers' interest in new retail banking loan and saving services, the factors that affect customers' decision to buy new retail banking loan and saving services, the influence of demographic characteristics on the importance that customers attribute to different factors, and finally explores the relationships between factors so as to reclassify them into smaller number of related subsets.

↓

**Chapter 5 Discussion**

This chapter summarizes and discusses the results of the statistical analysis of data as presented in chapter 4. It then proceeds into discussing how the results of the analysis could be incorporated into the new service development process in order to reach to a more customer oriented process that would lead to a higher probability of the new service's success.

↓

**Chapter 6 Conclusion**

This chapter summarizes the results of the research and addresses the research limitations and the future research topics.

### 1.8 Summary

This chapter provides an introduction to the topic under study. It starts with a background about retail banking, how innovation became inevitable for those banks who want to maintain a leading market position, and the important role that customers play in new service development and new service success. It then proceeds to discuss the research problem that could be summarized in finding the most important factors that affect customers' decision to buy new retail banking loan and saving services and then integrating them into the new service development process in order to introduce customer oriented successful new services. It then provides definitions for the most important terms used in the study such as financial services, retail banking services, service innovation, new services, and new service development. It also introduces the conceptual research model and the central research questions that led to the formulation of the generic research hypotheses. It finally discusses the importance of the study on both the academic and the empirical levels before it closes by describing the organization and content of the different chapters of the dissertation.

# Chapter 2 – Theoretical Foundations

This chapter reviews the available literature related to the problem under study. It starts by describing the characteristics of financial services and how they affect customers' behavior and the innovation process. It then proceeds with customers' behavior when dealing with financial services and the factors that affect customers' relationship with banks. Afterwards, it presents and discusses innovation in financial services, its forces, aims, types and strategies, and the new service development process with its different stages. The chapter then discusses available literature on customer orientation in new service development. Finally, it presents an overview of the retail banking market in Egypt. At the end of the chapter, a summary of the insights gained from this literature and how they are related to each other, as well as, the knowledge gap that came up from those insights and resulted in this research are presented.

## 2.1 Unique characteristics of retail financial services

Although retail financial services share many characteristics with other types of services such as intangibility, inseparability and simultaneity, and heterogeneity; they still have their own special characteristics that emerge from being a very special type of service that customers usually regard as sophisticated and risky. Those characteristics greatly affect the financial customers' buying behavior as well as the innovation process.

The most influential characteristics that retail financial services share with all other services are:

- **Intangibility:** As defined by Cowell (1988) and Burr (2006), this feature refers to the fact that services can not be tasted, felt, seen, heard or smelled before they are purchased. This also means that services can not be easily demonstrated, and while they are sold, no transfer of ownership happens (Normann, 2002). Therefore, when developing new services, a major challenge to the service provider is to design tangible characteristics as to reinforce the positioning of the service, as in the case of designing the tangible credit card to reflect the image of a high service quality (Meidan, 1996). Another challenge imposed by intangibility on service providers is the difficulty of testing the service concept before launch (Johne & Storey, 1998). Lievens, Moenaert, and S'Jegers (1999) found out that the higher the intangibility of the new financial service, the higher the perception of risk and uncertainty of the potential customers, and the higher the need for effective convincing communication. Therefore, the success of new financial services largely depends on conducting extensive market research before launch in order to clearly understand customers' needs, logic, and choice criteria of new services, as well as, on effectively communicating the right message to the customers.

- **Inseparability and Simultaneity:** Unlike goods, services can not be separated from the service provider (Cowell, 1988). They are simultaneously produced and distributed and require close interaction with customers as an indispensable external factor (Burr, 2006). Therefore, direct selling is very important and implies high cost and quality of contact personnel who should be properly trained and motivated, especially when developing new services. Customer orientation and involvement in NSD is also an important implication of this characteristic since most service delivery is represented by the employee customer interaction (Javalgi, Martin, & Young, 2006). Simultaneity implies that capacity planning is very important as demand must be promptly met or lost for ever. However, in retail financial services this is partially overcome by the use of ATMs, credit Cards, Home Banking, etc. (Meidan, 1996). McGoldrick & Greenland (1994) also argue that financial services are not simultaneously consumed when bought but are consumed over time or at one point of the future.

- **Heterogeneity:** This feature refers to the difficulty of achieving standardization in output (Hope & Muhlemann, 1997; Meidan, 1996), or ensuring the same level of output quality due to its reliance on who provides the service or when it is provided (Cowell,1988). Most service firms strive to achieve standardization; however, in trying to reinforce process orientation and uniformity, service personnel usually lose their customer orientation that is crucial for success.
  Lievens, Moenaert, and S'Jegers (1999) found out that when a new financial service is highly variable and requires a lot of information exchange between customer and service provider, customers' uncertainty increases, which requires effective communication to reduce their perception of risk and prevent service failure. Therefore, a major consideration now when developing new services is whether it is going to be people based or equipment based (e.g. ATMs) which allows for more uniformity (Meidan, 1996) and reduces customers' perception of risk.

- **Perishability:** Service products, unlike physical products, can not be stored (Burr, 2006). Thus, causing difficulties in matching supply with demand (Hope & Muhlemann, 1997). However, consumers are usually not convinced by this fact. They need cash when they run out of it regardless of whether the bank is closed or the ATM is out of service. Therefore, service organizations must be very careful and aware that unmet demand will be lost forever and excess supply would lead to wasted resources.

➢ **Difficulty of Patenting**: There are no copyrights in services, and therefore, any new advantage is short lived since other service providers can in no time imitate it (Meidan, 1996). As stated by Cowell (1988), this feature discourages R&D in services and places more focus on me- too services or service improvements rather than innovation. This ease of imitation also implies constant competitive pressure to develop new services or new features of existing services. Therefore, a cumulative history of innovation became crucial for financial service companies to develop the strategic attributes that lead to superior market and financial performance (Roberts & Amit, 2003).

In addition to these characteristics, retail financial services also have some unique characteristics that distinguish them from any other services offered in the market. These are:

➢ **Involvement of Risk**: Financial services in general have inherent risk. This risk is compounded by the fact that their outcome is sometimes not immediate like pension and insurance products (Beckett, Hewer & Howcroft 2000). It is even sometimes difficult for financial service providers to determine whether the newly launched service has been successful or not (Edgett & Snow, 1997). The fact that financial services usually represent major one–off purchase decision for customers compound this risk (Harrison, 2003). The implications of this characteristic of financial institutions and customers are as follows:

- Growth must be balanced with risk: Financial service providers have to keep good balance between growth, selling, and prudence (Meidan, 1996; El Khodeiry, 1999).
- Customers must trust their retail financial service provider: As money is one of customers' basic concerns, any known incident of loss for a bank may lead to lost customers' trust and end up with a large portion of customers switching their business to other banks (Lasheen, 1992; El Khodeiry, 1999). To develop trust in a new financial institution, customers usually rely on indicators such as size, image, and reputation (McGoldrick & Greenland, 1994)
- Fiduciary responsibility: Financial Service providers are responsible to protect the interests of their customers and to fulfill the promises they gave them when they initially adopted their services (Meidan, 1996).
- Highly individualized marketing system: Close direct relationship between the seller and the customers of financial services must exist. That is why direct distribution channels through branches are the most feasible choice (Meidan, 1996; Lasheen, 1992; El Khodeiry, 1999). Although new technology has to a great extent reduced this direct contact, it is still regarded important for both the seller and the buyer. Therefore, the financial sector is still highly labor intensive.

- **Wide range of services and geographical dispersion:** Retail financial service providers have to have a network of branches in order to be convenient to all customers (Meidan, 1996; El Khodeiry 1999). They also have to introduce a wide range of financial products that meet different needs for different customers (El Khodeiry 1999; Lasheen, 1992).

- **Lack of special identity:** Customers regard financial services as similar (Meidan, 1996). That is why the financial sector is characterized by intensive competition among different financial institutions as well as from other sectors like financial services provided by large retail stores (Lasheen, 1992). Therefore, financial service providers are in constant search for methods to create a special identity for their services that would distinguish them from their competitors. One of the most successful means of differentiation is innovation. Constant innovation enables the service provider to continuously create superior value to customers while at the same to build the company's innovation capabilities that over time establish its sustainable competitive advantage.

- **Close relationship with national economic and government policies**: The banking sector affects and is affected by the economic conditions through different monetary and credit policies that are set to achieve the national economic objectives (Lasheen, 1992). Demand for financial services fluctuates significantly according to the level of general economic activity.

The above mentioned characteristics impose very important qualities on new service development. Intangibility implies that services are highly perceptual; therefore, extensive market research must be done before launching any new service innovation to clearly understand customers' needs and choice criteria of new services. Inseparability, simultaneity and heterogeneity also imply that services cannot be developed in isolation of the customers who should extensively participate in the new service development (NSD) process. They also mean that there is a close interaction between the service provider and the customers, therefore, the proper training, motivation, and working conditions of human resources are essential for any new service to succeed. Perishability emphasizes the importance of capacity planning and the accurate estimation of demand in order to be able to accurately plan supply. It also requires greater inter-functional coordination in order to be able to quickly respond to changes in demand. The lack of patents implies that in order for leading companies to stay ahead of the market, they must engage in a continuous innovation process as their innovations could be copied within a very short time.

## 2.2 Financial consumer behavior

In the past, when banks where trying to drive the low margin retail banking away, customers had limited choices when regarding financial service providers, financial services, and delivery instruments (Foust & Natarajan, 2003). The rigid structure, government regulations, as well as the high fees imposed by banks on consumer banking forced consumers to accept the financial instruments and delivery channels offered to them. Switching between financial providers was costly, disruptive and did not yield any benefits. Therefore, customers were locked into buying patterns and their loyalty to their first financial service provider was high (Beckett, Hewer & Howcroft, 2000). However, the recent changes in the industry have created a very competitive market, one in which the same banks that were trying hard to drive consumer banking away are now fighting harder to attract their business. This change had a critical impact on consumers' buying behavior that changed a great deal during the last decade. Customers now have increased propensities to switch banks and make rational decisions in the purchase of certain products. They also play a central role in changing banks' strategies and policies, for example, customers increased dissatisfaction with limited working hours forced many banks to open on Saturdays, extend their service hours and operate 24 hours call center services (ING, Cap Gimini Ernst & Young, & European Financial Management and Marketing Association, 2004).

### 2.2.1 Factors affecting consumer behavior regarding financial services:

As mentioned above, customers now play a central role in shaping banks' strategies and policies. It is to what extent that the financial service provider meets their wants, needs, and evaluation criteria that formulate their decision to deal with a specific bank or buy a specific service. Therefore, it became imperative for those banks that want to maintain and expand their customer base to understand the factors that affect customers' buying behavior and evaluation criteria with regard to financial services. This will enable them, not only to react, but also to pro-act and even shape any changes in those factors that might affect customers.

As mentioned before, one of the most influential factors on financial consumers' buying behavior is the unique characteristics of financial services. For example, financial services are low in search qualities and high in experience and credence qualities (McKechnie, 1992), they also make information usually difficult to interpret, and evaluation more complex (Howcroft, Hewer & Hamilton, 2003). Other factors that interact to shape customers' behavior in financial services include:

- Internal factors such as psychological factors like motivation, perception, attitudes and beliefs (Meidan, 1996); and personal factors like life cycle, age, employment, economic standing, marital status (Meidan, 1996; Lasheen, 1992)
- External factors especially marketing factors such as services, pricing, distribution, and promotion; and environmental factors in terms of economic, technological, political and cultural aspects (Lasheen, 1992).

In addition, the type of the financial service purchased also influences consumers' behavior. Beckett, Hewer & Howcroft, (2000, pp. 15-18) divided consumers' behavior when buying financial services into four types according to two factors; first, involvement in the buyer-seller interchange as determined by customer control, participation, and level of contact; and, second, uncertainty or customers' perception of the risk associated with the service as determined by the complexity of the service and the certainty of outcome. The four ideal types of consumer behavior are as follows:

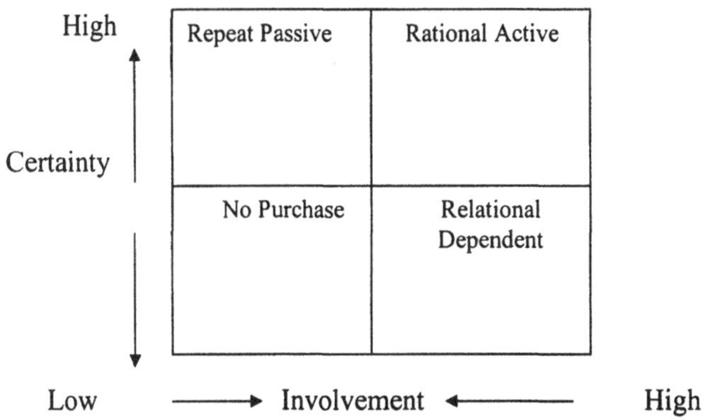


**Figure 2: Consumers' buying behavior in financial services (Beckett, Hewer & Howcroft, 2000)**

- Repeat Passive: This type is characterized by low level of involvement with the financial service and high level of certainty; therefore, consumers make repeated interactions without seeking alternatives. The choice of bank is determined by convenience, influence of friends and family, and finally by the image and reputation of the bank. Consumers in this type usually perceive little differentiation between banks' services and associate switching between banks with high costs. Consumers usually use this behavior to purchase simple financial services

- Rational Active: This type is characterized by high involvement and high certainty; therefore, consumers make carefully selected decisions after rationally comparing between alternatives. Consumers under this type are continuously looking for better and cheaper alternatives. They usually use this behavior to purchase transactional financial services and simple investment products.

- No Purchase: This type is characterized by low involvement and low certainty; therefore, consumers, who do have neither the ability nor the confidence, choose to make no purchases.

- Relational Dependent: This type is characterized by high involvement but also high complexity and low certainty; therefore, consumers who lack the information to make a rational decision seek advice and help from bankers or consultants. Trust, brand image and past performance are the main concerns of consumers under this category. They usually use this behavior to purchase complicated investment products.

As a result of these factors, consumers' purchasing process for financial services is different from any other product or service. It usually involves planned purchasing with a long decision making period, high loyalty (Although Meidan, (1996) reserved that customer loyalty has decreased recently), usually low levels of trial, single purchasing activities, joint decision making involving spouse or partners, absence of instant gratification, usually high price, and complex products (Hill, 1990). Devlin (2000) adds that due to the complexity of financial services, they are sometimes problematic in terms of consumer cognition.

### 2.2.2 Consumers' decision making process when buying financial services

Many researchers discussed the decision making process in financial services that we previously referred to as usually lengthy. Some researchers, such as Meidan (1996), El Khodeiry (1999), and Harisson (2003) described it as a sequential process that could be divided into phases. Others, such as McKechnie (1992) argued that it is not systematic and sequential in most of the times and that it should be considered within a more flexible, general, and interactive framework. Despite this difference and the difference in the number of phases identified by various researchers, the decision making process in financial services could be divided into three main stages as identified by Harisson (2003) as follows:

a. Pre Purchase information search: At this stage internal information, such as memory, knowledge, and experience, and external information, such as previous experience with product category, complexity of product and degree of uncertainty, are solicited (Harisson, 2003). Meidan (1996) and El Khodeiry (1999) identified four phases that could all be grouped under this broad stage of pre-purchase information search. These are cognition, awareness, information search, and knowledge. In a model developed by Guirdham (1987) for complex financial services, this stage is referred to as developing awareness and is divided into two phases: first, awareness of the general product type, and second, awareness of specific brand details (McGoldrick & Greenland, 1994, p. 73).

b. Evaluation of alternatives and decision: At this stage, consumers compare between alternative services and suppliers and make a decision. The three phases of evaluation behavior, preference, and decision as identified by Meidan (1996) and El Khodeiry (1999) could all be grouped under this broad stage. In Guirdham's model of complex financial services, this stage includes considering purchasing, starting to develop purchasing interest, forming the intention to buy, and finally taking the purchasing action. This stage is affected by many factors including customers' attitudes towards themselves, towards the general product type and towards the specific offer. It is also affected by their awareness of the offers and their details (McGoldrick & Greenland, 1994). Harisson (2003) suggests that more research need to be done in order to know how consumers evaluate financial services and what key attributes are sought.

c. Post purchase evaluation: After the decision, consumers evaluate products based on whether they fulfilled their needs or met their expectations as a way to build experience and knowledge. This stage is referred to as post purchase decision by Meidan (1996) and El Khodeiry (1999).

The most critical stage in the decision making process that all financial institutions should pay special attention to is the evaluation and decision making stage. This stage is usually difficult when considering financial services because of intangibility, complexity, and longitivity. Knowing the factors that customers consider in making the comparison and taking the purchasing decision is crucial for financial institutions because it can help them introduce successful services that attract customers and generate a high market share. They should understand customers' attitudes and motives, which direct them to the general product types, as well as perceptions and behavioral characteristics, which influence the brands and institutions that they select (McGoldrick & Greenland, 1994). Therefore, this research is seeking to identify some of the factors that are considered by customers when evaluating new financial services and affecting their decisions to buy them.

### 2.2.3 Factors affecting customers' choice in retail banking

Research around choice criteria in retail banking started almost two decades ago when retail banking started to develop and grow. At the beginning, when all banks were providing more or less the same narrow range of services, customers used to choose dealing with banks not buying services. Researchers then were trying to find out bank choice criteria. However, the retail banking industry witnessed a lot of development in the last few years. Bank loyalty decreased. The satellite product strategy, that involves developing stand alone services which customers could buy without even having to open an account in the bank, expanded. Finally, competition increased and resulted in the innovation race that banks started to engage in. As a result of these developments, customers started to consider services by themselves not as part of the bank, and researchers started to look into the factors that affect customers' choice of certain services. They also started to focus their efforts on new financial services and tried to explore factors affecting demand for new services, and what determines their success or failure. However, very limited research was conducted to address the factors that affect customers' decision to buy new retail banking services. As this decision is usually regarded as risky and complex, it may involve many aspects other than the service itself such as the offering bank, the competition, the legal environment, etc... Therefore, in order to be able to find out the factors that affect this decision, we will first start by identifying all the factors related to customers' choice when dealing with retail banks and their various products, then, at a later stage of this research, we will narrow them down through exploratory research into a limited number of relevant factors. The factors identified by researchers in the previously mentioned areas are as follows:

#### 2.2.3.1 Factors affecting choice of a bank

The factors affecting bank choice and bank choice criteria have been two of the areas that were extensively researched. Some researchers, such as Meidan (1996), and Kennington, Hill & Rakwaska (1996), tried to find general universal factors and criteria affecting customers allover the world, while others, such as Mylonakis, Malliaris & Siomkos (1998), Ulengin (1998), and TA, Huu Phuong & Har, Kar Yin (2000), tried to relate them to certain cultures, nations, or ethnic groups. By reviewing bank choice criteria in the literature, it becomes apparent that choice criteria has also changed and developed over time to reflect the general changes in the industry and the technology as follows:

El Bossat (1998) mentions that the factors that affect customers' decision to buy banking services can be divided into social, cultural and heritage, psychological, and personal factors; And, Hassan (1990) explain that Arab customers' decisions to deal with a bank are affected by three set of variables; personal variables (economic, social, and psychological), bank variables (product, price, promotion, distribution, information, services), and environmental variables (technological, economic, legal, political, social, geographic).

In a study conducted in the USA by Boyd, Leonard & White (1994), respondents identified reputation, interest on saving accounts, interest charged on loans, quick service and location in city as the most important criteria in the selection of a financial institution. When examining those criteria on different demographic segments, reputation is rated the most important criteria among almost all of them.

Meidan (1996) states that in general convenience of location and parents' bank are still the major factors determining customers' choice of a bank with product/ service considerations playing only a minor role. He explains that quality in financial services is measured in terms of reliability, professionalism, timeliness of service and ease of access, credibility and honesty, politeness and friendliness of staff, security and safety, and understanding and communication.

After reviewing several studies on the same topic, Kennington, Hill, and Rakwaska (1996) developed a set of universal criteria for bank selection which include reputation, price/cost, convenience, and service. In exploring the importance of those criteria in Poland, they found out that the Polish bank customers are more concerned with reputation and pricing than in many other countries. Convenience and service quality come directly after that.

Mylonakis, Malliaris, & Siomkos (1998) conducted a study on the Hellenic bank market and found out that location convenience and quality of services are the most influential factors followed by bank reputation and relatives' recommendations. Factors like advertising and location do not have much effect on the Greek customers.

In a study conducted by Ulengin (1998) about Turkish customers banking preferences, extended loyalty programs, continuous information flow from the bank, off site ATMs, maximum 5 minutes waiting time, and simple applications are found to be preferable for Turkish customers more than other aspects of product, delivery channels and customer relations. In terms of higher order constructs, delivery channels and customer relations are found to be more important than products.

El Khodeiry (1999) identifies variety of services offered, pricing of services compared to the market, conditions and restrictions imposed in order to get the service, time and effort exerted to get the service, bank branches' location and proximity, and effective advertising and personal selling as being important in customers' choice of a bank.

A study on bank selection decision in Singapore conducted by TA & Har (2000) found out that the most dominant factors in making the selection decision in Singapore are high interest rates, location convenience, quality of service and self banking facilities. These are followed by low charges, low loan rates, and long operating hours.

The study conducted by El Maioef (2001) in Saudi Arabia identifies that the most important choice criteria for Saudi customers are the network of branches, trust in the bank's competitive abilities, friendliness and helpfulness of employees, network of ATMs and finally bank reputation.

In a study based on the US market for the period 1993-1999, Dick (2002) found out that in choosing depository institutions, consumers base their decisions on deposit rates and to a lesser extent on account fees. In addition, they respond favorably to branch staffing, geographic density, bank's age, bank's size, and geographic diversification.

When examining retail banking choice criteria among customers with different levels of financial knowledge in the UK, Devlin (2002) found out that all customers, irrespective of their level of financial knowledge, rely primarily on extrinsic choice criteria, such as location or recommendations, in choosing a bank. However, they are more important to customers with low financial knowledge than to customers with high financial knowledge who also take into account intrinsic attributes such as service features, lower fees, and higher rate of return.

In a survey conducted in 2003 on 2,300 affluent decision makers from Asia and Europe, it was noticed that important factors considered when deciding which financial institution to deal with differed depending on whether this decision is for personal or business finances. When making business related decisions, financial strength, good reputation and solid establishment are considered the most important factors. When making this decision for personal finances, emotional factors such as trustfulness and being responsive to customers' needs are regarded as important (Banking on the Right Image, 2003)

Devlin & Gerrard (2004) analyzed the changes in consumers' choice criteria of a bank to see which factors are becoming more or less important. They found out that the most important criterion when making a bank choice has become recommendations by others. Offering of incentives, having a wide range of other products, and pricing factors have also increased in importance. Bank's image, reputation, and expectations concerning service quality has remained constant over time, while location factors have significantly decreased in importance, mainly due to technological developments such as internet and mobile banking that made accessibility of services much easier for customers.

Indian retail banking customers valued sound investment advice, lower waiting times, quick resolution of problems and a full range of products and services much more than convenience in terms of branch locations and hours of operations. 75% of Indian customers favor dealing with people rather than machines and 65% are hesitant to incur any debt. However, age and level of income affect those trends as for example younger and middle income consumers are more likely than others to take a mortgage (Joydeep & Renny, 2005).

In their study of retail banking choice criteria, Tank and Tyler (2005) found out that the most important choice criteria for UK students are recommendations by friends and family, reputation / image of the financial institution, level of interest rate, free cash incentives, and easiness of account opening. As for the most effective marketing communication tools, branch leaflets and bank's web site are regarded by the students as the most important in influencing their decisions. Findings also suggest that location convenience is no longer an important criterion.

Tank & Tyler (2005) also emphasized that the importance placed on each selection criterion in retail banking varies with the demographic characteristics of the population being tested. Along the same line, retail anthropologist Paco Underbill, as quoted by Schneider (2005), advised banks to watch demographic factors such as fathers with children and people living alone as these are very important in shaping the industry.

Several studies were conducted on the same problem in Egypt, the country subject of our research, and they show almost the same trend of changes in choice criteria as in other countries.

The first study was conducted by Gadallah (1979) to find out depositors' criteria in selecting their banks. He found out that the most important criteria are staff friendliness followed by location convenience, speed in service performance, and bank reputation. However, other important criteria were not included in the research as it was almost completely controlled by the government like interest and commission rates. Also then there was not much difference between the services offered by most banks. The same study was repeated by Lasheen (1992), who found out that the most important criteria for bank selection in Egypt are service speed, bank reputation, bank location, staff friendliness and trust. Customers who select public sector banks mainly care about bank reputation, bank location then trust. On the other hand, customers who select private sector and foreign banks care more about speedy service and staff friendliness.

In selecting specific services, Lasheen (1992) found out that pricing is ranked as the first criteria in selecting saving services.

Attia (1990) observed that the most important factors affecting customers' perception of quality are confidentiality, convenience in terms of availability of waiting areas and availability of a variety of saving services. However, the study was conducted in Port Said which is a small Egyptian city with limited number and smaller size of bank branches offering only limited range of services. Therefore, the sample might not be representative of the Egyptian bank customers.

Abdel Naby (1999) found out that the most important factors that affect public sector banks' customers choice of bank are a wide spread network of correspondences, availability of services not offered by other banks, good management that can take sound decisions, geographical dispersion of branches, qualified employees, and sound financial position. As for private sector banks customers, they rated good management as the most important factors, followed by availability of services not offered by other banks, qualified employees, network of correspondences, geographical dispersion, and finally sound financial position.

All customers of private and public sector banks agree on the importance of quality as measured by tangible aspects (such as layout, decoration, and employees' appearance), dependability (in terms of trust in employees, accuracy, and care in solving customers problems), response rate (in terms of quick services, quick response to questions and complaints), safety (in terms of confidentiality, accuracy of transactions, and ethics of employees), and sympathy (in terms of understanding, personalized treatment, and friendliness of employees) (Abdel Naby, 1999).

In summary, the importance that customers attribute to some of the factors that affect their choice of a bank has changed over time. For example, the location convenience factor's importance has diminished after the introduction of ATMs, internet banking, and mobile banking. However, there remain some factors that most researchers agree on as determinants of bank selection decisions. Those factors include bank reputation, service quality, range of services, effective communication, bank performance, and trustfulness. Therefore, and as our hypotheses include bank related factors as affecting customers' decisions to buy new retail banking services, those factors, among others, are included in our study.

### 2.2.3.2 Factors affecting demand for retail banking services

As mentioned before, retail banking started by the mid 90s to develop into a very competitive industry offering a wide range of services. It is since then that customers started to differentiate between financial services and do not consider them as homogeneous services offered by all banks. It is also since then that researchers started to realize that demand for financial services is affected by several other factors beside the offering bank. Some research findings in this are as follows:

Devlin (1998) conducted a research on retail banking customers to know what they perceive to be important in adding value to financial services; findings revealed that image and reputation are perceived to be the most important factors adding value to complex financial services, while price is more important in adding value to simple financial services. In 2000, he repeated the same research, but this time on retail bank managers and he found out that practitioners think that for more complex services, the features and quality of core services are more important in adding value followed by organizational factors such as image and reputation, on the other hand, pricing is perceived to be more important for simpler service offerings, as also perceived by customers (Devlin, 2000)

In his thesis titled "The impact of environmental variables on banking services planning strategy", Abdel Naby (1999) identified the following environmental factors as important determinants of demand for banking services:

- Economic variables such as inflation rate, overall economic condition (recession or boom), interest rate, GNP and economic growth. He clarifies that the more stable the economy is, the higher the demand on banking services.
- Legal variables such as laws and regulations that affect the banking sector, for example, foreign exchange and interest rate (liberalization). Meidan (1996) also adds government economic policy to those legal factors.

Beside those economic and legal factors, Meidan (1996) also identifies competition and political factors to be among the environmental non controllable factors that would affect demand for retail financial services.

As for demand for new retail banking services, the American Banker/Gallup found out in their survey conducted in 1999 that although 62% of respondents are interested in buying new nontraditional financial services from their banks, only 44% already did obtain those services. Those first time buyers tend to be relatively young, with lower incomes, and have no established service provider relationship (Garmhausen, 1999). El Khodeiry (1999) explains that the most important determinants of demand for new retail financial services are as follows:

**Factors related to the service itself**

- Degree of innovation in terms of the new advantages and benefits that the service offers to customers.
- Service sophistication in terms of familiarity of service type and easiness of understanding service features.
- Degree of match between the new service and the cultural values and traditions in terms of whether the bank has social and community service activities.
- Availability of information about the new services in terms of whether the bank offers informative advertising.

**Factors related to the offering bank**

- Bank size: The larger the bank, the more the resources it can allocate for new services.
- Market share: The higher the market share, the higher the bank's experience and ability to serve all types of customers.
- Bank's previous innovative activities: The more active the bank is in terms of introducing new service, the more capable it is to introduce successful services.
- Bank's experience and market reputation: The higher the bank's experience and the better its reputation in the market, the more confidence and trust the customers have in the success of its new services.

**Factors related to the market as a whole**

- Nature of competition in terms of success of competitive products offered by other banks or other financial institutions.
- Level of technology as technological innovations and the pace by which they diffuse affect to a great extent new banking service development.
- Customers in terms of customs, needs, income, preferences, etc...
- Local and international economic conditions as the current stage of economic cycle greatly affects innovative activities.
- Structure of the banking sector in terms of the existence of a strong central bank and different types of banks offering different services. The more solid the structure is, the more effective and organized the NSD effort will be.

This division of demand determinants for new retail banking services into factors related to the service, factors related to the bank, and factors related to the market constitute the basis on which our hypothesis is built on. However, the scope of factors covered in our research under each of these divisions is broadened by other factors mentioned in literature or identified through our exploratory research. In addition, the effect of demographic variables on customers' decisions to buy new retail banking services is also tested.

#### 2.2.3.3 Factors affecting success of new retail banking services

Since almost 70% of the resources devoted to developing new services are devoted to services that fail or are terminated before launch (Oldenboom & Abratt, 2000), researchers focused their attention on exploring the most important factors that lead to the success or failure of new services. Those factors could be divided into internal and external factors. Internal factors include such organizational factors as structure, strategy, management, culture, and workforce. They also include NSD success factors that are related to how to implement a well planned, systematic, and complete NSD process. External factors include environmental factors such as the political and legal system; and marketplace success factors that could be divided into factors related to the new service itself and factors related to how this service fit with the market in order to introduce a service that is considered as valuable and desirable by customers.

The following part will cover success factors in retail financial services with special emphasis on marketplace success factors which is crucial to know in order to understand why consumers value and desire certain new services more than others. NSD process success factors will be covered later with the NSD process in order to know how to carry out each and every phase of the process as professional and as successful as possible.

Easingwood & Storey (1993, p.44) identified the critical marketplace success factors of new retail financial services from the point of view of marketing managers. The following are the factors sorted in the order of importance:

- Total quality: This factor incorporates the organization's image, the service delivery, after sales service, the extensive branch network and the supporting tangible element of the service.
- Consistency of communication: This factor refers to the consistency in communicating the same image for the organization through all communication channels with its clients.
- Direct mail strength: This factor refers to the importance of using direct mail to target the desired segment.
- Unique Products: This factor refers to offering unique new benefits that were not previously introduced to the market. Differentiated services were found to be three times more successful than me too services (Cooper & Edgett, 1996).

- Adaptability: This factor refers to the organization's ability to adopt over time to different changes and to individual consumers' needs in order to sustain its competitive advantage.
- Distinct company positioning: This factor refers to the image and reputation of the financial service provider.

However, this research was based on the views of the marketing managers who might be biased to their side of business. In 1996, Storey and Easingwood also conducted another general study to find out determinants of new product performance in the financial service sector which resulted in identifying the following factors as major determinants of the success of new retail financial services (Storey and Easingwood, 1996, pp. 39-42):

- Overall company product fit or how do the product fit with the company's resources, expertise and existing range of products.
- Compatibility of the product with the corporate strategy and its high importance to the firm.
- Skills and knowledge of staff.
- Effective communication in creating awareness, convincing, and promoting brand image. Communication must be able to explain potential benefits of the service.
- Distribution strength that provides extensive access to target market.
- Product quality as measured by reliability, accuracy, consistency and the quality representation of the physical aspects of the product.
- Quality of service delivery as measured by the friendliness and efficiency of customer contact personnel.

Edgett & Parkinson (1994) and Cooper & Edgett (1996) identify service market synergy as one of the most important success factors of any service. They explain that those new services that exhibit synergy between service and market are five times as successful and achieve their objectives more than those with low synergy. They argue that synergy should be achieved in terms of how the new service responds to major changes in customers' wants, and fit with the customers' values, desires, and operating systems (Cooper & Edgett, 1996, p.35), as well as, how it fits the existing image of the company (Edgett & Parkinson, 1994, p.34).

Lievens, Moenaert, & S'Jegers (1999, p.39) found a direct positive relationship between the commercial success of new financial services and the extent to which communication to customers is able to create awareness of the new service, as well as realistic expectations of its performance and quality that would be consistent with the quality that will be actually delivered. Other factors are also found important to the success of new services such as market knowledge, extensive research, product champion, quick response, innovativeness, product distinctiveness, and customer understanding of the service.

Avlonitis & Papastathopoulou (2000) found out that successful innovative financial services are launched through the most integrated communication packages including print advertising, press coverage, direct mail, selling efforts at branches by a trained sales force and indoor advertising.

In their research about success factors in developing banking and insurance services in South Africa, Oldenboom & Abratt (2000, p.241) found out that the most important success factors are:

- Adequate skills and resources.
- Product advantage (mainly customers' perception of quality).
- Degree of service newness.
- Efficiency gaining consumer insight. In other words, understanding customers' wants and needs and how the purchase decision is made.

Out of those marketplace success factors, our research is concerned with those factors that are directly related to the customers and their evaluation of the new service. These include service quality, service uniqueness, effective and consistent communication, and finally how the service meets customers' needs and expectations.

### 2.2.3.4 Summary of factors affecting customers' choice in retail banking

Following is a summary of the relevant factors to our research question, measures identified for each, if any, as well as the researchers who identified them. As can be noted, identified bank related factors are much more comprehensive than identified environmental and service related factors. This is due to the same reasons mentioned before explaining why factors and criteria affecting choice of a bank are extensively covered while factors affecting choice a certain service is still not widely explored.

**Table 1: Summary of factors affecting customers' choice in retail banking**

| **Service Related Factors** | | |
|---|---|---|
| **Factor** | **Measurement** | **Identified by** |
| Pricing | | Lasheen (1992); Boyd et al (1994), Kinnington, Hill & Rakwaska, (1996); Ta & Har (2000); El Khodeiry (1999); |

| Factor | Measurement | Identified by |
|---|---|---|
| Pricing | | Dick (2002); Devlin & Gerrard (2004); Devlin (1998) |
| | Interest charged on saving accounts | Boyd et al (1994) ; Ta & Har (2000) ; Dick (2002) ; Devlin (2002) ; Tank & Tyler (2005) |
| | Interest charged on loans | Boyd et al (1994) ; Ta & Har (2000) |
| | Low fees and charges | Ta & Har (2000), Dick (2002); Devlin (2002) |
| Conditions & restrictions to get the service | | El Khodeiry (1999) |
| Service features | | Devlin (1998); Devlin (2002), Storey and Easingwood (1993) |
| | Tangible elements of the service | Storey and Easingwood (1993) |
| Service quality | Accuracy, reliability and consistency | Storey and Easingwood (1996); Devlin, (1998) |
| Degree of innova-tion | | El Khodeiry (1999); Olden-boom & Abratt (2000); Storey and Easingwood (1993) |
| | New advantages and benefits | El Khodeiry (1999), Olden-boom & Abratt (2000) |
| | Unique services | Storey and Easingwood (1993) |
| Service Sophistica-tion | Familiarity of service types<br>Easiness of undestand-ing service features | El Khodeiry (1999) |
| Degree of match with cultural values | | El Khodeiry (1999) |
| Availability of information | | El Khodeiry (1999), Lievens, Moenaert & S'Jegres (1999); Storey and Easingwood (1993); Avlonitis & Papastathopoulou (2000) |
| | Direct Mail | Storey and Easingwood (1993); Avlonitis & Papastathopoulou (2000) |
| | Print advertising | Avlonitis & Papastathopoulou (2000) |
| | Press coverage | Avlonitis & Papastathopoulou (2000) |

| Bank Related factors | | |
|---|---|---|
| **Factor** | **Measurement** | **Identified by** |
| Reputation and image | | Gadallah (1979); Lasheen (1992), Boyd et al (1994); Kinnington, Hill &Rakwaska, (1996); Mylonakis, Malliaris & Simokos, (1998);Devlin (1998); Maiouf (2001); Banking on the Right Image (2003); Devlin & Gerrard (2004); Tank & Tyler (2005); Storey and Easingwood (1993) |
| Bank size | | El Khodeiry (1999) |
| Market share | | El Khodeiry (1999) |
| Previous innovative activities | Frequency and success of previous new services | El Khodeiry (1999) |
| Trustfulness | | Maiouf (2001), Banking on the Right Image (2003); El Khodeiry (1999) |
| | Bank's competitive abilities | Maiouf (2001) |
| | Bank's experience | El Khodeiry (1999) |
| Adoptability | Ability to adopt to changing conditions | Storey and Easingwood (1993) |
| Good Management | | Abdel Naby (1999) |
| Financial Strength | | Banking on the Right Image (2003), Abdel Naby (1999) |
| Solid Establishment | | Banking on the Right Image (2003) |
| Quality of service | | Boyd et al (1994); Meidan (1996); Mylonakis, Malliaris & Simokos (1998); Ta & Har (2000); Devlin & Gerrard (2004); Abdel Naby (1999) Storey and Easingwood (1993) |
| | Quick service | Gadallah (1979); Lasheen (1992); Boyd et al (1994); Meidan (1996); Ulengin (1998); Joydeep & Renny (2005); Abdel Naby (1999) |

| Factor | Measurement | Identified by |
|---|---|---|
| | Reliability | Meidan (1996); Abdel Naby (1999) |
| | Professionalism | Meidan (1996) |
| | Ease of access | Meidan (1996) |
| | Credibility, honesty & confidentiality | Meidan (1996); Attia (1990) |
| | Friendliness of staff | Gadallah (1979); Lasheen (1992); Meidan (1996), Maiouf (2001); Abdel Naby (1999); Storey & Easingwood (1996) |
| | Staff qualifications and knowledge | Abdel Naby (1999); Storey and Easingwood (1996) |
| | Security and safety | Meidan (1996); Abdel Naby (1999) |
| | Understanding and communication | Meidan (1996); Abdel Naby (1999) |
| | Responsiveness to customers needs | Banking on the Right Image (2003) |
| | Quick resolution of problems | Joydeep & Renny (2005) |
| | Tangibles (such as decoration and layout) | Abdel Naby (1999) |
| Variety of services offered | | Attia (1990); El Kodeiry (1999); Devlin & Gerrard (2004); Ta & Har (2000); Joydeep & Renny (2005); Abdel Naby (1999) |
| | Self banking facilities | Ta & Har (2000) |
| Documentation | Simple applications | Ulengin (1998) |
| Sound investment advice | | Joydeep & Renny (2005) |
| Location convenience | | Gadallah (1979); Attia (1990), Lasheen (1992); Boyd et al (1994); Meidan (1996); Kinnington, Hill & Rakwaska (1996); Mylonakis, Malliaris & Simokos (1998); El El Khodeiry (1999); Ta & Har (2000); Maiouf (2001); Devlin (2002); Storey and Easingwood (1996) |

| Factor | Measurement | Identified by |
|---|---|---|
| | | |
| | Network of branches | Maiouf (2001), Abdel Naby (1999); Storey and Easingwood (1993) |
| | Offsite ATMs | Ulengin (1998), Maiouf (2001) |
| | Proximity | El Khodeiry 1999 |
| Long operating hours | | Ta, Huu Phuong & Har Kar Yin (2000) |
| Recommendations of others | | Meidan (1996); Mylonakis, Malliaris & Simokos (1998); Devlin (2002); Devlin & Gerrard (2004); Tank & Tyler (2005) |
| Extended loyalty programs | | Ulengin (1998) |
| Offering of incentives | | Devlin & Gerrard (2004); Tank & Tyler (2005) |
| Effective communication | | El Khodeiry (1999); Ulengin (1998); Tank & Tyler (2005) ; Storey and Easingwood (1996) |
| | Continuous information flow | Ulengin (1998) |
| | Personal selling | El Khodeiry (1999) |
| | Consistency in communication | Storey and Easingwood (1993) |
| **Market and Environmental Factors** | | |
| **Factor** | **Measurement** | **Identified by** |
| Economic conditions | Inflation rate, overall economic condition, interest rates, GNP and economic growth | Abdel Naby (1999); El Khodeiry (1999) |
| Legal conditions | Laws and regulations affecting the banking sector | Abdel Naby (1999) |
| | Government policy | Meidan (1996) |
| Nature of competition | Success of competitive services offered by other banks or other financial institutions | El Khodeiry (1999) |
| Level of technology | | El Khodeiry (1999) |

| Factor | Measurement | Identified by |
|---|---|---|
| Structure of the banking sector | Types of banks and services offered in the market | El Khodeiry (1999) |

**Demographic and Personal Factors**

| Factor | Measurement | Identified by |
|---|---|---|
| Age | | Joydeep & Renny (2005), Tank & Tyler (2005), Garmhausen (1999) |
| Level of income | | Joydeep & Renny (2005), Tank & Tyler (2005); El Khodeiry (1999) |
| Social variables | | Hassan (1994) |
| Needs, preferences, customs | | El Khodeiry (1999) |

## 2.3 Innovation in Financial Services

As evident from the change in the factors affecting customers choice of financial services over time, financial service customers are changing rapidly and getting more sophisticated and demanding. They are affected by and affecting this rapidly changing financial market with its shorter product life cycle, advancing technology, and growing competition. Within this turbulent environment, financial service institutions can no longer compete based on yesterday's value criterion and expect to be today's leaders. They became forced to constantly innovate and introduce new services not only to survive the changing environmental conditions, but also to take advantage of the opportunities that innovation offers such as invading new markets, increasing market shares, and growing profit margins. But, within the current global business arena where new services are rapidly imitated by others especially in the non- patentable service sectors, financial service institutions are now obliged to sustain their innovation effort in order to sustain their competitive advantage. In other words, it is continuous service innovation that establishes the firm's sustainable competitive advantage (Kandampully & Duddy, 1999).

As this thesis addresses the factors that affect customers' decisions to buy new retail banking services and then attempts to incorporate them into the new service development process in order to introduce successful new services, literature regarding financial service innovation, its forces, types, strategies, and development process are presented in the following section.

### 2.3.1 Innovation drivers in financial services

In today's dynamic world, many technological, environmental, and market changes occurred and made it impossible for financial service companies to continue doing business in their old ways. They became forced to continuously innovate and introduce new services in order to survive the continuously changing environmental conditions. They also became forced to keep track and even anticipate any changes in those forces in order to be able to pro-act to them before their services become obsolete. These forces include:

- **Competition:** Deregulation and the technological revolution in the financial service markets are driving fierce competition among banks, with other players in the financial service industry, as well as from other unexpected sources such as multiple retailers and tourism companies (Harborne, 2002). This led to shrinking margins, loss of market share and a shorter product life cycle, thus, creating a need for constant innovation (Meidan, 1996; Andrew 1986). Banks must at least introduce Me–too new services if they want to retain their current customers and must be more aggressive by introducing leading services if they want to increase their market share (Cowell, 1988). Customers who are not satisfied with their banks because they do not meet their expectations find it increasingly easy to switch to another (Edvardson and Olsson, 1996). The market is over saturated with new offerings. Therefore, finding the customer is becoming more and more difficult (Moskowitz & Krieger, 2001).

- **Changing customer behavior:** Customers are now becoming increasingly sophisticated, more demanding, more financially educated, more critical of services, and more cost and price conscious (Meidan, 1996 & Charofas, 1999). They demand convenience as they require anytime, anywhere delivery of services, information advice, and high level of technology (Frei, Harker & Hunter 1998; Lian, 1995). They also want to choose from many alternatives and require individualized solutions and they are becoming more mobile between competing financial service suppliers (Johannsen, 1992). They no longer wait for their banker to tell them what to buy, instead, they now tell their banker what to offer (Charofas, 1999). These changes greatly contributed to the emergence of demand led or customer driven retail banking strategies instead of the previously prevailing supply led strategies (Gardner, Howcroft & Williams, 1999).

- **Technological innovation:** The constant development in technology generates countless changes that affect the financial service sector especially the delivery channels, the nature of the banking relationship, the change in cost structure, and the comprehensive branch network (Frame

& White, 2002; Gardner, Howcroft & Williams, 1999; Hulshoof, Westhof, Kirchhoff J.J., Kirchhoff B.A.& Walsh, 1998). These technological innovations forced banks to introduce new services, new delivery channels, new payment systems, and new information systems to catch up with the modern banking world and to retain their customers who are increasingly becoming technology oriented (Meidan, 1996). Technology revolution also represents a great opportunity for banks to decrease their transaction costs. The cost per transaction decreases as the tendency to use electronic delivery channels increases along the ladder of branch, self service, telephone, internet, and mobile (Bainbridge & Meere, 2001). The impact of technology in the banking sector has become especially powerful compared to any other industry. This is due to the facts that it is almost changing every aspect of the industry including the following (Balling, Lierman & Mullinuex, 2003):

- The fundamentals of the business such as information, risk, customer interface, distribution, processing and monitoring.
- The structure of the market as it has an effect in lowering entry barriers, increasing the degree of contestability, and increasing economies of scale.
- Managerial decision making so far as it has introduced new decision making models.
- The organizational structure as it changed the traditional vertical integration structure and led to the introduction of subcontracting some banking processes.

➢ **Deregulation and consolidation of the financial service sector:** Government laws that reduced the barriers to competition and allowed for the introduction of many new services have created a pressure on financial service providers to fight the increasing competition from other sector competitors as well as from substitute services (Meidan, 1996). They also allowed for consolidation, a trend that was further fueled by the increasing competitive threats, the need to enlarge the scope of cross selling, and the need to exploit economies of scale in order to be able to decrease costs and invest heavily in new technologies (Frei, Harker & Hunter, 1998). Deregulation and competition also led to the increasing market orientation and the increasing emphasis on profitability and quality (Gardner, Howcroft & Williams, 1999).

➢ **Obsolescence**: As current service lines become obsolete or in their maturity stage of life cycle, financial service organizations must introduce new services, or at least add value added enhancements to their current services in order to survive (Cowell, 1988; Andrew, 1986).

- **Macroeconomic conditions**: Unstable macroeconomic conditions such as fluctuating interest and exchange rates, inflation, etc. creates risks for both financial institutions and customers and thus are likely to drive innovations in order to mitigate those risks. The greater the instability, the higher the innovation pace (Frame and White, 2002).

Besides those forces that constantly antiquating existing services and compel financial service institutions to introduce innovative services, there are other reasons that motivate them to do so. The following aims of introducing new services are identified by several researchers such as Cowell (1988), and Papastathopoulou, Avlonitis & Indounas (2001).

- **Spare capacity**: Financial service organizations sometimes introduce new services in order to utilize their spare capacities like introducing new retail banking loan services in order to invest excess funds.

- **Risk Reduction**: Financial service organizations may also introduce new services to diversify their service range, thus, reducing the risk of one service's failure on the whole organization.

- **Brand Leader Reasons**: People like to do business with well known names that bring higher degree of confidence, respectability, and quality. Being viewed by the market as a brand leader or at least as being always ahead of the market often attracts customers without much effort. This is particularly true in the case of banking due to the nature of financial services that involves risk and requires a high degree of trust

- **Opportunities:** Finally, service organizations may need to take advantage of market, technological, or legal opportunities that may arise.

Meidan (1996) also identified the following aims for new financial service development:

- **Cost reduction** that is mainly done via automation to introduce identical or more convenient services at lower personnel, training, or administration costs.
- **Expanding current market** i.e. attracting new customers from outside the current market.
- **Increasing sales in the existing market** by either cross selling to current customers, attracting core business from competitors, or developing products for sale to competitors' customers outside core business. The last option is easier than attracting competitors' customers core business, as in banking the tendency to buy is much stronger than the tendency to switch.

Johne & Storey (1998) added other aims of service innovations that include building a customer base, improving the loyalty of existing customers, increasing customers satisfaction, opening of new markets, increasing profits, complementing existing products, improving the organization's image, providing a platform for future new service products, enhancing competitive capabilities, enhancing team performance, and giving personal satisfaction to participating personnel. Social responsibility was added to those aims by Abou Seada (1995).

Oldenboom & Abratt (2000) argue that up till that date, most new service development efforts aimed at overcoming existing problems or avoiding failure rather then exploiting new opportunities

Although each of the above mentioned forces and aims has an effect on directing organizations' innovation efforts, they do not work on a stand alone basis. It is the dynamics of all of these forces and opportunities that actually lead to the emergence of new services. It is their interaction and influence on each other that makes it almost impossible to retain the status quo. For example, the emergence of new technologies such as computers changed customer's life style and expectations from their banks. This change along with the deregulation of the industry that lead to international level competition, and driven by bank's desire to retain their customers, excel, increase their market shares, and optimally utilize their resources usually drive banks to innovate and introduce new services, such as internet banking.

### 2.3.2 New Service development strategies

Whether the service firm is motivated to innovate in order to benefit from the prospects of innovation or is faced by compelling forces to do that greatly influences the strategy it adopts when introducing new services. Firms that would like to take advantage of market opportunities and prospects such as unmet demand or the discovery of new technologies would usually adopt the proactive strategies. On the other hand, firms that are forced to innovate to mitigate external threats such as competition or changing customer behavior would usually adopt the reactive strategies.

Kotler (1994) describes those two broad types of strategies according to their strategic intent as attacker who wants to lead the change or defender who wants to follow the lead of others (Johne & Storey, 1998). Serviceinnovationen (2005) describes them as the leader, who correctly understands customer needs and responds by offering new services, as such, he is the true innovator and the first in a newly created market; and the follower who either fully imitates the leader or only introduces minor modifications.

The leaders, or the pioneers, have the advantage of having an image of being innovative. Being first in the market, they can capture the highest market share and introduce entry barriers in front of competitors. These include patents, customer loyalty programs, or qualified motivated employees. On the other hand, followers or imitators, although cannot harvest the early fruits of innovation, still have the advantages of having less risk, and not having to bear the costs of research and development. In addition, they have the opportunity if they are fast followers to learn from the mistakes of the leaders to even introduce better services (Serviceinnovationen, 2005)

In their book "Retailing of Financial Services" McGoldrick and Greenland (1994) identified several strategies under those two broad strategic types as follows:

➢ **Proactive Strategies**

- R & D strategies: Conducting market research in order to identify customer needs and then introducing new services to fulfill those needs.
- Entrepreneurial strategies: Introducing new services using new inputs coming from entrepreneurs.
- Acquisition strategies: Building alliances and partnerships in order to introduce new joint services.

➢ **Reactive Strategies**

- Defensive strategies: Introduction of a new service in order to limit the damage resulting from a competitor's launching of a new service that can not be easily imitated.
- Imitative strategies: Copying competitors' innovation before they are able to achieve substantial competitive advantage.
- Fast follower strategies: Learning from competitors' mistakes in order to introduce similar but better services.

Although reactive strategies might allow service firms to sustain their customer base and survive market competition for sometime, followers will never be able to increase their market share or be market leaders. In addition, if they stick to these reactive strategies, even this survival will only be short term. They will gradually lose this customer base to leaders who, through their innovative services that satisfy customer needs and meet different demands, would be able to attract new segments and invade new markets. Overtime they will also be able to build a reputation of being true innovators and brand leaders, which customers translate into confidence, respectability, and quality. This is especially true in dynamic competitive markets such as retail banking where innovation became the norm. In those types of markets, firms who would like to have a leading position and a sustainable competitive advantage must continuously introduce successful innovations that customers regard as valuable.

For financial services, and due to their special characteristics and nature as an augmented service offering, Meidan (1996) identified the following three new service development strategies that are specific to financial services:

- The expansion strategy: expanding the services offered with the core financial service aiming to increase cross selling.
- The differentiation strategy: grouping core financial services into different packages targeting different segments.
- The satellite product strategy: the creation of separate stand alone products marketed separately aiming at generating sales to new customers without them having to switch or open an account.

Although both the expansion and the differentiation strategies might help financial service companies to achieve success, they may not actually lead to a real breakthrough. This is due to the fact that they both depend on exploiting current resources, either existing services or customer base, by introducing variations on how and to whom existing services should be offered. Real breakthroughs that actually establish financial service institutions as brand leaders and innovators are usually achieved through the satellite product strategy which enables the bank to introduce real innovations that easily attract new customers. As banks started to realize that, they started to offer an increasing number of new retail banking services under the satellite product strategy where any customer can easily buy the service without even having to open an account in the bank. This is evidenced by the fact that from the 55,000 subscribers of American Express first mutual fund in Egypt, less than 5% were bank clients. It is also evidenced from the advertising material, media, and delivery channels used when introducing new retail banking services that stress on the easiness of obtaining the service even through home delivery in some cases. Nevertheless, organizations must strive to create a balance between exploiting the advantages offered through successful existing services and exploring new success opportunities through innovative new services. They have to find the right mix of both strategies that would allow them to reap all the benefits of previous success and at the same time do not suffer from obsolescence. Kyriakopoulous & Moorman (2004) argue that a strong market orientation could act as a dynamic market linking capability that would facilitate integrating both strategies. This could be achieved through focusing on customer goals and facilitating market information flows between the two processes.

Regardless of the specific strategy that the financial institution is adopting when introducing new services, on the overall corporate level, innovative financial institutions must adopt what is described in a report by BAI, UNISYS

& Wharton Financial Institutions Center (2001) as the dynamic view of strategy. This view holds that the future is very difficult to predict and that the rapid environmental and market changes erode the traditional sources of competitive advantage. For those reasons, strategy makers must be very flexible and must focus primarily on identifying valuable resources and how to nurture and redeploy them over time. Those resources must stay flexible in order to be able to rapidly adapt to large scale changes that are mostly directed by a sound understanding of customers' changing needs, and motivations (BAI, UNISYS &Wharton, 2001).

### 2.3.3 Types of financial service innovation

Financial service innovations are categorized by different researchers along several dimensions. These include whether it is product or process oriented, whether it is a major innovation or only a minor amendment of existing services, or to which degree the new innovation affects customers. The following diagram summarizes some of the common innovation classifications:

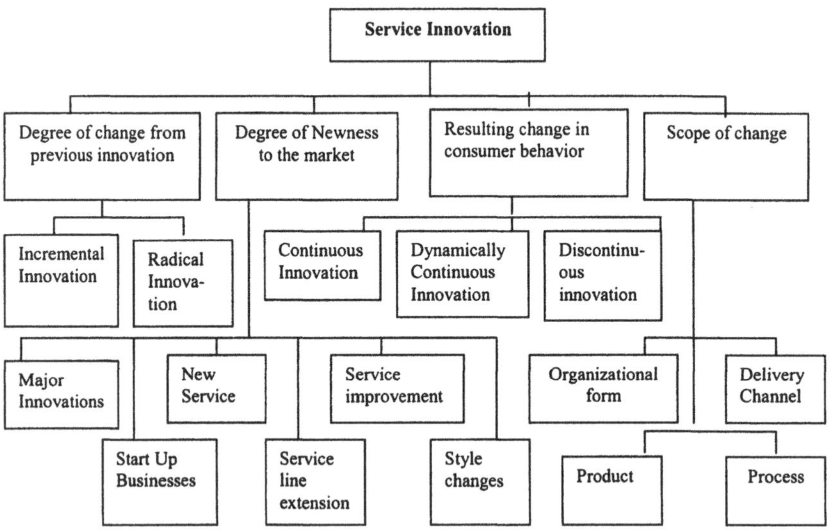


**Figure 3: Innovation Classifications**

Sciulli (1998) reported the following classifications of service innovation, as identified by a panel of retail banking executives, along two dimensions, degree of change and scope of change.

Along the first dimension, the following classifications are identified:

- **Incremental innovation**: This refers to a minor amendment in either a product or a process that do not result in noticeable changes such as adding "request a detailed statement" option to ATM machines.
- **Radical innovation**: This refers to a fundamental change that mandates revolutionary changes in product concepts or technological practices and usually represents a very high risk. Costanzo, Keasey & Short (2003, p. 277) define this type of innovation as the creation of unprecedented value. This unprecedented value is a mean of differentiation and creates a large gap between the organization and its competitors that allows it considerable time before the imitation process starts. The introduction of telephone banking by Midland bank in the early 90s is one example of radical innovation.

Along the second dimension, scope of change, Sciulli (1998) identify the following two categories:

- **Product innovation**: This type refers to a major "front stage" product introduction that customers feel and notice. These might include modifications, upgrades, extensions to existing lines or introducing a completely new service such as internet cards.
- **Process innovation**: This type refers to a major "back stage" process introduction that is introduced to ensure that service processes are conducted smoothly and efficiently. These might include process support, quality control, computerization, information processing or improved automation capabilities such as integrated database management system.

Along the same dimension of scope of change, Frame and White (2002) divide financial innovations into four categories:

a. **New products** including innovations such as adjustable rate mortgages or money market funds.
b. **New services** such as internet and mobile banking.
c. **New production processes** such as credit scoring or electronic record keeping for securities.
d. **New organizational forms** such as internet only banks.

And finally, Roberts & Amit (2003) divide retail banking innovation into three main categories:

a. **Distribution** such as ATMs, Mobile banking, PC banking, Private banking, and Telebanking.
b. **Process** such as centralization, equipment, and information technology.

c. **Product** such as accounts, deposit funds, annuities, credit cards, cash management accounts, investments, loans, and mortgages.

Along the dimension of resulting change in consumers' behavior, Warren, Abercrombie & Berl (1989) and McGoldrick & Greenland (1994) divide innovation types into three categories:

a. **Continuous innovation** which involves the alteration of existing products in a way that has the least effect on customers' behavioral patterns, for example paying credit cards using direct debit instead of having to go personally to pay.
b. **Dynamically continuous innovation** or introducing new products or modifications of existing products that cause slight changes in behavioral patterns, for example, using cheque payments instead of cash payments.
c. **Discontinuous innovation** which involves introducing a new product that introduces a new pattern of behavior, for example the introduction of internet banking.

The word "new services" might also describe a whole range of services on the innovation spectrum; most of the time the dimension of newness to the firm and the market is mentioned. Cowell (1988) classified new services along this dimension as follows:

- **Major innovations**: These are services that are introduced to still undefined markets. These include new types of services such as first internet service provider, as well as, new service delivery systems such as ATM machines that were first introduced by chemical bank in 1969.
- **Start up businesses**: These are services that are introduced to markets where other services that meet the same generic needs are available. An example of that is First Education Bank that was established in the USA in 2002 with the sole purpose of offering education loans.
- **New services**: These are services offered by the service organization for the first time, but are offered by other competitors, such as insurance services offered by banks, or banks adding credit cards to their service lines.
- **Service line extensions:** These are additions to the existing service range or lines or different way of delivering services. An example of that would be increasing the number and type of retailers participating in a credit card scheme.
- **Service improvements**: These are additions to some features of the service in order to improve its performance such as extended opening hours.
- **Style changes:** These are visible changes to indicate a different style, such as changing the interior decoration of a branch to reflect a more formal setting.

Some classifications introduced new variations along the previously mentioned dimensions. For example, Veryzer (1998) classified innovation based on the degree to which the new product provides new features and benefits to customers as well as the extent to which new technology is used to provide those benefits as follows:

- **Continuous product innovations** are those products offering technological and product features similar to current products.
- **Technologically discontinuous innovations** are those products offering new technological features and capabilities.
- **Commercially discontinuous innovations** are those products perceived as really new by the customers.
- **Technologically and commercially discontinuous innovations** are those products that offer new technological features and are perceived as really new by the customers.

Another variation was introduced by Avlonities and Papastathopoulou (2001) as well as Debackere, Van Looy & Papastathopoulou (1998). They described three types of financial service innovation projects according to the content of the service and the delivery process:

- **Breakthrough projects** are those projects that involve radical changes in both the service and the delivery process. (e.g. electronic banking)
- **Platform projects** are those projects that involve major product market extensions and the introduction of new services, new delivery processes or both (e.g. electronic banking for corporations, for SMEs and finally home banking)
- **Derivative projects** are those projects that involve small changes either in the service itself, the service delivery processes or both (e.g. developing new saving accounts)

Because each of the above classifications looks at new financial services from a different angle, they obviously overlap. For example, a product innovation could be radical or incremental and could cause a dramatic or only a slight change in consumer behavior. Nevertheless, they all share one central theme, which is that innovation involves a new idea (whether a product, a process or just a feature) that challenges the existing systems, products or processes (of the firm, the consumer, or the market).

This research is addressing product/ service innovations, that could be major innovations, start up businesses, or new services. In other words, it tackles those retail banking products/ services that are offered by the financial institution for the first time regardless of whether it is already available in the market or not.

### 2.3.4 New service development process

Although some researchers like McGoldrick and Greenland (1994) thought of the innovation process as an evolutionary process driven by the previously mentioned forces, most researchers stated that successful new services never emerge from mere coincident, and that in order for the new services to be successful, a well planned, systematic, and complete NSD process should be executed (Edgett & Parkinson (1994); Edgett (1994); Cooper & Edgett, (1996); Storey and Easingwood, (1996); Zahn, Foschiani, Lienhard, & Meyer (2003)). Cooper & Edgett (1996) further illustrated this by stating that a stage-gate process that provides a roadmap from new concept to market should be used. This means having a high quality, well defined, systematic and formal new service development process with well defined stages and activities described within each stage. Quality control check points should be built into the process, and 'Go/ Kill' decision points should be identified in order to decide, based on definite criteria, whether to proceed with or to terminate the project.

At the beginning, researchers working in the field of new product development like Booz-Allen & Hamilton (1982) did not distinguish between goods and services. They used almost the same traditional process of new product development even in services like banking. It was not until the late eighties that researchers started to realize that services have distinguishing characteristics that necessitate the development of a different process for new services, and they already started to propose different processes for new service development. Some of the early work on the subject goes back to Andrew (1986) who proposed a traditional process for developing new banking services that is mainly based on previous research conducted on new product development processes. It was not until 1988 when the special characteristics of services were really integrated into the NSD process when Cowell (1988) introduced a new service development process that was considered the cornerstone on which all work addressing new service development was built on thereafter.

Although researchers agreed on the importance of a systematic well defined NSD process with well defined stages, they failed to agree on the stages of this process. Each of them identified a different sequence of steps that he/she thinks will lead to the most successful services. The evolution of NSD processes as proposed by different researchers is summarized in figure 4.

Figure 4: Summary of NSD Processes as presented by different researchers

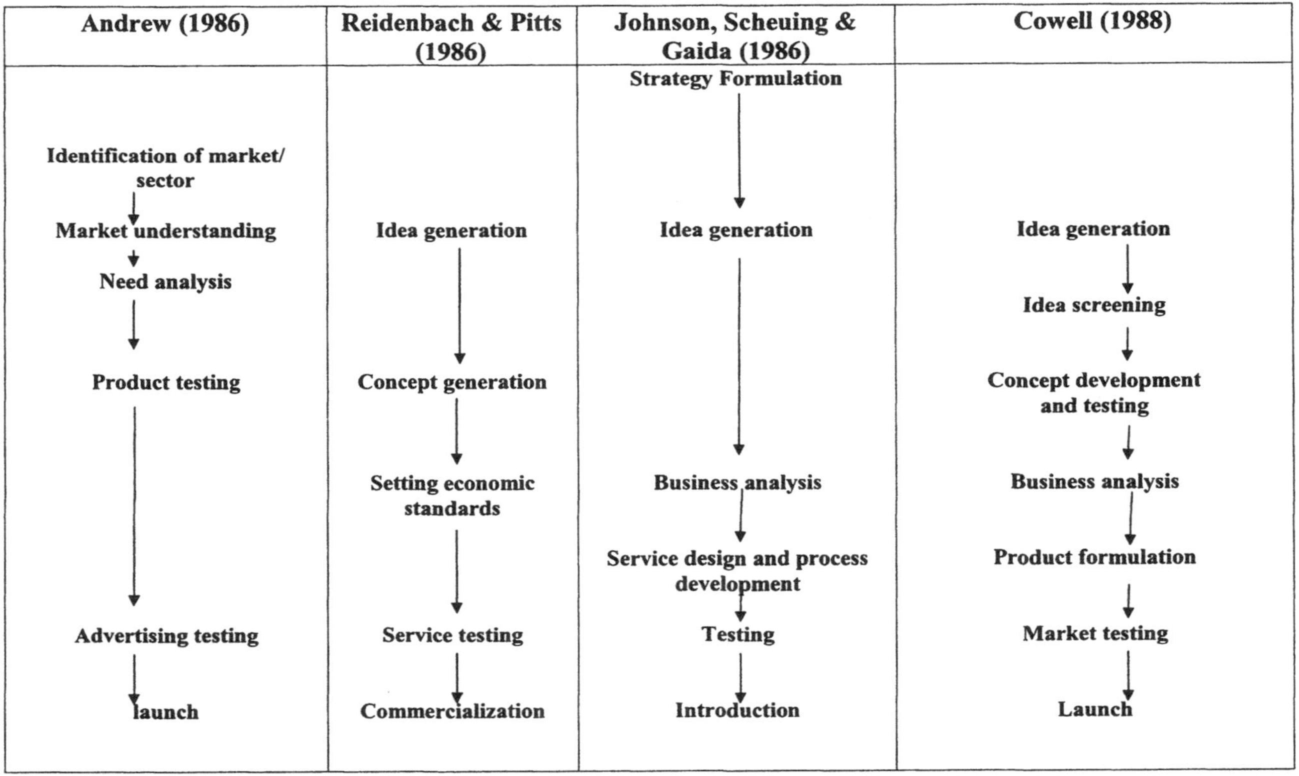

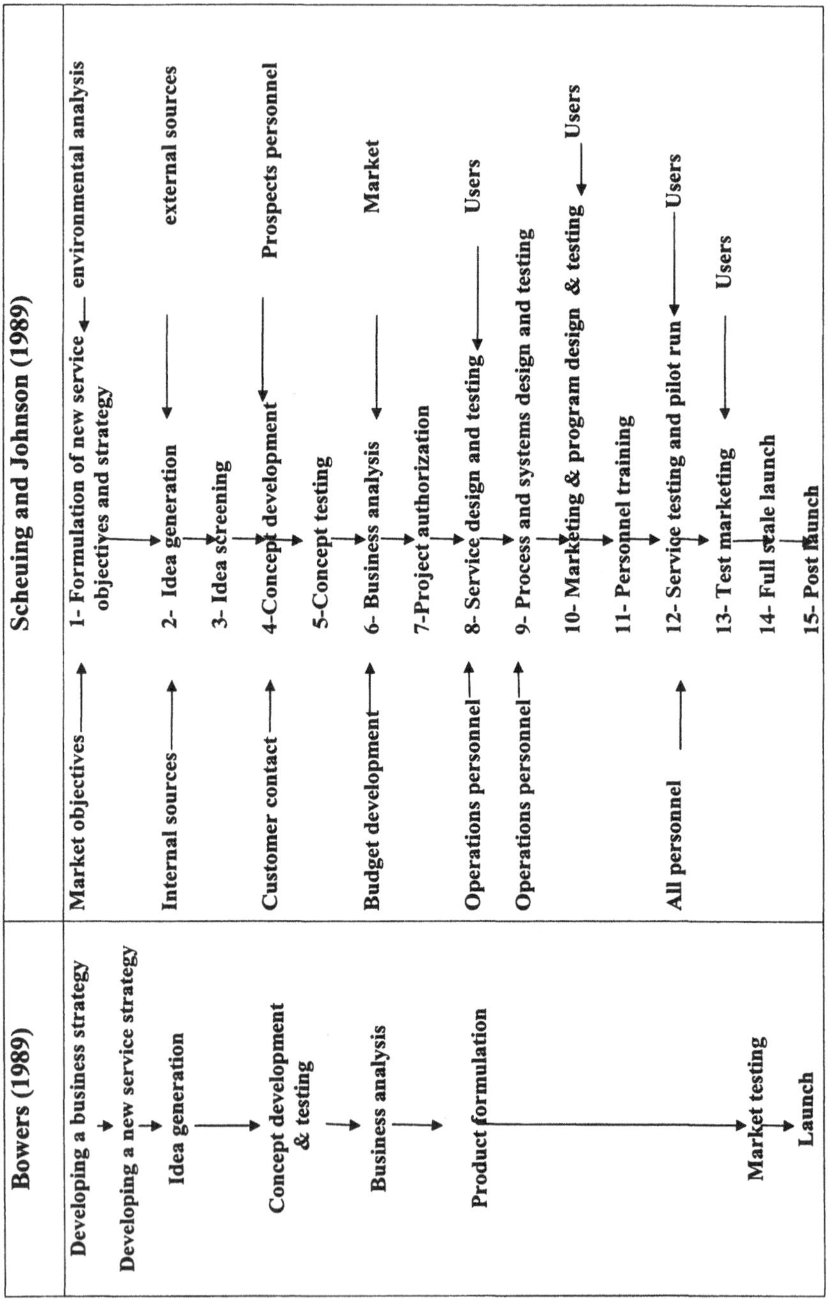

Bowers (1989)
Developing a business strategy
Developing a new service strategy
Idea generation
Concept development & testing
Business analysis
Product formulation
Market testing
Launch
Scheuing and Johnson (1989)
Market objectives
Internal sources
Customer contact
Budget development
Operations personnel
Operations personnel
All personnel
1- Formulation of new service objectives and strategy
2- Idea generation
3- Idea screening
4-Concept development
5-Concept testing
6- Business analysis
7-Project authorization
8- Service design and testing
9- Process and systems design and testing
10- Marketing & program design & testing
11- Personnel training
12- Service testing and pilot run
13- Test marketing
14- Full scale launch
15- Post launch
environmental analysis
external sources
Prospects personnel
Market
Users
Users
Users
Users

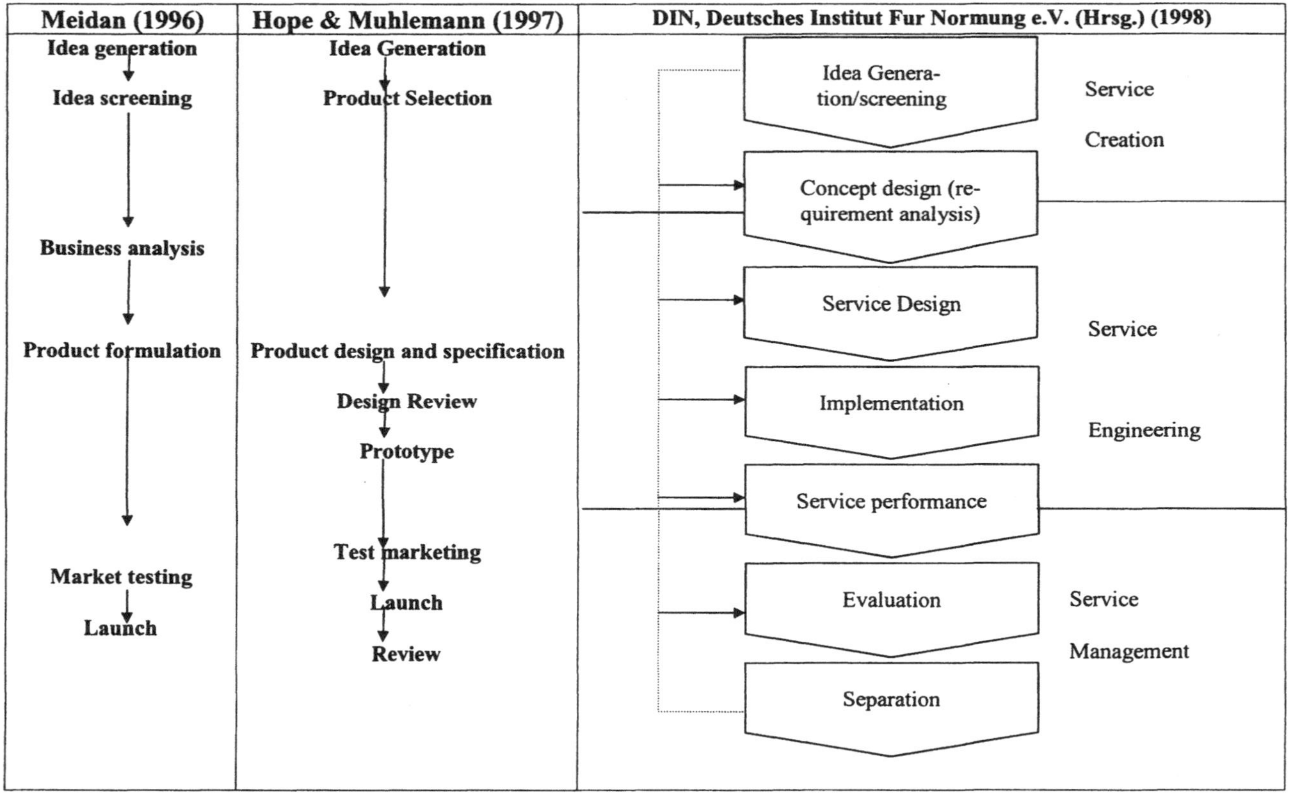
Meidan (1996)
Idea generation
Idea screening
Business analysis
Product formulation
Market testing
Launch
Hope & Muhlemann (1997)
Idea Generation
Product Selection
Product design and specification
Design Review
Prototype
Test marketing
Launch
Review
DIN, Deutsches Institut Fur Normung e.V. (Hrsg.) (1998)
Idea Generation/screening
Concept design (requirement analysis)
Service Design
Implementation
Service performance
Evaluation
Separation
Service Creation
Service Engineering
Service Management

| **Papastathopoulou, Avlonitis, & Indounas (2001)**<br>**Pre-development Activities** | **Alam & Perry (2002)**<br>**Sequential Model (for large financial institutions)** |
| --- | --- |
| **Formulation of new service development strategy**<br>↓<br>**Market problems and needs exploration**<br>↓<br>**Idea generation**<br>↓<br>**Idea screening**<br>↓<br>**Concept development**<br>↓<br>**Concept testing**<br>↓<br>**Business analysis** | **Strategic Planning**<br>→ Go/kill<br>↓<br>**Idea Geneation**<br>→ Go/kill<br>↓<br>**Idea screening**<br>→ Go/kill<br>↓<br>**Business Analysis**<br>→ Go/kill<br>↓<br>**Formation of cross functional teams**<br>→ Go/kill<br>↓<br>**Service design and process system design**<br>→ Go/kill<br>↓<br>**Personnel training**<br>→ Go/kill<br>↓<br>**Service testing and pilot run**<br>→ Go/kill<br>↓<br>**Test marketing**<br>→ Go/kill<br>↓<br>**Commercialization** |

| Alam & Perry (2002)<br>Parallel Model (for small financial institutions) | Thomke (2003) |
| --- | --- |
| 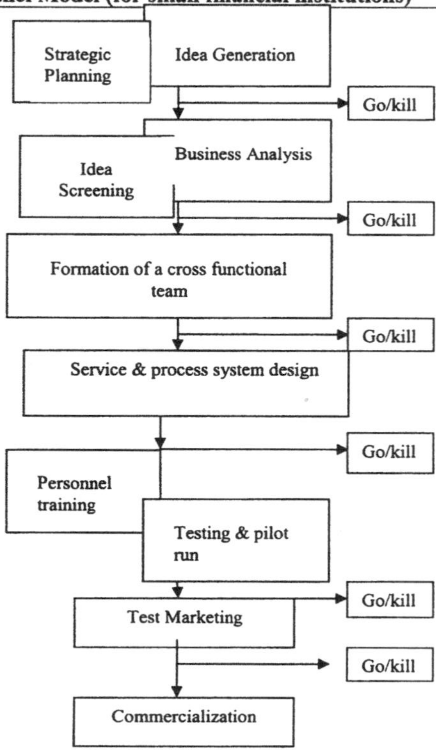 | 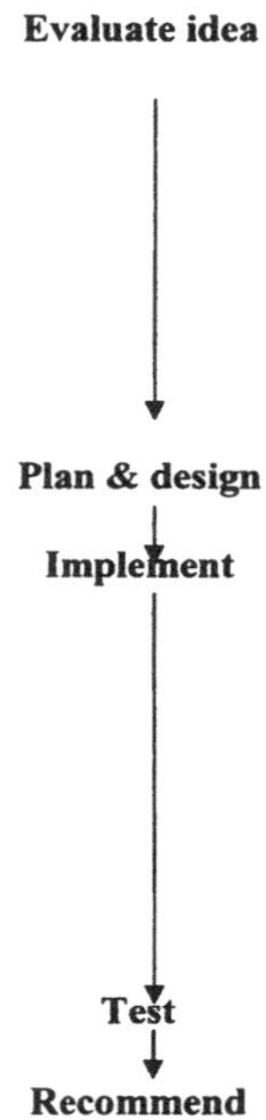 |

Most of the previously presented NSD processes as proposed by different researchers share some steps that can be considered the most important and that together compose a complete process that can be adopted for all types of new services. Variations on those steps by different researchers are meant to make the process more detailed, such as adding the steps of formation of cross functional teams and personnel training by Alam & Perry (2002); to focus on some steps that are considered the most important, as in the case of pre- development activities presented by Papastathopoulou, Avlonitis & Indounas (2001); to incorporate the role of important parties such as customers and customers' contact staff as in process presented by Scheuing & Johnson (1989); or to present a real life process, such as that adopted by Bank of America and presented by Thomke (2003). However, the following sequence of steps, as proposed to be used in our research, composes the cornerstone and most comprehensive steps that have to be systematically, completely, and proficiently carried out in order to ensure the success of any new service effort.

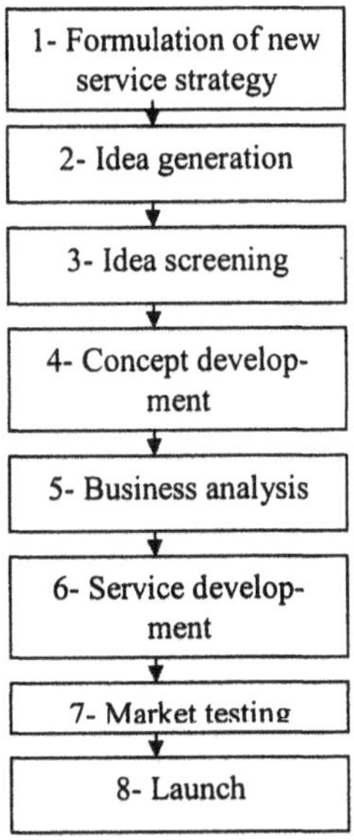


**Figure 5: Proposed NSD process**

**Formulation of new service strategy**: This step involves setting a plan for the type of new services to be developed (Bowers, 1989). Papastathopoulou, Avlonitis & Indounas (2001), stated that this stage should identify the strategic goals of the whole effort, the best research categories to explore, and the best NSD process to be used. To be able to do that, historical performance and strategic roles should be examined and individual roles and responsibilities should be assigned.

**Idea generation**: The purpose of this stage is to identify high potential new service ideas. It is considered by researchers to be one of the critical success activities and by managers to be the most important in the whole process (Alam & Berry, 2002). Papastathopoulou, Avlonitis & Indounas (2001) identify customers, competitors, and industry experts as the basic external sources of ideas. Cowell (1988) adds suppliers, overseas markets, and environmental changes to those sources. Besides those external sources, Papastathopoulou, Avlonitis & Indounas (2001) identify the marketing department, top management and line managers as important internal sources of ideas. Meidan (1996) adds employees to those internal sources. McGoldrick and Greenland (1994) identify the same internal and external sources of ideas, however, they clarify that most innovations are either competitively driven, technology driven or market driven. Andrew (1986) identifies six idea generation techniques. These include brainstorming and synectics (which is similar to brainstorming except in that the discussion in centered around a general idea that is related to the problem no to the problem itself). They also include futurology (which involves creating an environment that would reflect the future in order to enable people to have a realistic vision about new products), technological developments, past failures, and ideas borrowed from elsewhere. In their study of a leading Greek bank, Papastathopoulou, Avlonitis & Indounas (2001) also add to these techniques problem inventory analysis, and the application of new services for new functions. Zahn, Foschiani, Lienhard, & Meyer (2003) suggest that service firms must keep a structured idea data bank to collect and document previously generated ideas in case they could be revitalized under changed conditions. Reidenbach & Pitts (1986) clarify that it is statistically proven that from over 60 new banking product ideas, only one is translated to an actual product. In order to implement this step successfully, Bowers (1989) suggests that idea generation should be routinely and systematically carried out in order to constantly scan the environment for potential opportunities and gaps in customer's needs. Crosby, Johnson & Winslow (2003) suggest that customers should be put in the forefront of the idea generation effort.

**Idea screening**: Cowell (1988) explained that this stage involves ranking ideas according to a preset evaluation criteria in order to check whether they justify the time and expense of further study. Papastathopoulou, Avlonitis & Indounas (2001) identify ranking, checklists and scoring models, and numerical weighting models as the most common screening techniques. They group criteria into five major categories being consumer screens, operational screens, strategic screens, technological screens, and market screens. McGoldrick and Greenland (1994) add to those criteria market opportunity, competitive edge, capabilities and resources, congruence (development in accord with overall image and objectives), financial projections, and legal and government regulations. In order to implement this stage successfully, Crosby, Johnson, & Winslow (2003) explain that screening standards should be applied consistently and fairly to select only those ideas that match the firm's capabilities and core value propositions to the marketplace. Hope & Muhlemann (1997, P. 129) suggest that while selecting the new service, the following functions must be involved:

- Marketing: Who should have inputs about future demand.
- Operations: Who should have inputs about issues such as resource availability, capacity, etc..
- Finance: Who should have inputs about the availability of cash/ capital.
- HRM: Who should have inputs about staffing.

Hope & Muhlemann (1997) also recommend that the following factors should be considered when selecting the product to be introduced (P. 129):

- Probability of success that can be measured from different angles such as the location, size of target market, etc…
- Feasibility in terms of cost, technology, logistics, and physical constraints.
- Compatibility with existing operations

**Concept development and testing**: This stage involves translating the idea into a specific consumer meaning and testing target customers' reaction to it (Cowell, 1988). Reidenbach & Pitts, (1986, p. 123) described the concept as a "detailed statement of what the new product will be and do", while, Papastathopoulou, Avlonitis & Indounas (2001, p. 150) explained it as "a description of the customers' needs and how they are to be satisfied in the form of the context of the service". They stress that at this stage, not only core attributes of the service should be developed, but also the supplementary variables of the service. This stage also involves evaluating the concept in light of the bank's objectives, strengths, resources, new product criteria, and market conditions. If serious deficiencies are found, the idea is terminated.

**Business analysis**: This stage involves analyzing the business attractiveness of the idea and chances of success or failure (Cowell, 1988) and also the feasibility and profitability of the product (Meidan, 1996). Papastathopoulou, Avlonitis & Indounas, (2001) suggest that at this stage forecasts for market opportunities, sales, and financials should be prepared. Reidenbach & Pitts (1986) call this stage setting economic standards which means conducting cost/ benefit analysis for the new idea.

The previously mentioned pre-development activities do not waste, but actually save time, as product specifications are accurately defined, thus, reducing time to market. In addition, if those stages are carried out properly, failures could be identified early enough so as to save the organization the effort and resources that would be wasted if the idea is further developed.

In order to maximize chances of success of pre development activities, researchers identify the following steps that should be properly implemented in terms of attention, time, and funds:

- Market assessment to reach quick scoping of the market and determine market existence, size, and expected product definition should be conducted early in the process and must be properly funded and executed (Edgett, 1994; Cooper & Edgett 1996).

- Market research based upon a solid definition of the service concept should be conducted. It should involve a large research sample, use a formal design, and use consistent data collection procedures (Edgett & Parkinson, 1994). Market studies might include user wants and needs studies, value in use studies (what economic value the new service will bring to the customers), competitive analysis, and concept tests (testing the proposed service to estimate interest, liking, and purchase intent) (Edgett,1994; Cooper & Edgett, 1996).

- A thorough technical assessment should also be conducted early in the process and should be properly funded with enough time and effort allocated. This involves the conceptual work to reach technical appraisal of system feasibility, identify likely system solutions, deal with technical risks, identify operations requirements, and assess development cost, time and risks. The early and proper market and technical assessments will allow the organization to drop or modify the new service early enough without wasting resources (Cooper & Edgett 1996).

- A comprehensive business assessment should also be conducted to define the business proposition, justify the project, identify potential risks and prepare detailed financial analysis, business risk assessment, and legal / regulatory assessment (Cooper & Edgett, 1996).

**Development:** This stage involves making all necessary investments to translate the idea into an actual service. In order to implement this step successfully, Bowers (1989) recommends that both customers and contact personnel must be deeply involved in order to discover problems early.

**Testing**: Testing is mainly concerned with market acceptance of the service. It might involve test marketing or launching the product for a selected target market like a selected territory, or use testing by introducing the product to a group of customers who are aware of the test. Hope & Muhlemann (1997) suggest introducing a prototype to test the new idea through a trial run to see whether the service will be successful or not and to be able to identify potential problems that might come up during implementation. Zahn, Foschiani, Lienhard, & Meyer (2003) recommend developing different prototypes that are tested and modified in generations until a final satisfactory design is reached. In all cases, the amount of testing is influenced by the time pressure, initial investment cost, and risk associated with the launch (Meidan, 1996). Cowell (1988) adds that given the inseparability character of service, and the lack of patenting in services, testing is not usually carried out by service organizations for high cost and fear of imitation. Despite this fact, researchers agree that testing is one of the very important steps of the process that gives the bank a chance to see the real performance of the new service and to take corrective actions when necessary. Some of the testing related recommendations that researchers gave in order to improve chances of success are as follows:

- Enough time and effort must be spent on conducting thorough testing to ensure that the new service is properly designed and accepted (Edgett, 1994). The marketing mix of the new service should also be exposed to market testing in order to make sure it will work in the marketplace (Bowers, 1989). Testing techniques might include field trials, test marketing, and preference tests (Cooper & Edgett, 1996).

- Testing should also include all technical and information technology aspects of the project in order to make sure that they are working properly with no technical deficiencies (Edgett & Parkinson, 1994).

**Commercialization**: This stage involves market introduction by establishing external relationships between the service provider and other organizations such as advertising agencies or intermediaries and then full scale launch of the service (Reidenbach & Pitts, 1986). Quality of Launch greatly distinguishes between successful and failing services. A well planned, strongly supported market launch in terms of money, time, and people is usually a characteristic of successful new services (Cooper & Edgett, 1996). The following are some of the components of high quality launch:

- There is a real detailed marketing launch plan that is carefully crafted and outlines all the actions needed for launch. Part of the plan, there should be a formal advertising, promotion, marketing communication, training and internal and external marketing program backed with sufficient resources (Cooper & Edgett, 1996; Edgett & Parkinson, 1994).

- The communication effort must be well targeted at the right customers. It should be effective in creating awareness, convincing, and promoting brand image, and must be able to explain potential benefits of the service and to create realistic expectations (Lievens, Moenaert, & S'Jegers, 1999; Storey & Easingwood, 1996). It must be consistent over time, with the rest of the marketing plan and with the company's other services (Storey & Easingwood, 1993). Finally, various communication materials should be ready and in place so that the new good service does not have a hard time succeeding (Edgett, 1994).

- Quality of service delivery, as measured by the friendliness and efficiency of customer contact personnel, is high (Storey & Easingwood, 1996). Customer contact staff must be well trained on the new service and must posses all the necessary marketing and selling skills and knowledge before launch (Cooper & Edgett, 1996). The new service should be extensively marketed to them internally to ensure their buy in and support (Cooper & Edgett, 1996). There is also a control system to ensure that frontline staff is committed to sell the new service (Edgett, 1994). This is vital given the intangibility of services that makes it difficult for consumers to judge the quality of the service before purchase and consequently base their purchase decision on the service expertise.

- Distribution is extensive enough so as to provide widespread access to target market (Storey & Easingwood, 1996). Customers should be trained on their roles in service delivery and should know exactly what is required from them. Surprisingly, in a research conducted in the US, it was found out that 30% of customer dissatisfaction is a result of their own inadequate performance.

Despite this great importance attributed to the systematic process in new services success, Bowers (1989) and Johne & Storey (1998) noted that, in reality many service companies skip large parts of the process, and even when steps are carried out, they are not proficiently done. The steps that are often skipped according to Bowers are formalized idea generation, product development and testing, and market testing, those usually skipped according to Johne & Storey (1998) are product screening, concept testing and product and marketing testing, while Alam & Berry (2002) identified test marketing as the least performed stage . The observed common characteristic between all skipped steps is that they are those steps that need customers' involvement. This might be attributed to:

- ➢ The intangibility of services which makes concept testing very difficult as it is very difficult to ask people to articulate the benefits that they expect from an imaginary intangible service.

- The ease of copying by competitors that discourages external customers' involvement as the new idea could be used by competitors even before the originator is able to launch his new service.

Even if it is difficult and sometimes risky to implement those steps, they are crucial to the success of the process as they test the acceptability of the market and the customers to the product.

## 2.4 Customer orientation in new service development

Customer orientation is one component of the broader term marketing orientation which also encompasses competitor orientation and inter-functional coordination (Esteban, Millan, Angel, Molina & Martin-Consuegra, 2002; Javalgi, Martin, & Young, 2006). Customer orientation is defined by Esteban, Millan, et al., p. 3 as "the knowledge of what is wanted or needed before the marketing process begins" and by Deshpande et al. (1993, p.13) as "the set of beliefs that puts the customers' interest first, while not excluding those of other stakeholders such as owners, managers, and employees, in order to develop a long term profitable enterprise"

The importance of customer orientation is highlighted by many researchers. Brady & Cronin (2001) explain that customer oriented firms outperform competitors by responding to consumer needs with services that they perceive have higher value and lead to greater satisfaction. Being customer oriented allows firms to acquire and use the information necessary to design strategies that result in more favorable customer outcomes. They argue that customers' perception that a certain organization is customer oriented is positively associated with higher quality, which is in turn associated with higher satisfaction. This increases customer loyalty, repurchase, and positive word of mouth recommendations.

Spitler (2005, p.59) terms the organization's ability to define major differences in consumer preferences and tailoring their responses accordingly as "the new survival skill". He explains that through practical inquiries into such issues as consumer preferences in products, organizations can focus their resources, achieve differentiation and exploit new opportunities.

If customer orientation is important in new product development as customers now are the ones who drive the process, it is even more important in new service development because of the extensive involvement of customers in services (Alam & Perry, 2002). Therefore, customers' needs, wants, and assessment criteria must be the point of departure for any new service development, taking into consideration that customers, who are the ultimate judge of any new service, are becoming more sophisticated, demanding, and knowledgeable.

Several researchers identify customer's involvement in new service development as one of the critical success factors. Martin & Horne (1994) proved that direct customer participation is higher in more successful service innovations. They explained that the more the customers' participation is in the development process, the less the surprises that can be expected from the market place. Han, Kim & Srivastave (1998) and Oldenboom & Abratt (2000), confirm that a strong marketing and customer orientation, i.e. understanding customers and responding to their needs, is very important for the success of any new service.

In summarizing the key activities that researchers mention as critical to new service success, Johne & Storey (1998) identify the following customer related activities:

- Market knowledge and market orientation;
- Customers' knowledge, familiarity and understanding of the product;
- Customers' participation in the development process, especially idea generation phase, as well as in delivery;
- Explicitly communicating the advantages of the new service to customers in a language that they understand.

They emphasize on the importance of front line personnel participation in the NSD process as they are more aware of customers' needs and will prevent efficiency considerations to overwhelm them. Although they asserted that customers' involvement in the NSD process is directly related to service success, they explained that most researchers found that customers' involvement in service development is relatively low. The same conclusion was reached by Martin and Horne (1994) who proved that despite its close association with success, direct customer participation was not considered important when developing new services.

Bowers (1989) highlights the lack of attention that service organizations give to the marketplace when developing new services and noted that usually consumers see services for the first time during commercialization. This is supported by the studies conducted by Scheuing & Johnson (1989) and Avlonities & Papastathopoulou (2001) that prove that service companies place less emphasis on market testing while focus on the development, process design and launch phases of the NSD process.

On the other hand Andrew (1986), Storey & Easigwood (1996) and Demoranville, Kaminski, Ridnour & Young (1999) identify the lack of understanding of customers as a major cause for new financial services failure. Bortree (1991) identifies this as the reason why 9 out of every 10 new financial products fail in meeting their objectives. He clarifies that when banks introduce new services, they look around for inexpensive enhancements and competitors' offerings, look inside for capacity planning, and then put together a product that they think can sell. Even large banks that conduct some research do that to segment customers based on their demographic profiles, but never try to understand their needs, attitudes, or buying behavior.

Edvardson and Olsson (1996), Meidan (1996), Lasheen (1992), and Costanzo, Keasey & Short (2003) argue that the first task of any new service development is to create services that customers regard as having added value. Laurino (1993, p.2) further extends this to banks by stating that for banks "all plans should begin and end with the customer". In order to do that, service providers have to have a thorough understanding of customers' needs, expectations, and logic through continuing research. They also have to involve customers in the process of creating new services and specifically when formulating and testing the service concept and developing service processes. Alam & Perry (2002) assert that although managers of financial institutions are well aware that customer involvement is necessary to develop a superior service in the shortest possible time, they do not have a systematic reliable tool to do that.

Despite this agreement on the importance of customer orientation and involvement in new service development, in practice, only limited tools such as customers' complaint management systems or customer questionnaires are used (Zahn, Foschiani, Lienhard, & Meyer, 2003). Literature is almost silent on the details of NSD stages and how they should interface with the customers, therefore, the picture of how new customer oriented services should be developed is incomplete. Some researchers suggested different methods to incorporate customer voice in different stages of the NSD process, while only two tried to find a systematic way to incorporate customers' voice throughout the whole NSD process and determine the roles played by customers in each stage. The methods through which researchers suggested involving customers in different stages of NSD process are as follows for each stage:

- In setting the new service strategy, Zahn, Foschiani, Lienhard, & Meyer (2003) recommend integrating the customer requirements with the enterprise competences to come up with the new customer oriented service strategy.

- During **idea generation** Bowers (1989, p. 18) encourages a formal active process for searching for new ideas from outside the organization. He identifies focus groups and front line employees who are in constant contact with customers as one of the most important sources of ideas as they are more aware of customers' needs. Meidan (1996) and Scheuing & Johnson (1989) identify customers as the first external source of new product ideas. And Alam & Perry (2002) identify idea generation as one of the activities that report the highest frequency of customer input. Zahn, Foschiani, Lienhard, & Meyer (2003) suggest that customers must be involved in the very early stages of the process so that they can co-influence the origin of the new service.

- During **Idea screening** Meidan (1996, p. 99) suggests that ideas must be evaluated against customers' needs and behavior as the success of NSD is based upon how well the new products suit customers' needs.

- During **Business analysis** Meidan, (1996, p. 99) and Scheuing and Johnson (1989, p.32), also identify market research as a tool to measure the feasibility and profitability of the planned product. Martin & Horne (1994) also associate the use of customers' information at this stage with the success of the new service innovation.

- During **Service development and evaluation** Median (1996, p.99) explains that a very important step of product development is to develop the ways in which the product and its benefits will be explained to target customers in the promotion materials, contract forms, contact personnel, etc. Bowers (1989) suggests that the developed new service definitions, policies, procedures, and standards of performance should be evaluated by the customer contact personnel as they are more knowledgeable of the customers and might identify problems that no other departments pay attention to. Scheuing and Johnson (1989) stated that users must be actively involved in service design and testing, and Martin and Horne (1994) found out that successful service innovation are characterized by greater customers' involvement in the preparation of the marketing plan. This stage was reported as one of the stages that heavily involve customers by Alam and Perry (2002).

- During **Market testing**, Meidan (1996, p. 101) states that even with prior market research, market testing is very important via test marketing (limited launch of the product) or use testing (testing by limited no. of customers) as market failure of financial products might be very costly and risky. Bowers (1989, p. 19) recommends limited scale tests like offering the product to employees or testing the effectiveness of the promotional campaign on a selected group of customers so as to avoid imitation. Scheuing and Johnson (1989, p. 33) suggest users'involvement in test marketing, and service testing and pilot runs. Alam and Perry (2002), also identified this stage to be among the ones in which customers are heavily involved.

It should be noted, however, that the above mentioned stages are exactly the five stages reported by researchers as the most skipped phases of the NSD process for the reasons mentioned earlier.

The two researches who tried to come up with a systematic way to incorporate customer's voice throughout the financial service development process were carried out by Bortree (1991) and Alam & Perry (2002). Bortree (1991, p.14) suggests a different consumer based methodology that relies on the sequential input of most likely consumers to develop and position new bank services as follows:

**Stage 1: Understanding the target consumer**

using attitudinal segmentation instead of demographics or behavior. This can be achieved using focus groups that can highlight what consumers are looking for in the new service and the most important attitudes that impact their behavior and may be relevant to the purchasing decision. After identifying the attitudes of the target segment, quantifying the size of this attitudinal segment can be done through more extensive research via mail.

**Stage 2: Product and positioning development**

Also using focus groups, the bank can ask the identified target segment to list the desirable product features, delivery channels, benefits hierarchies, effective communication channels,—etc. in order to decide which of several benefits will promote consumers' interest in the new service. The final task is to put together the strongest elements into alternatives of product, positioning and trade mark.

**Stage 3: Product and positioning refinement**

Also using focus groups, the most appealing alternative of product, positioning and trade mark to the target market will be identified.

Alam & Perry (2002, p. 527) suggested the model demonstrated in figure (6) for incorporating customers' input into the NSD process. This model suggests a very extensive role of customers that extend even to selection of project team members. In reality, this might not be very practical as there are other considerations that should be regarded.

| Stage | Customers' role |
|---|---|
| 1- Strategic Planning | Feedback on financial data. |
| 2- Idea Generation | State needs, problems and their solutions, criticize existing services, identify gaps in the market; provide a wish list (service requirements), state new service adoption criteria. |
| 3- Idea Screening | Suggest rough sales guide and market size, suggest desired features, benefits and attributes, show reactions to the concept, liking, preferences, and purchase intent of all the concepts, help the producer in go/kill decision. |
| 4- Business Analysis | Limited feedback on financial data, including profitability of the concept, competitors' data. |
| 5- Formation of cross-functional teams | Join top management in selecting team members. |
| 6- Service design and Process system design | Review and jointly develop the blueprints, suggest improvements by identifying fail points, observe the service delivery trial by the firm personnel. |
| 7- Personnel training | Observe and participate in mock service delivery process, suggest improvements. |
| 8- Service testing and pilot run | Participate in a simulated service delivery process, suggest final improvements and design change. |
| 9- Test marketing | Comments on the marketing plan, detailed comments about their satisfaction of marketing mixes, suggest desired improvement. |
| 10- Commercialization | Adopt the service as a trial, feedback about overall performance of the service along with desired improvements, if any, word of mouth communication to other potential customers. |

**Figure 6: NSD Model presented by Alam & Perry (2002)**

## 2.5 Retail Banking in Egypt

Before the mid 90s, retail banking in Egypt was dominated by the public sector banks mainly because of their large network of branches (Mohieldin, 2001). They introduced very limited range of services that were mainly copied from foreign banks not initiated by the bank based on deep understanding of the customers and the environment (Lasheen, 1992). The Central Bank of Egypt was then imposing ceilings on interest rates and restricting fees and charges which discouraged innovation and made competition not worthwhile. Private sector and joint venture banks with their limited network of branches and staff were then focusing on the large volume corporate business that was considered the main revenue and profit generator.

It was not before the mid 90s when retail banking started to gain popularity in the Egyptian market. Banks started to focus on the high end retail banking services as a result of the reduced margins and repayment problems of corporate business. They also realized that they have to find a substitute to long term lending as companies found cheaper sources of investment finance through bond and share issues (Euromoney Instiutional Investor PLC, 2001). At the beginning, banks did not have proper strategies, planning, or services; they were just trying something different from corporate banking (Oteify, 2003). Later on, they realized that retail banking is more stable, more profitable, and less risky and it developed to be the most important business segment of most banks that is growing at a very high speed. As a result, most banks started to enlarge their range of retail banking services such as mutual funds, private banking, insurance, personal loans, and others

Although banks started to target specific market segments and to offer an increasingly sophisticated range of services, the retail banking market in Egypt is still far from maturity in terms of both customers and banks. To start with, the market potential is still huge; it is estimated that out of the 25-30 million potential market, only 7-8 million Egyptians hold bank accounts and only for simple purposes (Oteify, 2003). Services such as mutual funds, credit cards, ATM cards, and even checks are still considered only for the rich. The market penetration rate for simple retail banking services such as credit cards is still very low (1.34% of total population) (Aboul Enin & Hanna, 2004).

As for banks, there are more than 40 banks in Egypt offering retail banking services without any systematic planning. They have not developed a range of services that could in any way reflect the market potential (Hubband, 1999, Euromoney Instiutional Investor PLC 2001). They offer services that are not differentiated and do not have unique value added benefits (Oteify, 2003). They compete for credit customers without even knowing how much they borrow from other banks. In addition, those banks spend huge amounts of money on unplanned branch expansions and advertising, while only a small amount, if any, is spent on research to understand customer needs. As a result, banks use incredibly underdeveloped techniques in developing their retail business and they do what they guess is a good thing without having any evidence that this is the case. The end result is product led rather than market led banks with no understanding of the market or the customers. This approach caused the corporate business problems in the past, and if not corrected as soon as possible, will lead to the same problems in the retail banking business. In addition, the same forces that are driving innovation worldwide are pressuring the Egyptian banks to introduce new services. However, if those new services are haphazardly introduced without carefully studying customer needs, wants, and assessment criteria, and without employing a systematic NSD process that incorporates those needs into the new service in order to develop a successful service that is valued by customers with the least possible resources, both resources and opportunities will be wasted on introducing failing or at least moderately successful services.

As per the latest Central Bank of Egypt report issued in 2006, there are 43 banks operating in Egypt; 40 commercial banks including one Islamic bank, and three specialized banks for industry, agriculture and real estate. In terms of ownership, there are 7 public commercial and specialized banks, 29 private and joint venture banks, and 7 offshore banks. Retail banking services are offered by the following three types of banks:

1. **State Owned banks:** These are the biggest four banks in Egypt, which are National Bank of Egypt, Bank of Alexandria, that was privatized by the end of 2006, Baque Du Caire, and Misr Bank. They hold almost 65-70% share of retail banking market through more than 900 branches all over the country (Abdel Naby, 1999). Customers select those banks mainly because of their reputation, security and trust. In addition, they have the largest branch network of all other types. In general those banks' customers have lower income than the other types of banks as they don't require a minimum account balance and don't charge high fees on their services. Although customer satisfaction with those banks is generally low with 77.5% of customers complaining about slow service and crowded branches, customers still think that public sector banks are more trustworthy and secure than others (Lasheen,1992).

2. **Private sector banks:** These are either local banks (e.g. Commercial International Bank) or joint ventures between local investors and international banks (e.g. National Societe Generale Bank). These hold almost 27% share of the retail banking market. Customers select those banks mainly because of their speedy services, friendly staff, and solid reputation. Customers of those banks generally have higher income than public sector bank customers. Those banks' customers are more satisfied than public sector banks' customers with only 10% of them complaining about few aspects of service quality (Lasheen, 1992).

3. **Branches of foreign banks:** These are fully owned by foreign banks such as American Express, and Citibank. They hold 3-7% share of retail banking market. Customers select those banks mainly because of their speedy services, friendly staff, and convenient locations. Although customers of those banks generally have higher income than all other bank types, they have only moderate satisfaction with 26% of them complaining about service quality (Lasheen, 1992). This might be attributed to their high expectations from such reputable international banks.

The market is mainly divided into three segments, the first is the middle income mass market targeted by the public sector banks, the second is the middle to high income group targeted by private and joint venture banks and the third is the high income segment which is a small segment for which most banks have developed a specific policy. (Oteify, 2003)

## 2.6 Summary of theoretical foundations

Most of the available studies related to the problem in question were conducted to examine the criteria affecting customers' choice of a bank (Ta & Har 2000; Ulengin 1998; El Maiouf 2001), factors affecting demand for retail banking service (Devlin 2002; El Khodeiry 1999), consumer buying behavior in financial services (Harrison 2003; Beckett, Hewer, & Howcroft 2000), sources, types and models of innovation in retail banking (Moskawitz & Krieger 2001; Papaststhopoulou, Avlonities & Indounas 2001; Scheuing & Johnson 1989; Cowell 1988; John & Storey 1998) or to examine success and failure factors for new banking services (Storey & Easingwood 1996 & 1993; Oldenboom & Abratt 2000, Martin & Horne 1994). Although many researches highlighted the importance of customer involvement in new service development process, very little research was conducted to develop a NSD process that systematically incorporate customers' needs and choice criteria into its stages. There is lack of studies aiming to identify the factors affecting customers' decisions to buy new retail banking services, or to relate these factors to the development process of those services. This shortage of related studies is mainly due to the following:

- First, the difficulty of conducting research in services. As services are intangible and highly perceptual, it is already difficult to ask customers about their opinions or preferences for existing services (Thomke, 2003). It is even more difficult to ask them to articulate what benefits they expect from a service innovation and what elements should this service consist of (Cowell, 1988; Johne & Storey, 1998). In addition, given the ease of copying of services, most service organizations use competitors not customers as their primary source of new ideas and refine from bearing the extra cost of research (Johne & Storey, 1998). The wide range of services and service types compounded by the difficulty of defining service categories also add to the difficulties that research face in this area. Finally, the highly private and confidential nature of financial services also encompasses a major obstacle in front of customers' involvement (Johne & storey, 1998).

- Second: up till mid 90's, customers' loyalty in the banking sector was very high and most of them used to deal with only one bank that used to introduce the standard package of services offered by almost all other competitors. However, with the introduction of the new technologies that reduced the importance of the previously predominant convenience factor, the changing customers' needs and profiles, the deregulation that allowed the introduction of satellite services, i.e. separate stand alone services that does not even require an account to be opened in the bank, and the consequent increasing competition, customer loyalty in the financial service sector declined (Johne & Storey, 1998). Customers became increasingly inclined to buy services from several institutions to satisfy different needs; however, if those customers are satisfied with the one service they bought from a new bank, they may eventually switch all their business to this bank (Johne & Storey 1998). Therefore, knowing the factors that affect their selection of a new service offered in the market, an area that was rarely researched, became as important as the factors that affect their selection of a bank, an area that was extensively researched. Those factors must be incorporated in the NSD process in order to design services that can really attract those customers. However, those factors are much more comprehensive than the factors affecting the choice of a bank due to the grater variety and options involved in the decision especially given the risky nature of the service.

Moreover, given the young age and relatively recent attention given to retail banking in Egypt, this service industry in general is still not sufficiently studied by researchers. Therefore, our research aims at identifying the different factors that affect customers' decision to buy new retail banking services, with special emphasis on loan and saving services, and to incorporate those factors into the new service development process in order to develop successful new services that customers desire and value. In reaching this aim, the research answers the following central questions:

- Do demographic variables affect customers' interest in new retail banking loan and saving services?

- What are the factors that affect customers' decision to buy new retail banking loan and saving services?

- Which factors are considered the most important in taking the decision to buy new retail baking loan and saving services?

- Do the most important factors affecting customers' decision to buy new retail banking loan services differ from those affecting their decision to buy new retail banking saving services?

- How do demographic variables affect the importance that customers attribute to different factors for both new retail banking loan and saving services?

- How can we integrate the most important factors affecting customers' decision to buy new retail banking loan and saving services into the new service development process in order to ensure the market success of the new service?

# Chapter 3 – Methodology

As previously identified, the objectives of this research are (1) to identify the factors that affect customer's interest and decisions to buy new retail banking loan and saving services and then (2) to incorporate those factors into the new service development process in order to introduce customer oriented services that are considered valuable and desirable by customers. The first objective will be achieved through an empirical study conducted on the Egyptian market. This chapter discusses the methodology and procedures used to carry out this study. The second objective will be achieved by integrating the findings of this empirical study into the new service development process as described in the literature. This objective will be reached in the discussion chapter of this dissertation.

The empirical side of this research will be conducted in Egypt as one of the growing markets for retail banking. The fact that the study is conducted in one country is not considered to be a constraining factor as the Egyptian market follows the trends occurring in most markets such as deregulation, new technology and international competition. Slight differences in the importance attributed to different factors may appear if the study is conducted on other markets due to cultural differences or to the stage of market development, which will affect the managerial implications for the study. However, the general framework will remain the same.

## 3.1 Research hypotheses

As previously mentioned in chapter 1, the following are the research hypotheses tested in the study:

Hypothesis 1: The demographic variables of (a) gender, (b) age, (c) level of education (d) marital status, (e) number of children, (f) employment status, and (g) level of income affect customers' interest in buying new retail banking loan and saving services.

Hypothesis 2: The following sets of factors are important for customers when taking the decision to buy new retail banking loan and saving services.

A. **Service related factors:** (1) service uniqueness (2) service sophistication, (3) pricing, (4) tenor, (5) liquidity, (6) service risk, (7) documentation required, (8) availability of information and (9) previous positive experience with new retail banking services.

b. **Bank related factors:** (1) bank performance, (2) Service quality, (3) convenience, (4) availability of a wide range of other services,

(5) availability of technologically advanced services, (6) performance of previous new services, (7) bank reputation, (8) previous positive experience with the bank, and (9) ownership/ nationality of bank.

c. **Environment related factors:** (1) level of competition, (2) overall performance of the banking sector, (3) country's economic performance, (4) legal stability, and (5) political stability.

Hypothesis 3: Some factors are considered more important for customers when taking the decision to buy new retail banking loan and saving services than others.

Hypothesis 4: Most important factors affecting customers' decisions to buy new retail banking loan services are different from those affecting their decision to buy new retail banking saving services.

Hypothesis 5: The demographic variables of (a) gender, (b) age, (c) level of education, (d) marital status, (e) number of children, (f) employment status, and (g) income affect the importance that customers attribute to different factors when taking their decision to buy new retail banking loan and saving services.

## 3.2 Research design

Since the objective of this research is to know the most important factors that affect customers' decisions to buy new retail banking loan and saving services, a survey by means of questionnaires was found to be the most appropriate design for this study.

As previously mentioned this area of factors affecting customers' choice of new retail banking services is relatively new and is still considered to be under researched. In addition, as there are greater variety and options involved especially with satellite service introductions, the list of factors affecting the decision to buy new retail banking services are expected to be much more comprehensive than those affecting choice of a bank. Therefore, several methods had to be used in order to ensure the completeness and relevance of the identified list of factors that will be studied. These methods were conducted in the following sequence:

**Step 1**: A review of academic literature related to retail financial services, customers' buying behavior in financial services, criteria and factors affecting customers' choice of banks and financial services, and factors affecting market success of new services was conducted.

**Step 2**: A study of popular financial services and business magazines was carried out to find articles and features addressing new retail financial loan and saving services and their market and technical performance.

**Step 3**: A review of available marketing material for new services (such as leaflets, newspapers ads, internet ads, and direct marketing material) was conducted to examine which service features banks think are the most important to advertise. These ads reflect their point of view regarding the most important features that customers care about for both loan and saving services.

**Step 4**: Personal interviews with six retail banking managers from three different banks were conducted to identify, from their experience, who are interested customers in new loan and saving services. They were also asked about the factors that they think mostly affect those customers' decision to buy the new service, and how could each of these factors be measured for both loan and saving services.

**Step 5:** A comprehensive list with all factors that might be involved in the purchasing decision of both loan and saving new financial services was developed along with their measures.

**Step 6:** Exploratory research through unstructured interviews with 6% of the sample (30 retail banking customers; 15 for loan and 15 for saving services) from three different banks, in different age categories, and with different incomes and gender was conducted to:

1. Explore customers' interest in new financial loan and saving service.
2. Explore interested customers point of view of what they think is important when making the purchasing decision of new services.
3. Expose the customers to the comprehensive list of factors previously prepared in order to see which ones are really considered in their decisions and how would they measure them.

Finally, the previously prepared list of factors and measures was trimmed by means of narrowing down. Only those factors that were reported as important by at least 80% of the interviewed customers, and only those measures that were fully agreed on, were included in the questionnaire. Other factors, such as recommendations of others that were not considered important by the interviewed sample, were removed. The factors that are included in the questionnaire are:

**(1) - New service related factors**

- Service uniqueness (in terms of service offering of a unique advantage or fulfillment of an unsatisfied need);
- Service sophistication (in terms of familiarity of service type and understanding of features and operating mechanisms);
- Pricing (in terms of competitiveness and stability of interest and commission rates);
- Tenor (in terms of flexibility of deciding on service duration);
- Liquidity (in terms of ability to decide on service amount without restrictions);
- Service risk ( in terms of expected consequences of new service failure and level of guarantees provided from the bank);
- Documentation required (in terms of amount and legal responsibility of signed documentation);
- Availability of information (in terms of availability of informative advertising through different media);
- Previous positive experience with new retail banking services either directly or through trusted acquaintances.

**(2) - Bank related factors**

- Bank performance (as measured by market share, strength of financial position and profitability growth);
- Reputation of service quality (as measured by staff friendliness, efficiency and accuracy of transactions and speedy services);
- Convenience (in terms of coverage and location convenience of network of branches and ATMs);
- Availability of a wide range of other services;
- Availability of technologically advanced services;
- Performance of previous new services;
- Bank's reputation (in terms of brand name and continuity in the market);
- Previous positive experience with the bank either directly or through trusted acquaintances;
- Ownership/ nationality of the bank

**(3) - Environmental related factors**

- Level of competition (in terms of availability of competitive and substitute services);
- Overall performance of the banking sector (in terms of sector investments and profitability growth);
- Country economic performance (in terms of overall economic conditions, economic forecasts, and stability of interest and exchange rates);

- Legal stability (in terms of stability of economic legislations and banking policies);
- Political stability (in terms of absence of internal and external political turmoil).

### 3.3 Population

Based on the above, the population for the research should be the target market for retail banking in Egypt which is estimated at 25-30 million Egyptians, including the upper and medium – upper income brackets, youth, and people with jobs (Oteify, 2003).

### 3.4 Sample design

The research was conducted in three banks, one from each of the previously mentioned three types of banks; public sector banks, private sector banks, and branches of foreign banks. The survey was conducted in Cairo, the capital of Egypt with the largest population and most concentrated business and banking activities. The sample covered three branches of each selected bank with locations chosen to cover middle, upper middle, and high income segments, as well as, to achieve the highest geographic dispersion. The banks and branches chosen were as follows:

- **National Bank of Egypt (NBE):**

NBE is the oldest and largest public sector bank in Egypt, the 5th among the top 100 Arab banks, and the 311th among the top 1000 world banks. With its 200 branches around the country, NBE is trying to upgrade its retail services to compete with what private banks offer (www.NBE.com.eg, retrieved 2006). It currently offers credit cards, secured loans, different types of deposit certificates, installment cards, internet cards, and ATMs. The bank accounts for 45.8% of all cards issued in Egypt (Oteify, 2003). The branches in which the survey was conducted are located in Nasr City, Capital branch (downtown), and Mohandseen.

- **National Societe Generale Bank (NSGB):**

NSGB is a joint venture between Societe Generale Bank– France and the National Bank of Egypt that was established in 1978, and is currently considered as the largest private bank in Egypt as it merged with Misr International Bank in 2006. Since its establishment, NSGB traditionally focused on corporate banking with large clients, but recently, it decided to go into the retail business and, therefore, expand its branch network to include the currently available 54 branches (www.NSGB.com.eg, retrieved 2006). The bank offers loans for cars, education and durable goods, different types of accounts, ATMs and debit cards and a certificate of deposit for 7 years. It also introduces GSM banking which allows customers to access information about their accounts from their mobiles. The branches in which the survey was conducted are in Maadi, Pyramids area, and Heliopolis.

- **American Express Bank Egypt**

As a branch of American Express Bank International, AMEX Egypt was one of the highly reputable banks in Egypt offering retail banking services to high income segments. Through its limited network of branches, 6 branches, the bank offered credit and debit cards, secured loans, different types of mutual funds, different types of accounts and ATMs. In June 2005, the bank merged with its affiliate, the Egyptian American Bank, in which it was the major shareholder. The branches in which the survey was conducted were in Giza, Garden City, and Zamalek.

A sample of 500 customers who have personal bank accounts were randomly selected and asked to participate in the survey while waiting for their service to be delivered in bank branches. 250 questionnaires were administered for loan services and 250 questionnaires for saving services. Sample was distributed in the three types of banks prorate to their market share as follows:

- **National Bank of Egypt (Public sector)**: 68% of sample (i.e. 340 questionnaires, 170 for loan and 170 for saving services)
- **National Societe Genrale Bank (Joint venture)**: 26% of sample (i.e. 130 Questionnaires, 65 for loan and 65 for saving services)
- **American Express Bank Egypt (Branch of a foreign bank)**: 6% of sample (i.e. 30 Questionnaires, 15 for loan and 15 for saving services)

## 3.5 Instrument development

The data was collected though two survey questionnaires developed by the researcher; one for loan services and the other for saving services. The questionnaires start by checking the interest of bank customers in new retail loan/or saving services, they then proceed to asking interested customers about the degree of importance attributed to the above mentioned factors using a five point likert scale. While measures for constructs were developed based on previous literature and exploratory research, other factors were assessed using single indicator (please refer to appendix A for a chart showing questionnaire items measuring different factors for both loan and saving services). Factors were divided into service related factors, where all of the difference between loan and saving questionnaires lies, bank related factors, which is the same for both, and environmental related factors which is also the same for both questionnaires. The third part of the questionnaire identifies the demographic variables of respondents.

The questionnaires were first developed in English and then translated into Arabic by the researcher with translation reviewed by a professional translator, a Banking specialized university professor, and two retail banking managers (Please refer to appendix B for the English and Arabic versions of the questionnaires).

### 3.6 Instrument validity and reliability

As mentioned before, new services research is not easy to conduct as it is difficult to ask participants to articulate intangible benefits that they expect from a new service, therefore, extensive testing for the instrument was required in order to make sure that it is valid and reliable

#### Validity

The content validity of the instrument was evaluated by three professional judges from the banking sector (retail banking managers from the three different banks in which the survey was conducted). The judges were independently asked to evaluate whether the questions asked accurately measure the factors researched and whether they are essential and comprehensive. They also evaluated the format and wordings of the questions to clear out any confusion and make sure they will be understandable by retail banking customers. Only one question related to the tangible aspects of service quality was removed for being rated as unessential by two of the judges.

#### Pilot testing

A sample of 30 questionnaires (15 for loan and 15 for saving services) was administered by the researcher to selected members of the population in order to clear any ambiguities in the questions and make them at the technical level understood by the general public. Some questions were reformulated (such as question No. 9 related to liquidity, question no. 15 related to advertising, and question no. 30 related to technologically advanced services), examples were added to other questions to further clarify the meaning (such as question no. 4 related to familiarity of service, question no. 25 related to location convenience, and questions no. 44 & 45 related to legislations), and finally the order of some of the questions was changed in order to allow for a consistent flow of ideas (such as the order of environmental factors that was changed to competitive environment, sector performance, economic performance, stability of legislations, and finally, political stability) .

**Reliability: Test – retest**

A test-retest procedure was carried out on a sample of 40 members of the population in order to measure the reliability of the instrument. Three weeks were selected as a time span between the test and the retest as this period will not allow participants to remember their original test answers, at the same time, it will not allow any major change in their mindsets towards the important factors that would affect their decisions to buy new retail banking services. The answers of the 28 (70%) returned questionnaires were coded, compiled and analyzed using the SPSS statistical analysis software. Considering the known difficulty of articulating expected benefits from a new intangible service, the following correlations between the test and the retest results for different factors are considered reliable.

**Table 2: Results of test – re-test measure of reliability**

| Item | Correlation |
|---|---|
| Interest in new retail financial services | **0.74** |
| **Product related factors** | |
| Service uniqueness | **0.58** |
| Service sophistication | **0.77** |
| Pricing | **0.54** |
| Tenor | **0.74** |
| Liquidity | **0.51** |
| Service Risk degree | **0.61** |
| Documentation required | **0.67** |
| Availability of information. | **0.58** |
| Previous positive experience with new retail banking services either directly or through trusted acquaintances | **0.68** |
| **Bank related factors** | |
| Bank performance | **0.62** |
| Service quality | **0.62** |
| Convenience | **0.73** |
| Availability of a wide range of other services | **0.69** |
| Availability of technologically advanced services | **0.92** |
| Performance of previous services | **0.73** |

| | |
|---|---|
| Bank 's reputation | **0.59** |
| Previous positive experience with the bank either directly or through trusted acquaintances | **0.83** |
| Ownership/ Nationality of bank | **0.64** |
| **Environment related factors** | |
| Level of competition | **0.54** |
| Overall performance of the banking sector | **0.63** |
| Country Economic performance | **0.59** |
| Legal stability | **0.72** |
| Political stability | **0.54** |

Questions with lower correlations were reconstructed to be clearer and able to be understood. Two questions were added to have a more reliable measurement of the liquidity and risk degree factors (question no. 9 related to flexibility of loan drawings or purchase of extra investment and saving instruments and question no.11 related to expected risk in case of new service failure).
Finally, the English versions of the questionnaires were amended accordingly and reviewed by two retail banking professionals.

### 3.7 Data collection

Data was gathered in 2005/2006 from the nine branches of the three banks mentioned before. The data was collected by the researcher on different days during banks' operating hours to avoid any time related biases. Equal number of days was devoted to each branch in each bank. Random sampling was used as all the customers who happened to enter the branch on that day were asked to participate in the survey during their waiting time to receive their services. Thus, any demographic related biases are also avoided. Loan and saving questionnaires were sorted interchangeably, (i.e. one for loan followed by one for saving, etc...) for equal distribution in all branches. The questionnaire and the purpose of study were first introduced by the researcher to each respondent through a face to face interview and then respondents were asked to answer the questions while waiting inside the branch and to hand in the questionnaire on their way out.

426 questionnaires were returned, of which 373 questionnaires were complete and acceptable for analysis (i.e. 74.6% response rate). Of the total number of valid questionnaires, 261 were from the national bank of Egypt (NBE) (i.e. 77% response rate), 91 from National Societe Generale Bank (NSGB) (i.e. 70% response rate), and 21 from American Express Bank Egypt (AMEX) (i.e. 70% response rate). As for the division of valid questionnaires between loan and saving services, 201 questionnaires were valid for saving ser-

vices (i.e. 80.4% response rate) and 172 questionnaires were valid for loan services (i.e. 68.8% response rate).

**Table 3: Valid returned questionnaires by type and bank**

| | | TYPE | | | % |
|---|---|---|---|---|---|
| | | Loan | saving | Total | |
| BANK | National Bank of Egypt (NBE) | 121 | 140 | 261 | 70 |
| | National Societe Generale Bank (NSGB) | 40 | 51 | 91 | 24.4 |
| | American Express Bank (Amex) | 11 | 10 | 21 | 5.6 |
| Total | | 172 | 201 | 373 | |
| % | | 46.1 | 53.9 | | 100 |

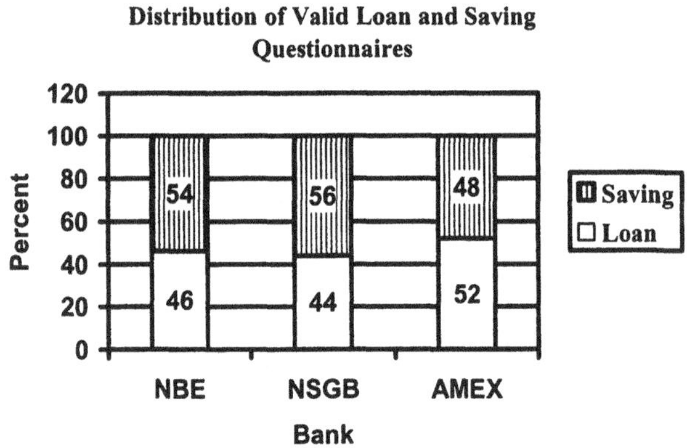


**Graph 1: Distribution of valid loan and saving questionnaires**

### 3.8 Data analysis

The procedure for data analysis was mainly divided into two phases as follows:

(a)- Data preparation: The aim of this phase was to assure the accuracy of the data and convert it into a classified format that could be analyzed. This included editing the collected questionnaires, coding, and data entry on the SPSS statistical analysis software. This phase was performed by the researcher and revised by a specialized university professor.

(b)- Data Analysis: At this stage, the researcher performed statistical analysis on the SPSS version 11 software. The analyses conducted were as follows:

- First, frequency distribution analysis was conducted to describe the demographic characteristics of the sample.

- Second, frequency distribution analysis was carried out to examine the demographic characteristics of uninterested respondents in new retail banking loan and saving services. Chi Square analysis was performed to test the significance of the impact of demographic variables on customers' interest in new retail banking loan and saving services. Logistic regression analysis was then performed in an attempt to predict customers' interest in new services from their demographic variables.

- Third, frequency distribution and descriptive statistics were performed to describe interested customers' response to different questionnaire items in terms of frequencies, mean and variability.

- Fourth, one sample t- test was used to determine whether the different factors mentioned are considered important for customers when taking a decision to buy new loan and saving services.

- Fifth, a two sample t -test was used to determine the difference between importance attributed to different factors for both loan and saving services.

- Sixth, discriminant analysis was performed to isolate the discriminating factors between loan and saving services.

- Seventh, analysis of variance (ANOVA) was used to determine the most important factors that customers consider when taking the decision to buy new retail banking loan and saving services.

- Eighth, Analysis of variance (ANOVA) was also used to investigate the effect of demographic variables on customers' response to different factors for both loan and saving services.

- Finally, ninth, factor analysis was used to examine the relationship between factors in an attempt to redefine them into fewer number of subsets for both loan and saving services

### 3.9 Summary of methodology

To achieve the objectives of this research, an empirical study on the Egyptian retail banking market to identify the factors that affect customer's interest and decision to buy new retail banking loan and saving services was conducted. This chapter discussed the procedures employed in order to carry out this study including research design, population, sample, instrument development, testing, data collection and finally statistical analysis used to reach the final results. The second objective of incorporating the findings into the new service development process will be discussed in chapter V based on previous literature conducted on the subject.

## Chapter 4- Results

This chapter contains a discussion of the results of the statistical analysis of the data, as well as an examination of the hypotheses of the study. The level of significance was set at 0.05 for all tests in the study. The statistical analyses that were carried out are as follows:

- First, frequency distribution analysis was conducted to describe the demographic characteristics of the sample.
- Second, frequency distribution analysis was carried out to examine the demographic characteristics of uninterested respondents in new retail banking loan and saving services. Chi Square analysis was performed to test the significance of the impact of demographic variables on customers' interest in new retail banking loan and saving services. Logistic regression analysis was then performed in an attempt to predict customers' interest in new services from their demographic variables.
- Third, frequency distribution and descriptive statistics were performed to describe interested customers' response to different questionnaire items in terms of frequencies, mean and variability.
- Fourth, one sample t- test was used to determine whether the different factors mentioned are considered important for customers when taking a decision to buy new loan and saving services.
- Fifth, a two sample t -test was used to determine the difference between importance attributed to different factors for both loan and saving services.
- Sixth, discriminant analysis was performed to isolate the discriminating factors between loan and saving services.
- Seventh, analysis of variance (ANOVA) was used to determine the most important factors that customers consider when taking the decision to buy new retail banking loan and saving services.
- Eighth, Analysis of variance (ANOVA) was also used to investigate the effect of demographic variables on customers' response to different factors for both loan and saving services.
- Finally, ninth, factor analysis was used to examine the relationship between factors in an attempt to redefine them into fewer numbers of subsets for both loan and saving services

As mentioned before, out of the 373 returned valid questionnaires, 201 were for saving services with 80.4% response rate, and 172 were for loan services with 68.8% response rate. This difference of response rate between loan and saving services may be attributed to the following:

- Loan services are considered relatively new to the retail banking market in Egypt. Customers are not yet accustomed to the idea of borrowing to buy personal items. Even the rate of penetration of credit cards in the market is still considered very low.

- As an Islamic country with more then 85% Muslim population, many Muslims hold the belief that paying interest is forbidden by Islam, especially if the loan is utilized for personal not business purposes.

## 4.1 Demographic characteristics of the sample: Frequency distribution analysis:

The results of the cross-tabulation of the demographic characteristics of respondents for both loan and saving services are presented in Table (4) as follows:

### Gender

There were 111 male respondents for loan services representing 64.5% of total loan respondents and 61 female respondents representing 35.5%. As for saving services, there were 124 male respondents representing 61.7% of total saving respondents and 77 female respondents representing 38.3%. On the overall, there were 235 male respondents representing 63% of total sample and 138 female respondents representing 37% of total sample. This greater percentage of male respondents may be attributed to the fact that financial and banking decisions and relationships are usually considered major family decisions, and therefore, they should be handled by males. It could also be that males are more willing to participate in such research than females. Further research on the subject is needed.

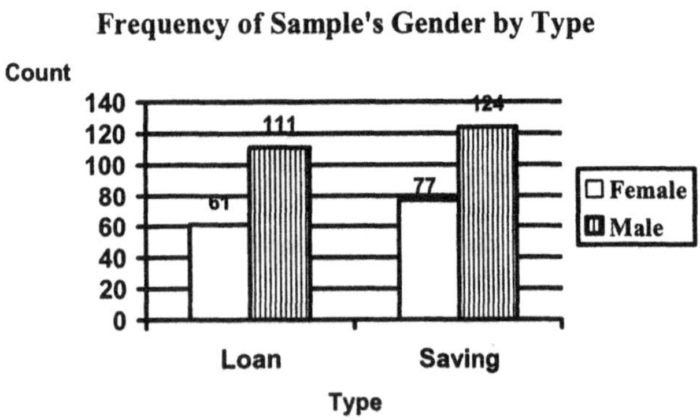


**Graph 2: Frequency of sample's gender for both loan and saving services**

**Age**

There were 39 respondents for loan service questionnaires at the age of 21-30, 48 respondents at the age of 31-40, 42 respondents at the age of 41-50, 33 respondents at the age of 51-60, and 10 respondents above 60 years old. These represent 22.7%, 27.9%, 24.4%, 19.2%, and 5.8% of the total loan respondents respectively. As for saving services, there were 43 respondents at the age of 21-30, 45 respondents at the age of 31-40, 43 respondents at the age of 41-50, 41 respondents at the age of 51-60, and 29 respondents above 60 years old. These represent 21.4%, 22.4%, 21.4%, 20.4% and 14.4% of total saving respondents. Overall, there were 82 respondents at the age of 21-30, 93 respondents at the age of 31-40, 85 respondents at the age of 41-50, 74 respondents at the age of 51-60, and 39 respondents above 60 years old. These represent 22%, 24.9%, 22.8%, 19.8%, and 10.5% of total sample. It is worth noting that the frequency distribution of different age categories is almost equal for saving services with slight decline at the above 60 category. On the other hand, the distribution of age categories in loan services is more variable with somehow sharper decline at the above 60 age. This could be attributed to the fact that most banks set a maximum age of 55 to grant personal loans. It could also be attributed to older peoples' lack of interest in loan services as they may not be accustomed to the idea for personal or religious reasons, or may think do not have enough future cash flow to repay the loan.

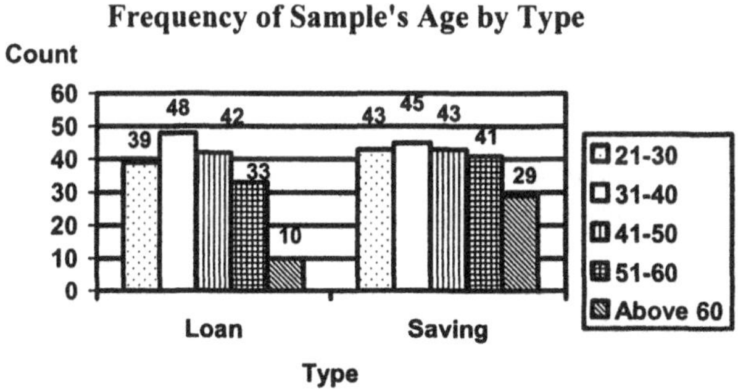


**Graph 3: Frequency of sample's age for both loan and saving services**

**Level of education**

There were 2 respondents with basic education for loan services, 8 respondents with high school certificate, 126 respondents with bachelor degrees and 36 respondents with master/PhD. These represent 1.2%, 4.7%, 73.3%, and 20.9% of total loan respondents respectively. As for saving services, there were no respondents with basic education, 14 respondents with high school certificates, 152 respondents with bachelor degrees, and 35 respondents with master/PhD. These represent 0%, 7%, 75.6%, and 17.4% of total saving respondents respectively. Overall, there were 2 respondents with basic education, 22 with high school certificates, 278 with bachelor degrees, and 71 with Master/PhD. These represent 0.5%, 5.9%, 74.5%, and 19% of total sample respectively.

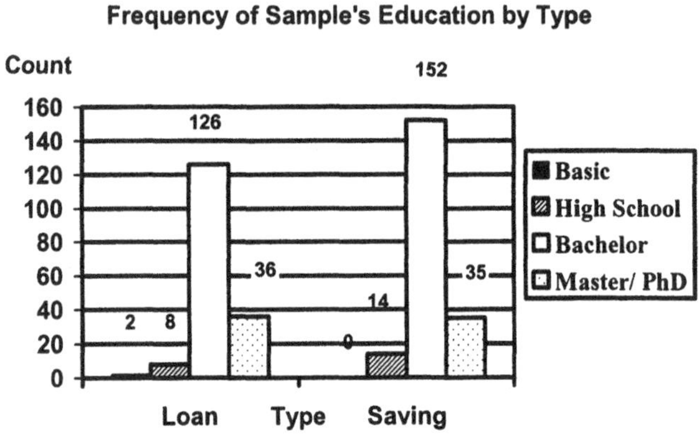


**Graph 4: Frequency of sample's education for both loan and saving services**

**Marital status**

There were 35 single respondents for loan services, 131 married respondents, 4 widowed, and 2 divorced. These represent 20.3%, 76.2%, 2.3%, and 1.2% of total loan respondents respectively. As for saving services, there were 37 single respondents, 145 married respondents, 15 widowed respondents, and 4 divorced respondents. These represent 18.4%, 72.1%, 7.5%, and 2% of total saving respondents respectively. Overall, there were 72 single respondents, 276 married respondents, 19 widowed respondents, and 6 divorced respondents. These represent 19.3%, 74%, 5.1%, and 1.6% of total sample respectively.

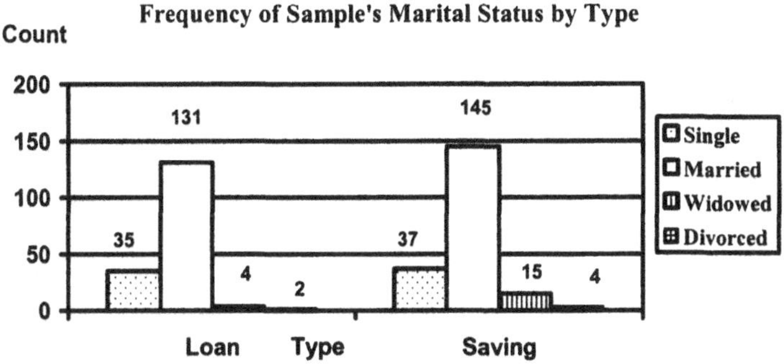


**Graph 5: Frequency of sample's marital status for both loan and saving services**

**Number of children**

There were 42 respondents with no children for loan services, 26 respondents with 1 child, 48 respondents with 2 children, 39 respondents with 3 children, and 17 respondents with more than 3 children. These represent 24.4%, 15.1%, 27.9%, 22.7%, and 9.9% of total loan respondents respectively. As for saving services, there were 46 respondents with no children, 25 respondents with 1 child, 66 respondents with 2 children, 40 respondents with 3 children, and 24 respondents with more than 3 children. These represent 22.9%, 12.4%, 32.8%, 19.9%, and 11.9% of total loan respondents respectively. Overall, there were 88 respondents with no children, 51 respondents with 1 child, 114 respondents with 2 children, 79 respondents with 3 children, and 41 respondents with more than 3 children. These represent 23.6%, 13.7%, 30.6%, 21.2%, and 11% of the total sample respectively.

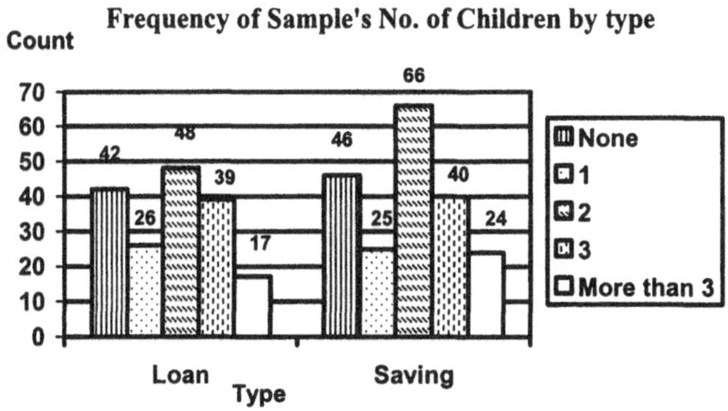


**Graph 6: Frequency of sample's no. of children for both loan and saving services**

**Employment status**

There were 53 respondents for loan services working for the private sector, 48 respondents working for the public sector, 33 respondents having their own private business, 20 respondents unemployed, and 17 respondents having other employment status such as people working abroad or on pension. These represent 31%, 28.1%, 19.3%, 11.7%, and 9.9% of total loan respondents respectively. As for saving services, there were 59 respondents working for the private sector, 47 respondents working for the public sector, 39 respondents having their own private business, 33 respondents unemployed, and 23 respondents having other employment status. These represent 29.4%, 23.4%, 19.4%, 16.4%, and 11.4% of total saving respondents respectively. Overall, there were 112 respondents working for the private sector, 95 respondents working for the public sector, 72 respondents having their own private business, 53 respondents unemployed, and 40 respondents having other employment status. These represent 30.1%, 25.5%, 19.4%, 14.2%, and 10.8% of total sample respectively.

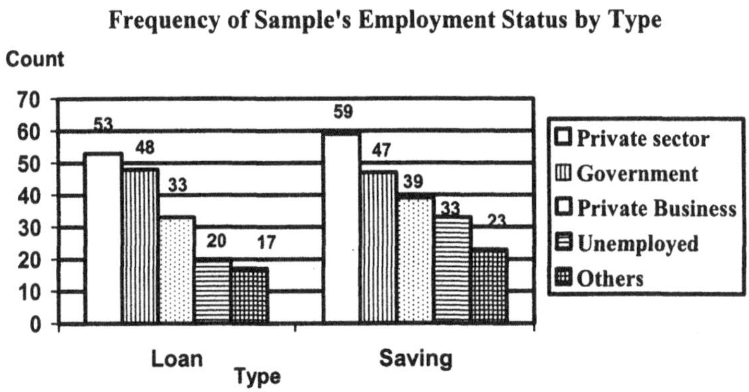


**Graph 7: Frequency of sample's field of work for both loan and saving services**

**Level of income**

There were 47 respondents for loan services with less than 2000 Egyptian pounds (LE) of monthly income, 75 respondents with monthly income in the range of LE 2000-LE 5000, 23 respondents with monthly income in the range of LE 5000- LE 10000, and 17 respondents with monthly income exceeding LE 10000. These represent 29%, 46.3%, 14.2%, and 10.5% of total loan respondents respectively. As for saving services, there were 71 respondents with less than LE 2000 monthly income, 76 respondents with monthly income in the range of LE 2000- LE 5000, 29 respondents with monthly income in the range of LE 5000- LE10000, and 19 respondents with monthly income exceeding LE 10000. These represent 36.4%, 39%, 14.9%, and 9.7% of total saving respondents respectively. Overall, there were 118 respondents with less than LE 2000 monthly income, 151 respondents with monthly income in the range of LE 2000-LE 5000, 52 respondents with monthly income in the range of LE 5000-LE 10000, and 36 respondents with monthly income exceeding LE 10000. These represent 33.1%, 42.3%, 14.6%, and 10.1% of total sample respectively. It is worth noting that response rate for this item was 95.7% with 4.3% of respondents not wishing to reveal their income.

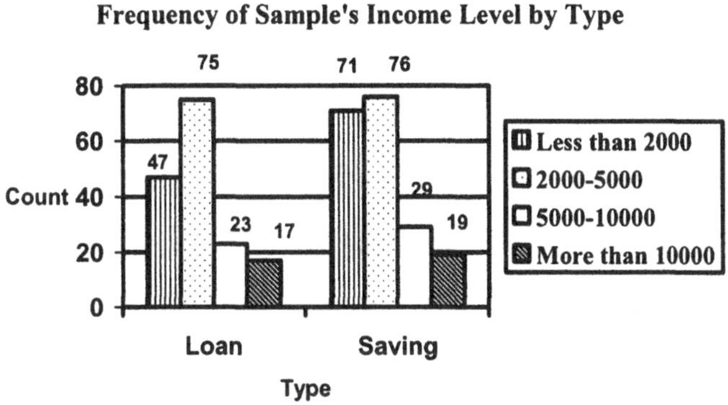


**Graph 8: Frequency of sample's income for both loan and saving services**

## Summary profile

Based on the percentage distribution of sample, the typical questionnaire respondent for both loan and saving services is a male, at the age of 31-50, with a bachelor degree, married with two children, employed by the private sector and having a monthly income of LE 2000-5000.

**Table 4: Demographic characteristics of the Sample**

| Variable | Loan N. 172 | Loan % | Saving N. 201 | Saving % | Total N. 373 | Total % |
|---|---|---|---|---|---|---|
| **Gender** | | | | | | |
| Male | 111 | 64.5 | 124 | 61.7 | 235 | 63 |
| Female | 61 | 35.5 | 77 | 38.3 | 138 | 37 |
| Age | | | | | | |
| 21- 30 | 39 | 22.7 | 43 | 21.4 | 82 | 22 |
| 31- 40 | 48 | 27.9 | 45 | 22.4 | 93 | 24.9 |
| 41- 50 | 42 | 24.4 | 43 | 21.4 | 85 | 22.8 |
| 51- 60 | 33 | 19.2 | 41 | 20.4 | 74 | 19.8 |
| Above 60 | 10 | 5.8 | 29 | 14.4 | 39 | 10.5 |

| | | | | | | | |
|---|---|---|---|---|---|---|---|
| **Level of Education** | | | | | | | |
| | Basic | 2 | 1.2 | 0 | 0 | 2 | 0.5 |
| | High School | 8 | 4.7 | 14 | 7 | 22 | 5.9 |
| | Bachelor | 126 | 73.3 | 152 | 75.6 | 278 | 74.5 |
| | Masters/ PhD | 36 | 20.9 | 35 | 17.4 | 71 | 19 |
| **Marital Status** | | | | | | | |
| | Single | 35 | 20.3 | 37 | 18.4 | 72 | 19.3 |
| | Married | 131 | 76.2 | 145 | 72.1 | 276 | 74 |
| | Widowed | 4 | 2.3 | 15 | 7.5 | 19 | 5.1 |
| | Divorced | 2 | 1.2 | 4 | 2 | 6 | 1.6 |
| **Number of Children** | | | | | | | |
| | 0 | 42 | 24.4 | 46 | 22.9 | 88 | 23.6 |
| | 1 | 26 | 15.1 | 25 | 12.4 | 51 | 13.7 |
| | 2 | 48 | 27.9 | 66 | 32.8 | 114 | 30.6 |
| | 3 | 39 | 22.7 | 40 | 19.9 | 79 | 21.2 |
| | More than 3 | 17 | 9.9 | 24 | 11.9 | 41 | 11 |
| **Employment Status** | | | | | | | |
| | Private Sector | 53 | 31 | 59 | 29.4 | 112 | 30.1 |
| | Public sector | 48 | 28.1 | 47 | 23.4 | 95 | 25.5 |
| | Private Business | 33 | 19.3 | 39 | 19.4 | 72 | 19.4 |
| | Unemployed | 20 | 11.7 | 33 | 16.4 | 53 | 14.2 |
| | Others | 17 | 9.9 | 23 | 11.4 | 40 | 10.8 |
| **Level of monthly Income** | | | | | | | |
| | Less than LE 2000 | 47 | 29 | 71 | 36.4 | 118 | 33.1 |
| | LE 2000- LE 5000 | 75 | 46.3 | 76 | 39 | 151 | 42.3 |
| | LE 5000- LE 10000 | 23 | 14.2 | 29 | 14.9 | 52 | 14.6 |
| | More than LE 10000 | 17 | 10.5 | 19 | 9.7 | 36 | 10.1 |

## 4.2 Customers' interest in buying new retail banking loan and saving services

At the beginning of the questionnaires, a question was asked to identify those customers who are not interested in trying new retail banking loan or saving services. Having filtered those customers who tried a new service before but no longer have the interest, the remaining customers are those risk averse customers who are not even interested to know about new retail banking services. These were 79 respondents representing 21% of total sample, of which 55 respondents were for loan services (32% of total respondents for loan services), and 24 respondents were for saving services (12% of total respondents for saving services). The higher percentage of customers who are not interested in new loan services further supports the argument why response rate was lower for loan services. The justifications mentioned were:

- Loan services are considered relatively new to the Egyptian retail banking customers who are not yet accustomed to the idea of borrowing to buy personal items.
- As an Islamic country with more then 85% Muslim population, many Muslims hold the belief that paying interest is forbidden by Islam, especially if the loan is utilized for personal not business purposes.

### 4.2.1 Frequency distribution analysis: The demographic characteristics of uninterested customers in buying new retail banking loan and saving services

The results of the cross tabulation of the demographic characteristics of uninterested customers in buying new loan and saving services are presented in table (5) as follows:

#### Gender

For loan services, there were 26 male respondents representing 47.3% of total uninterested customers in buying new loan services, and 29 female respondents representing 52.7%. As for saving services, there were 12 male respondents and 12 female respondents representing 50% each. Overall, there were 38 male respondents representing 48.1% of total uninterested respondents and 41 female respondents representing 51.9%

#### Age

For loan services, there were 9 uninterested respondents at the age of 21- 30, 17 respondents at the age of 31-40, 11 respondents at the age of 41-50, 12 respondents at the age of 51-60, and 6 respondents above 60 years old. These represent 16.4%, 30.9%, 20%, 21.8% and 10.9% of total uninterested respondents in buying new loan services respectively. As for saving services, there were 8 respondents at the age of 21-30, 8 respondents at the age of 31-40, 2 respondents at the age of 41-50, 5 respondents at the age of 51-60, and only 1 respondent above 60 years old. These represent 33.3%, 33.3%, 8.3%, 20.8%, and 4.2% of total uninterested respondents in buying new saving services respectively. Overall, there were 17 respondents at the age of 21-30, 25 respondents at the age of 31-40, 13 respondents at the age of 41-50, 17 respondents at the age of 51-60, and 7 respondents above 60 years old. These represent 21.5%, 31.6%, 16.5%, 21.5%, and 8.9% of total uninterested customers respectively.

**Level of Education**

For loan services, there were 4 uninterested respondents with high school certificates, 34 with bachelor degrees, and 17 with Master/PhD. These represent 7.3%, 61.8%, and 30.9% of total uninterested customers in buying new loan services respectively. For saving services, there were 4 uninterested respondents with high school certificates, 18 respondents with bachelor degrees and 2 respondents with Master/PhD. These represent 16.7%, 75%, and 8.3% of total uninterested customers in buying new saving services respectively. Overall, there were 8 uninterested respondents with high school certificates, 52 respondents with bachelor degrees and 19 respondents with PhD/Masters. These represent 16.7%, 75%, and 8.3% of total uninterested customers respectively. The high percentage of uninterested respondents with Master/PhD degrees in buying new loan services (30.9%) relative to those uninterested in buying new saving services (8.3%) and relative to the percentage of respondents having master/PhD degrees to total loan respondents (20.9%) is worth noting.

**Marital Status**

Out of uninterested respondents in buying new loan services, 9 were single, 43 were married, 2 were widowed and 1 was divorced. These represent 16.4%, 78.2%, 3.6%, and 1.8% of uninterested customers in buying new loan services respectively. As for saving services, 7 were single, 13 were married, and 4 were widowed. These represent 29.2%, 54.2%, and 16.7% of uninterested respondents in buying new saving services respectively. Overall, there were 16 single uninterested respondents, 56 married, 6 widowed and one divorced. These represent 20.3%, 70.9%, 7.6%, and 1.3% of total uninterested respondents respectively. The fact that the percentage of married respondents who are not interested in buying new loan services (78.2%) is considered high compared to those not interested in saving services (54.2%) is worth noting. On the other hand, the percentage of single respondents who are not interested in buying new saving services (29.2%) is also considered high compared to those not interested in buying new loan services (16.4%).

**Number of Children**

Out of uninterested respondents for loan services, 9 have no children, 8 have one child, 13 have 2 children, 14 have 3 children, and 11 have more than 3 children. These represent 16.4%, 14.5%, 23.6%, 25.5%, and 20% of total uninterested respondents in buying new loan services respectively. As for saving services, out of those uninterested in buying new services 8 have no children, 3 have 1 child, 7 have 2 children, 3 have 3 children and 3 have more than 3 children. These represent 33.3%, 12.5%, 29.5%, 12.5%, and 12.5% of uninterested customers in buying new saving services respectively. Overall, out of total uninterested respondents 17 have no children, 11 have one child, 20 have 2 children, 17 have 3 children and 14 have more than 3 children. These represent 21.5%, 13.9%, 25.3%, 21.5%, and 17.7% of total uninterested respondents respectively. It is worth noting that the percentage of uninterested respondents who have 3 children or more for loan services is 45.5%, while for those in saving services is only 25%. This is reflected on the fact that 33.3% of uninterested respondents in buying new saving services have no children corresponding to only 16.4% for loan services.

**Employment Status**

Out of uninterested respondents for loan services, 7 are employed by the private sector, 24 by the public sector, 9 have their own private business, 11 are unemployed and 4 have other employment status. These represent 12.7%, 43.6%, 16.4%, 20% and 7.3% of uninterested respondents in buying new loan services. As for new saving services, out of uninterested respondents, 10 are employed by the private sector, 4 by the public sector, 6 have their own private business, and 4 are unemployed. These represent 41.7%, 16.7%, 25%, and 16.7% of uninterested respondents in buying new saving services respectively. Overall, there were 17 respondents employed by the private sector, 28 by the public sector, 15 having their own private business, 15 are unemployed, and 4 are having other employment status. These represent 21.5%, 35.4%, 19%, 19%, and 5.1% of total uninterested respondents respectively. The composition of uninterested respondents employed by the public sector and the private sector is worth noting. For loan services, 12.7% were private sector employees and 43.6% were public sector employees compared to 31% and 28% of total loan respondents respectively. For saving services, 41.7% were private sector employees and 16.7% were public sector employees compared to 29.4% and 23.4% of total saving respondents respectively

**Level of Income**

Out of uninterested respondents for loan services, there were 18 respondents with less than LE 2000 monthly income, 24 with monthly income in the range of LE 2000-LE 5000, 3 with monthly income in the range of LE 5000-LE10000 and 6 with more than LE 10000 monthly income. These represent 35.3%, 47.1%, 5.9% and 11.8% of uninterested respondents in buying new loan services respectively. For saving services, there were 10 uninterested respondents with less than LE 2000 monthly income, 7 with monthly income in the range of LE 2000-LE 5000, and 7 with monthly income in the range of LE 5000-LE 10000. These represent 41.7%, 29.2%, and 29.2%of uninterested respondents in buying new saving services respectively. Overall, there were 28 uninterested respondents with less than LE 2000 monthly income, 31 with LE 2000- LE 50000 monthly income, 3 with LE 5000 – LE 10000 monthly income, and 6 with more than LE 10000 monthly income. These represent 37.3%, 41.3%, 13.3%, and 8% of total uninterested respondents respectively. It is worth noting that four uninterested respondents were reluctant to reveal their income level. The fact that 11.8% of uninterested respondents in loan services earn more than LE 10000 compared to 0% in saving services is also worth noting.

**Table 5: Demographic characteristics of uninterested respondents**

| Variable | Loan N. 55 | Loan % | Saving N. 24 | Saving % | Total N. | Total % |
|---|---|---|---|---|---|---|
| **Gender** | | | | | | |
| Male | 26 | 47.3 | 12 | 50 | 38 | 48.1 |
| Female | 29 | 52.7 | 12 | 50 | 41 | 51.9 |
| **Age** | | | | | | |
| 21- 30 | 9 | 16.4 | 8 | 33.3 | 17 | 21.5 |
| 31- 40 | 17 | 30.9 | 8 | 33.3 | 25 | 31.6 |
| 41- 50 | 11 | 20 | 2 | 8.3 | 13 | 16.5 |
| 51- 60 | 12 | 21.8 | 5 | 20.8 | 17 | 21.5 |
| Above 60 | 6 | 10.9 | 1 | 4.2 | 7 | 8.9 |
| **Level of education** | | | | | | |
| Basic | 0 | 0 | 0 | 0 | 0 | 0 |
| High school | 4 | 7.3 | 4 | 16.7 | 8 | 10.1 |
| Bachelor | 34 | 61.8 | 18 | 75 | 52 | 65.8 |
| Masters/ PhD | 17 | 30.9 | 2 | 8.3 | 19 | 24.1 |
| **Marital status** | | | | | | |
| Single | 9 | 16.4 | 7 | 29.2 | 16 | 20.3 |
| Married | 43 | 78.2 | 13 | 54.2 | 56 | 70.9 |
| Widowed | 2 | 3.6 | 4 | 16.7 | 6 | 7.6 |
| Divorced | 1 | 1.8 | 0 | 0 | 1 | 1.3 |
| **Number of children** | | | | | | |
| 0 | 9 | 16.4 | 8 | 33.3 | 17 | 21.5 |
| 1 | 8 | 14.5 | 3 | 12.5 | 11 | 13.9 |
| 2 | 13 | 23.6 | 7 | 29.2 | 20 | 25.3 |
| 3 | 14 | 25.5 | 3 | 12.5 | 17 | 21.5 |
| More than 3 | 11 | 20 | 3 | 12.5 | 14 | 17.7 |
| **Employment status** | | | | | | |
| Private sector | 7 | 12.7 | 10 | 41.7 | 17 | 21.5 |
| Public sector | 24 | 43.6 | 4 | 16.7 | 28 | 35.4 |
| Private business | 9 | 16.4 | 6 | 25 | 15 | 19 |
| Unemployed | 11 | 20 | 4 | 16.7 | 15 | 19 |
| Others | 4 | 7.3 | 0 | 0 | 4 | 5.1 |
| **Level of monthly income** | | | | | | |
| Less than LE 2000 | 18 | 35.3 | 10 | 41.7 | 28 | 37.3 |
| LE 2000- LE 5000 | 24 | 47.1 | 7 | 29.2 | 31 | 41.3 |
| LE 5000- LE 10000 | 3 | 5.9 | 7 | 29.2 | 10 | 13.3 |
| More than LE 10000 | 6 | 11.8 | 0 | 0 | 6 | 8 |

### 4.2.2 Chi- square analysis: Impact of demographic variables on customers' interest in buying new retail banking loan and saving services

In order to examine whether the above mentioned demographic variables have a significant influence over customers' interest in buying new retail banking loan and saving services, one sample chi- square analysis was found to be the most appropriate test. Chi- square is a non parametric measure of association that is used to assess the significance of the relationship between nominal data in cross tabulations. It could be used for one sample, two independent samples, or many independent samples. The test statistic is as follows:

$$X^2 = \sum_{i=1}^{K} \frac{(O_i - E_i)^2}{E_i}$$

Where $O_i$ is the observed number of cases in the *i*th category, $E_i$ is the expected number of cases in the *i*th category under H*0*, and k is the number of categories.

The null hypothesis that will be tested is as follows:
H*0*: "The demographic variables of (a) gender, (b) age, (c) level of education (d) marital status, (E) number of children, (F) employment status, and (G) level of income don't affect customers' interest in buying new retail banking loan and saving services"

The test was performed for loan and saving services separately. The results of the test are presented in table (6) and show the following:

#### Gender

The results of chi- square analysis reveal that gender has a significant impact on customers' interest in buying new retail banking loan services. It was not found to have a significant impact on their interest in buying new saving services. For loan services, males represent 64.5% of the sample, while they only represent 47.3% of uninterested respondents; on the other hand, females represent 35.5% of the sample while they represent 52.7% of uninterested respondents. This indicates that males are more interested in buying new retail banking loan services than females.

#### Age

Results reveal that age does not have a significant impact on customers' interest in buying new retail banking services. This result is valid for both loan and saving services.

**Level of education**

Results reveal that level of education does not have a significant impact on customers' interest in buying new retail banking services. This is valid for both new loan and new saving services.

**Marital status**

Marital status was not found to have a significant impact on customers' interest in buying new retail banking services. This is valid for both loan and saving services

**Number of children**

Number of children was found to have a significant impact on customers' interest in buying new retail banking loan services. However, it was not found to have a significant impact on their interest in buying new saving services. Although respondents with no children represent 42% of total sample, they represent only 16.4% of uninterested respondents; and although respondents with 3 or more children represent 32.6% of total sample, they represent 45.5% of uninterested respondents. This indicates that customers with no children are more interested in buying new loan services than customers with 3 children or more.

**Employment status**

Results reveal that Employment status has a significant impact on customers' interest in buying new retail banking loan services. However, it was not found to have a significant impact on their interest in buying new saving services. For loan services, privately employed respondents represent 31% of total sample and 12.7% of uninterested respondents; public sector employees represent 28.1% of total sample and 43.6% of uninterested respondents; respondents having their own private business represent 19.3% of the sample and 16.4% of uninterested respondents; and unemployed represent 11.7% of total sample and 20% of uninterested respondents. This indicates that private sector employees and private business owners are more interested in buying new loan services than public sector employees and unemployed people.

**Level of income**

Level of income was not found to have a significant impact on customer's interest in new retail banking services. This is valid for both loan and saving services.

**Summary of chi – square analysis**

In Summary, chi-square analysis reveals that, for new loan services, gender, number of children and employment status have a significant impact on customers' interest. For new saving services, none of the demographic variables tested have a significant impact on customers' interest.

**Table 6: Effect of demographic variables on customers' interest in buying new retail banking services: Chi- square analyses results**

| | Demographic variable | Chi- Square | Df* | P- value |
|---|---|---|---|---|
| **Loan services** | | | | |
| | Gender | 10.527 | 1 | 0.001** |
| | Age | 6.230 | 4 | 0.183 |
| | Level of education | 5.587 | 2 | 0.061 |
| | Marital status | 0.792 | 1 | 0.373 |
| | No. of children | 11.342 | 4 | 0.023** |
| | Employment status | 21.450 | 4 | 0.000** |
| | Level of income | 4.761 | 3 | 0.190 |
| **Saving services** | | | | |
| | Gender | 1.576 | 1 | 0.209 |
| | Age | 7.439 | 4 | 0.114 |
| | Level of education | 4.975 | 2 | 0.083 |
| | Marital status | 2.100 | 1 | 0.147 |
| | No. of children | 2.169 | 4 | 0.705 |
| | Employment status | 5.493 | 4 | 0.240 |
| | Level of Income | 7.310 | 3 | 0.063 |

*df = k-1

### 4.2.3 Logistic regression analysis: Predicting customers' interest in buying new retail banking loan and saving services from their demographic variables

In order to be able to predict the probability of customers' interest in buying new retail banking loan and saving services using their demographic variables, logistic regression analysis was performed. Logistic regression is a statistical tool used to predict a categorical variable, such as interest in buying new retail banking services, from a set of predictor variables that could be a mix of both continuous and categorical variables, such as customers' demographic variables (www2.chass.ncsu.edu/garson/PA765/logistic.htm.) To accomplish this, a model is created that includes all predictor variables that are useful in predicting the response variable. The regression model will be predicting the logit, that is, the natural log of the odds of having made one or the other decisions, that is

$$\ln(ODDS) = \ln\left(\frac{\hat{Y}}{1-\hat{Y}}\right) = a + bX$$

where $\hat{Y}$ is the predicted probability of being uninterested, $1-\hat{Y}$ is the predicted probability of the other decision (being interested), and X is the predictor variable.

The results of logistic regression for loan services as shown in table (7) reveal that the test that all slopes are zero is statistically significant with a p-value of 0.001. This indicates that the model is a good predictor of customers' interest in new loan services. Out of those variables, gender proved to have a significant partial effect with a p-value of 0.004, and an odds ratio of 0.3 indicating that, when holding all other variables constant, a man is 3.3 times more likely to be interested in buying a new loan service than a woman.

**Table 7: Logistic regression analysis results- loan services**

| **Predictor** | **Coefficient** | **p-value** | **Odds ratio** |
|---|---|---|---|
| Gender | -1.1876 | 0.004** | 0.30 |
| Age | 0.0988 | 0.655 | 1.10 |
| Education | 0.7781 | 0.051 | 2.18 |
| Marital | -1.1914 | 0.082 | 0.30 |
| Children | 0.4498 | 0.057 | 1.57 |
| Work | 0.0524 | 0.742 | 1.05 |
| Income | -0.1774 | 0.435 | 0.84 |

Test that all slopes are zero: G = 23.958; DF = 7; p-Value = 0.001

As for saving services, results of logistic regression as presented in table (8) confirm the findings of the chi square analysis that none of the demographic variables can predict customers' interest in new loan services. The test that all slopes are zero proved to be not significant indicating that the model is a poor predictor to customers' interest in new saving services.

**Table 8: Logistic regression analysis results- saving services**

| **Predictor** | **Coefficient** | **p-value** | **Odds ratio** |
|---|---|---|---|
| Gender | -0.4798 | 0.311 | 0.62 |
| Age | -0.3892 | 0.106 | 0.68 |
| Education | -1.1045 | 0.049 | 0.33 |
| Marital | -0.3333 | 0.673 | 0.72 |
| Children | 0.1269 | 0.625 | 1.14 |
| Work | -0.1424 | 0.454 | 0.87 |
| Income | 0.0859 | 0.742 | 1.09 |

Test that all slopes are zero: G = 11.671; DF = 7; p-Value = 0.112

### 4.2.4 Summary of demographic factors affecting customers' interest in new loan and saving services

In addition to the general typical profile of the respondents for both loan and saving services given above that indicates that they are typically males, at the age of 31-50, with a bachelor degree, married with two children, employed by the private sector and having a monthly income of LE 2000-5000; the following could be added based on our analysis of the effect of demographic variables on customers' interest in buying new retail banking services:

**For new loan services**, males would be three times as interested as females in a new loan service. They would typically be employed by the private sector or have their own business, and would have two or less children.

**For new saving services**, none of the above mentioned demographic variable proved to have a significant effect on customers' interest. Therefore, the above mentioned general profile of respondents applies to those interested in new savings services.

## 4.3 Factors affecting customers' decisions to buy new retail banking loan and saving services

There were 294 interested respondents in buying new retail banking services representing 79% of total sample, of which 117 were respondents for new loan services representing 68% of total loan respondents, and 177 were respondents for new saving services representing 88% of total saving respondents. Those respondents were asked to identify the degree of importance they attribute to the following factors when taking a decision to buy new loan or saving services.

a) **Service related factors:** (1) service uniqueness, (2) service sophistication, (3) pricing, (4) tenor, (5) liquidity, (6) service risk, (7) documentation required, (8) availability of information, and (9) previous positive experience with new retail banking services.

b) **Bank related factors:** (1) bank performance, (2) service quality, (3) convenience, (4) availability of a wide range of other services, (5) availability of technologically advanced services, (6) performance of previous services, (7) bank reputation, (8) previous positive experience with the bank, and (9) ownership/ nationality of the bank.

c) **Environment related factors:** (1) level of competition, (2) overall performance of the banking sector, (3) country Economic performance, (4) legal stability, and (5) political stability.

### 4.3.1 Frequency distribution and descriptive statistics

Frequency distribution and descriptive statistics for the data revealed the following results:

**a) Service related factors**

Frequency distribution and descriptive statistics for service related factors are presented in table (9) for loan services and table (10) for saving services

**1- Service uniqueness**

Questions 1 and 2 were the questions measuring the degree of importance that customers attribute to the uniqueness of the service in terms of its offering of new advantages or fulfillment of unsatisfied needs that no other service fulfils in the market. Frequency distribution analysis indicates that for both loan and saving services, more than 85% of respondents consider this factor either "1 = extremely important" or "2= important" with a mean of 1.62 for loan services and 1.67 for saving services. The variation of customers' response to the importance of this factor is higher in saving service than in loan services.

**2- Service sophistication**

Questions 3 and 4 were the questions measuring the degree of importance that customers attribute to the level of service sophistication in terms of familiarity of service type and easily understood service features. More than 90% of customers considered easily understood service features as either "1 = extremely important" or "2= important" for both loan and saving services with slightly less importance attributed to familiarity of service type in both services. The mean for this factor is 1.62 for loan services and 1.71 for saving services with less variability in loan services. This reflects customers' concern about knowing all service details and features in loan services as they are relatively new in the market which further adds to their risky nature.

**3- Pricing**

Questions 5 -7 were the questions related to the importance that customers attribute to the factor of pricing in terms of competitive interest (debit or credit) relative to the market, competitive service fees, and stability of interest and commission rates. The majority of customers in both loan and saving services considered this factor as "1 = extremely important" with competitiveness of interest rate considered extremely important by a higher percentage of customers for both services. The mean for this factor is 1.37 for loan services vs. 1.56 for saving services with lower variability in customers' response for loan services.

### 4- Tenor

The majority of respondents considered the flexibility of deciding on saving service tenor as "1 = extremely important" with a mean of 1.5 and low variability of response. On the other hand, the mean of having flexible repayment tenors for loan services was 1.9 with much higher variability of responses. This might be attributed to the higher variation of purposes that saving services are used to, while loans are granted for usually only one purpose with repayment tenor specifically tailored to satisfy this purpose.

### 5- Liquidity

Questions 9 and 10 are the questions measuring the importance that customers attribute the new service's liquidity. Liquidity, for both loan and saving services, is measured in terms of ability to increase or decrease service amount without restrictions or extra costs. The majority of respondents considered this factor as "1 = extremely important" for both loan and saving service. However, the mean for loan services (1.44) is lower than that for saving services (1.56). This is mainly attributed to the fact that 72% of respondents considered the option for loan prepayment without extra fees as extremely important. Variability of response to this item was also lower than all other questions.

### 6- Service risk

Questions 11 and 12 were the questions concerned with measuring the importance that respondents attribute to the new service risk in terms of expected consequences of service failure and level of guarantees provided from the bank for saving services, and consequences of default and level of guarantees provided to the bank for loan services. Importance attributed to this factor is much higher in saving services with majority of respondents considering it as extremely important and with less variability than in loan services. This is specifically true for the level of guarantees required that 74% of respondents regarded as extremely important for saving services compared to 44% for loan services. Overall, factor mean for saving services is 1.43 as compared to 1.78 for loan services. This may be attributed to the fact that in loan services, risk is pre calculated and controlled to a great extent by the customer himself and is usually limited to the loss of guarantees. On the other hand, in saving services, customers do not control the outcome and are usually not provided with enough guarantees from the bank.

### 7- Documentation

Questions 13 and 14 were the questions measuring the importance that customers attribute to the amount and legal responsibility of the documentation they have to sign in order to get the service. The majority of respondents for loan and saving services considered this factors either "1 = extremely important" or "2 = important" with a mean of 1.64 for loan services and 1.75 for saving services. More respondents consider the legal responsibility of loan documents as extremely important as banks sometimes exaggerate in their documentation requirements to guarantee their rights. This might reach the degree of making customers sign blank checks to be kept with the bank till full repayment.

### 8- Availability of information

Questions 15 through 17 were concerned with the importance attributed to the availability of information about the new service. This is measured in terms of availability of informative advertising through different media, availability of brochures and printed material, and direct selling effort. Although the majority of respondents considered this factor as either "1 = extremely important" or "2 = important" for both loan and saving services, factor mean was 1.82 for loan services and 1.94 for saving services. The higher importance attributed to this factor by loan respondents agree with the importance they attribute to understanding service features.

### 9- Positive experience with new services

The majority of respondents considered this factor as "2 = important" with a mean of 2.1 for loan services and 2.0 for saving services, and with high variability in response for both services.

### b) Bank related factors

Frequency distribution and descriptive statistics for bank related factors are presented in table (11) for loan services and table (12) for saving services and show the following results:

### 1- Bank performance

Questions 19 through 21 were the questions measuring the importance that respondents attribute to the performance of the offering bank in terms of solid market share, strong financial position and growing profitability. The majority of respondents considered this factor as either "1 = extremely important" or "2 = important" with higher importance attributed and lower variability of answers in saving than loan services. The mean for this factor is 1.71 for saving services compared to 2.01 for loan services. This higher importance attributed to this factor in saving services might be justified by the fact that customers consider the bank's satisfactory performance as a signal that they can trust it with their money. For loan services, however, customers would not need this trust as much, so they would not care a lot about bank performance.

**2- Service quality**

Questions 22 to 24 were concerned with the importance that customers attribute to service quality in terms of staff friendliness and helpfulness, accuracy of transactions, and prompt services. The majority of respondents considered this factors as "1 = extremely important" with a mean of 1.34 for loan services and 1.31 for saving services and with low variability of answers.

**3- Convenience**

Questions 25 through 28 where the questions measuring the importance of convenience in terms of extended opening hours, and location and network of branches and ATMs. The majority of respondents considered this factor as "1 = extremely important" for both loan and saving services with a mean of 1.57 for loan services and 1.62 for saving services. Network of ATMs was considered particularly important in saving services with a slightly higher variability in answers. This might be attributed to the higher frequency of using ATM machines in saving services to withdraw interest, check balance, or carry out any other transaction.

**4- Availability of other services**

Although most of the respondents considered the availability of a wide range of other services as either "1 = extremely important" or "2 = important", the mean for this factor was 1.89 for loan services and 2.05 for saving services. This relatively lower importance attributed to the other services offered by the bank is justifiable given the expansion of the satellite service strategy that allows customers to buy the banking service without having even to open an account. This made customers look at each service on a stand alone basis without considering the other services offered by the same bank

**5- Availability of technologically advanced services**

Although most of the respondents considered the availability of technologically advanced services such as internet and mobile banking as either "1 =

extremely important" or "2 = important", the mean for this factor was 1.94 for loan services and 2.14 for saving services with a high variability in answers. This relatively lower importance might be a result of the novelty of such services and their still low penetration rate in the market.

**6- Performance of previous services**

Satisfactory performance of previous services introduced by the same bank was considered either "1 = extremely important" or "2 = important" by the majority of respondents. The mean for this factor was 1.85 for loan services and 1.77 for saving services with almost the same degree of variability in answers for both services.

**7- Bank reputation**

Questions 32 and 33 were the questions measuring the importance that customers attribute to bank's reputation in terms of bank's brand name and its stability and continuity in the market. More than 70% of the customers considered this factor as "1 = extremely important" for saving services compared to only around 57% for loan services. The mean for this factor is 1.34 for saving services compared to 1.55 for loan services with higher variability of response for loan. This might be attributed to the fact that, again, when customers deposit their money with a bank, they need to trust this bank. A solid reputation, a strong brand name, and market continuity all signal a trustworthy bank. For loan services, this trust is not as important as customers do not face the risk of losing their money.

**8- Previous positive experience with the bank**

Although the majority of respondents considered this factor as either "1 = extremely important" or "2 = important" for both loan and saving services, it was attributed greater importance with a mean of 1.72 for saving services than for loan services with its mean of 1.93. This goes back again to the trust and assurance that customers need to have in the banks in which they will deposit their money.

**9- Ownership/ nationality of the bank**

Ownership/ nationality of the offering bank are again associated with the level of trust that customers have for different banks. That is why this factor was considered more important in saving services with a mean of 1.87 than in loan service with a mean of 2.16. Variability of responses was also much higher in loan services. When asked to state which type of banks they prefer to deal with, those customers who consider this factor as either "1 = extremely important" or "2 = important" had different preference for loan than saving services. For loan services, 53% preferred public sector banks, 36% preferred joint venture and private sector banks, and 9% preferred foreign branches. For saving services, 66.5% preferred public sector banks, 23.5% preferred private sector and joint venture banks, and 10% preferred foreign branches. The higher preference for public sector banks in saving services goes back again to customers' trust in government owned institutions than private or foreign ones.

**c) Environment Related Factor**

Frequency distribution and descriptive statistics for environment related factors are presented in table (13) for loan services and table (14) for saving services and show the following results:

**1- Competition**

Questions 36 and 37 were concerned with measuring the degree of importance that customers attribute to the availability of other substitute and competitive services when taking a decision to buy new retail banking loan and saving services. The majority of respondents considered this factor either "2 = important" or "3 = neutral" with a mean of 2.3 for loan services and 2.4 for saving services and with a high variability of answers for both.

**2- Performance of the banking sector**

Questions 38 and 39 were the questions measuring the importance that customers attribute to the overall performance of the banking sector in terms of growth and profitability. Although the majority of respondents considered this factor as either "1 = extremely important" or "2 = important" for both loan and saving services, factor mean for loan services is 2.07 and for saving services is 1.77. This indicates that customers of saving services consider the current performance of the sector as an indication of future performance, and thus, if the sector is growing and facing no problems, this trend is most likely to continue in the future, and the new service is more likely to succeed.

**3- Country economic performance**

Questions 40 through 43 are the questions measuring the importance that customers attribute to the overall economic performance of the country in terms of overall economic condition, positive forecasts, and stability of interest and exchange rates. The majority of respondents considered this factor as either "1 = extremely important" or "2 = important" with a mean of 1.84 for loan services and 1.72 for saving services.

**4- Legal stability**

Questions 44 and 45 were measuring the importance that customers attribute to the legal stability in terms of the stability of economic and banking policies and laws. The majority of respondents for both loan and saving services considered this factor as extremely important with a mean of 1.65 for loan services and 1.62 for saving services.

**5- Political stability**

Questions 46 and 47 were concerned with the importance that customers attribute to the internal and external political stability. The majority of respondents considered this factor as extremely important with a mean of 1.40 for saving services as compared to 1.59 for loan services. This indicates that although customers of both saving and loan services consider the absence of internal or external political turbulence as an extremely important prerequisite for trying a new service, saving customers who are more threatened with the risk of losing their money when they actually need it, give it even more importance than loan customers.

### 4.3.2 One sample t- test: Identifying important factors affecting customers' decisions to buy new retail banking loan and saving services

In order to determine whether the factors under study are considered important for customers when taking the decision to buy new loan and saving services, a one sample t -test was performed. The null hypothesis that will be tested is that customers do not consider the following factors as important ($H_0$: $\mu>2$), versus the alternative hypothesis that they do consider them important ($H_1$:$\mu$=2).

a) **Service related factors:** (1) service uniqueness, (2) service sophistication, (3) pricing, (4) tenor, (5) liquidity, (6) service risk, (7) documentation required, (8) availability of information, and (9) previous positive experience with new retail banking services.

b) **Bank related factors:** (1) bank performance, (2) service quality, (3) convenience, (4) availability of a wide range of other services, (5) availability of technologically advanced services, (6) performance of previous services, (7) bank reputation, (8) previous positive experience with the bank, and (9) ownership/ nationality of the bank.

**Table 9: Service related factors frequency and descriptive statistics- Loan services**

| Factor | item | Frequency | | | | | | | | | | Descriptive Statistics | | |
|---|---|---|---|---|---|---|---|---|---|---|---|---|---|---|
| | | 1 | % | 2 | % | 3 | % | 4 | % | 5 | % | Mean | S. D. | Factor mean |
| Uniqueness | Q1 | 63 | 53.8 | 37 | 31.6 | 14 | 12 | 3 | 2.6 | 0 | 0 | 1.63 | .794 | 1.62 |
| | Q2 | 57 | 48.7 | 51 | 43.6 | 8 | 6.8 | 1 | 0.9 | 0 | 0 | 1.60 | .657 | |
| Sophistication | Q3 | 68 | 58.1 | 38 | 32.5 | 10 | 8.5 | 1 | 0.9 | 0 | 0 | 1.52 | .690 | 1.62 |
| | Q4 | 56 | 47.9 | 44 | 37.6 | 12 | 10.3 | 4 | 3.4 | 1 | 0.9 | 1.72 | .849 | |
| Pricing | Q5 | 97 | 82.9 | 14 | 12.0 | 4 | 3.4 | 2 | 1.7 | 0 | 0 | 1.24 | .597 | 1.37 |
| | Q6 | 83 | 70.9 | 26 | 22.2 | 6 | 5.1 | 2 | 1.7 | 0 | 0 | 1.38 | .666 | |
| | Q7 | 79 | 67.5 | 24 | 20.5 | 9 | 7.7 | 4 | 3.4 | 1 | 0.9 | 1.5 | .847 | |
| Tenor | Q8 | 54 | 46.2 | 33 | 28.2 | 20 | 17.1 | 8 | 6.8 | 2 | 1.7 | 1.9 | 1.029 | 1.9 |
| Liquidity | Q9 | 75 | 64.1 | 27 | 23.1 | 9 | 7.7 | 6 | 5.1 | 0 | 0 | 1.54 | .846 | 1.44 |
| | Q10 | 85 | 72.6 | 26 | 22.2 | 5 | 4.3 | 1 | 0.9 | 0 | 0 | 1.33 | .602 | |
| Risk | Q11 | 62 | 53 | 33 | 28.2 | 16 | 13.7 | 4 | 3.4 | 2 | 1.7 | 1.73 | .943 | 1.78 |
| | Q12 | 51 | 43.6 | 43 | 36.8 | 16 | 13.7 | 5 | 4.3 | 2 | 1.7 | 1.84 | .937 | |
| Documentation | Q13 | 55 | 47 | 39 | 33.3 | 19 | 16.2 | 4 | 3.4 | 0 | 0 | 1.76 | .847 | 1.64 |
| | Q14 | 77 | 65.8 | 26 | 22.2 | 9 | 7.7 | 4 | 3.4 | 1 | 0.9 | 1.51 | .847 | |
| Information | Q15 | 54 | 46.2 | 42 | 35.9 | 13 | 11.1 | 6 | 5.1 | 2 | 1.7 | 1.8 | .949 | 1.82 |
| | Q16 | 61 | 52.1 | 38 | 32.5 | 14 | 12 | 3 | 2.6 | 1 | 0.9 | 1.68 | .849 | |
| | Q17 | 53 | 45.3 | 35 | 29.9 | 14 | 12 | 11 | 9.4 | 4 | 3.4 | 1.96 | 1.125 | |
| P. experience | Q18 | 40 | 34.2 | 45 | 38.5 | 18 | 15.4 | 9 | 7.7 | 5 | 4.3 | 2.09 | 1.091 | 2.1 |

1= Extremely important 2= Important 3= Neutral 4 =Not important 5= Not important at all

**Table 10: Service related factors frequency and descriptive statistics- Saving services**

| Factor | item | Frequency | | | | | | | | | | Descriptive Statistics | | |
|---|---|---|---|---|---|---|---|---|---|---|---|---|---|---|
| | | 1 | % | 2 | % | 3 | % | 4 | % | 5 | % | Mean | S. D. | Factor mean |
| Uniqueness | Q1 | 96 | 54.2 | 59 | 33.3 | 18 | 10.2 | 2 | 1.1 | 2 | 1.1 | 1.62 | .804 | 1.67 |
| | Q2 | 81 | 45.8 | 72 | 40.7 | 18 | 10.2 | 3 | 1.7 | 3 | 1.7 | 1.73 | .843 | |
| Sophistication | Q3 | 99 | 55.9 | 63 | 35.6 | 11 | 6.2 | 3 | 1.7 | 1 | 0.6 | 1.55 | .738 | 1.71 |
| | Q4 | 73 | 41.2 | 68 | 38.4 | 25 | 14.1 | 8 | 4.5 | 3 | 1.7 | 1.87 | .935 | |
| Pricing | Q5 | 138 | 78.0 | 30 | 16.9 | 7 | 4.0 | 2 | 1.1 | 0 | 0 | 1.28 | .593 | 1.56 |
| | Q6 | 98 | 55.4 | 49 | 27.7 | 15 | 8.5 | 9 | 5.1 | 6 | 3.4 | 1.73 | 1.040 | |
| | Q7 | 104 | 58.8 | 43 | 24.3 | 18 | 10.2 | 7 | 4.0 | 5 | 2.8 | 1.68 | 1.002 | |
| Tenor | Q8 | 102 | 57.6 | 63 | 35.6 | 10 | 5.6 | 2 | 1.1 | 0 | 0 | 1.50 | .658 | 1.50 |
| Liquidity | Q9 | 106 | 59.9 | 55 | 32.1 | 9 | 5.1 | 7 | 4.0 | 0 | 0 | 1.53 | .769 | 1.56 |
| | Q10 | 105 | 59.3 | 49 | 27.7 | 16 | 9.0 | 4 | 2.3 | 3 | 1.7 | 1.59 | .875 | |
| Risk | Q11 | 113 | 63.8 | 49 | 27.7 | 10 | 5.6 | 3 | 1.7 | 2 | 1.1 | 1.49 | .777 | 1.43 |
| | Q12 | 132 | 74.6 | 29 | 16.4 | 11 | 6.2 | 3 | 1.7 | 2 | 1.1 | 1.38 | .776 | |
| Documentation | Q13 | 80 | 45.2 | 56 | 31.6 | 27 | 15.3 | 10 | 5.6 | 4 | 2.3 | 1.88 | 1.013 | 1.75 |
| | Q14 | 102 | 57.6 | 49 | 27.7 | 20 | 11.3 | 2 | 1.1 | 4 | 2.3 | 1.63 | .896 | |
| Information | Q15 | 82 | 46.3 | 55 | 31.1 | 26 | 14.7 | 11 | 6.2 | 3 | 1.7 | 1.86 | .998 | 1.94 |
| | Q16 | 82 | 46.3 | 62 | 35 | 20 | 11.3 | 11 | 6.2 | 2 | 1.1 | 1.81 | .946 | |
| | Q17 | 63 | 35.6 | 56 | 31.6 | 34 | 19.2 | 15 | 8.5 | 9 | 5.1 | 2.16 | 1.152 | |
| P. experience | Q18 | 67 | 37.9 | 64 | 36.2 | 30 | 16.9 | 11 | 6.2 | 5 | 2.8 | 2.00 | 1.028 | 2.0 |

1= Extremely important 2= Important 3= Neutral 4 =Not important 5= Not important at all

**Table 11: Bank related factors frequency and descriptive statistics – Loan services**

| Factor | item | Frequency | | | | | | | | | | Descriptive Statistics | | |
|---|---|---|---|---|---|---|---|---|---|---|---|---|---|---|
| | | 1 | % | 2 | % | 3 | % | 4 | % | 5 | % | Mean | S. D. | Factor mean |
| Bank performance | Q19 | 39 | 33.3 | 36 | 30.8 | 27 | 23.1 | 13 | 11.1 | 2 | 1.7 | 2.17 | 1.07 | 2.01 |
| | Q20 | 54 | 46.2 | 35 | 29.9 | 19 | 16.2 | 7 | 6.0 | 2 | 1.7 | 1.87 | 1.01 | |
| | Q21 | 47 | 40.2 | 35 | 29.9 | 23 | 19.7 | 8 | 6.8 | 4 | 3.4 | 2.03 | 1.09 | |
| Service quality | Q22 | 82 | 70.1 | 30 | 25.6 | 3 | 2.6 | 1 | 0.9 | 1 | 0.9 | 1.37 | .664 | 1.34 |
| | Q23 | 80 | 69 | 31 | 26.7 | 4 | 3.4 | 1 | 0.9 | 0 | 0 | 1.37 | .640 | |
| | Q24 | 86 | 73.5 | 26 | 22.2 | 4 | 3.4 | 0 | 0 | 1 | 0.9 | 1.32 | .627 | |
| Convenience | Q25 | 67 | 57.3 | 30 | 25.6 | 18 | 15.4 | 2 | 1.7 | 0 | 0 | 1.62 | .808 | 1.57 |
| | Q26 | 67 | 57.3 | 34 | 29.1 | 13 | 11.1 | 3 | 2.6 | 0 | 0 | 1.59 | .790 | |
| | Q27 | 66 | 56.4 | 36 | 30.8 | 12 | 10.3 | 3 | 2.6 | 0 | 0 | 1.59 | .779 | |
| | Q28 | 68 | 58.1 | 39 | 33.3 | 6 | 5.1 | 2 | 1.7 | 2 | 1.7 | 1.56 | .814 | |
| Range of services | Q29 | 36 | 30.8 | 49 | 41.9 | 23 | 19.7 | 7 | 6.0 | 2 | 1.7 | 2.06 | .950 | 2.05 |
| Technological services | Q30 | 48 | 41 | 39 | 33.3 | 20 | 17.1 | 7 | 6.0 | 3 | 2.6 | 1.96 | 1.03 | 1.94 |
| Performance of previous services | Q31 | 45 | 38.5 | 48 | 41 | 20 | 17.1 | 3 | 2.6 | 1 | 0.9 | 1.86 | .850 | 1.85 |
| Reputation | Q32 | 68 | 58.1 | 39 | 33.3 | 7 | 6.0 | 1 | 0.9 | 2 | 1.7 | 1.55 | .793 | 1.55 |
| | Q33 | 66 | 56.4 | 41 | 35 | 5 | 4.3 | 3 | 2.6 | 2 | 1.7 | 1.58 | .833 | |
| P. experience | Q34 | 45 | 38.5 | 45 | 38.5 | 19 | 16.2 | 5 | 4.3 | 3 | 2.6 | 1.94 | .976 | 1.93 |
| Ownership/nation | Q35 | 46 | 39.3 | 28 | 23.9 | 26 | 22.2 | 11 | 9.4 | 6 | 5.1 | 2.17 | 1.20 | 2.16 |

| | | | | | | | | | |
|---|---|---|---|---|---|---|---|---|---|
| Preferred type of bank | Public sector | 39 | 53% | J.V.s & private sector | 26 | 36% | Branches of foreign banks | 7 | 9% |

1= Extremely important 2= Important 3= Neutral 4 =Not important 5= Not important at all

**Table 12: Bank related factors frequency and descriptive statistics – Saving services**

| Factor | item | Frequency | | | | | | | | | | Descriptive Statistics | | |
|---|---|---|---|---|---|---|---|---|---|---|---|---|---|---|
| | | 1 | % | 2 | % | 3 | % | 4 | % | 5 | % | Mean | S. D. | Factor mean |
| Bank performance | Q19 | 78 | 44.1 | 53 | 29.9 | 31 | 17.5 | 11 | 6.2 | 4 | 2.3 | 1.93 | 1.03 | 1.71 |
| | Q20 | 117 | 66.1 | 31 | 17.5 | 19 | 10.7 | 9 | 5.1 | 1 | 0.6 | 1.56 | .915 | |
| | Q21 | 102 | 57.6 | 45 | 25.4 | 23 | 13 | 4 | 2.3 | 3 | 1.7 | 1.65 | .912 | |
| Service quality | Q22 | 124 | 70.1 | 44 | 24.9 | 6 | 3.4 | 2 | 1.1 | 1 | 0.6 | 1.37 | .663 | 1.31 |
| | Q23 | 133 | 75.1 | 38 | 21.5 | 6 | 3.4 | 0 | 0 | 0 | 0 | 1.28 | .522 | |
| | Q24 | 142 | 80.7 | 27 | 15.3 | 4 | 2.3 | 1 | 0.6 | 2 | 1.1 | 1.26 | .641 | |
| Convenience | Q25 | 95 | 53.7 | 58 | 32.8 | 17 | 9.6 | 4 | 2.3 | 3 | 1.7 | 1.66 | .872 | 1.62 |
| | Q26 | 93 | 52.5 | 65 | 36.7 | 15 | 8.5 | 3 | 1.7 | 1 | 0.6 | 1.61 | .762 | |
| | Q27 | 85 | 48 | 74 | 41.8 | 15 | 8.5 | 2 | 1.1 | 1 | 0.6 | 1.64 | .733 | |
| | Q28 | 115 | 65.3 | 36 | 20.5 | 15 | 8.5 | 8 | 4.5 | 2 | 1.1 | 1.56 | .912 | |
| Range of services | Q29 | 67 | 37.9 | 71 | 40.1 | 31 | 17.5 | 7 | 4 | 1 | 0.6 | 1.89 | .869 | 1.89 |
| Technological services | Q30 | 67 | 37.9 | 51 | 28.8 | 32 | 18.1 | 21 | 11.9 | 6 | 3.4 | 2.14 | 1.15 | 2.14 |
| Performance of previous services | Q31 | 74 | 41.8 | 74 | 41.8 | 24 | 13.6 | 4 | 2.3 | 1 | 0.6 | 1.78 | .806 | 1.78 |
| Reputation | Q32 | 124 | 70.1 | 45 | 25.4 | 6 | 3.4 | 1 | 0.6 | 1 | 0.6 | 1.36 | .635 | 1.34 |
| | Q33 | 131 | 74 | 38 | 21.5 | 5 | 2.8 | 2 | 1.1 | 1 | 0.6 | 1.33 | .644 | |
| P. experience | Q34 | 79 | 44.6 | 77 | 43.5 | 14 | 7.9 | 5 | 2.8 | 2 | 1.1 | 1.72 | .817 | 1.72 |
| Ownership/nation | Q35 | 92 | 52 | 40 | 22.6 | 28 | 15.8 | 10 | 5.6 | 7 | 4.0 | 1.87 | 1.12 | 1.87 |

| | | | | | | | | | |
|---|---|---|---|---|---|---|---|---|---|
| Preferred type of bank | Public sector | 88 | 66.5 | J.Vs & private sector | 31 | 23.5 | Branches of foreign banks | 13 | 10 |

1= Extremely important 2= Important 3= Neutral 4 =Not important 5= Not important at all

**Table 13: Environment related factors frequency and descriptive statistics- Loan services**

| Factor | item | Frequency | | | | | | | | | | Descriptive Statistics | | |
|---|---|---|---|---|---|---|---|---|---|---|---|---|---|---|
| | | 1 | % | 2 | % | 3 | % | 4 | % | 5 | % | Mean | S. D. | Factor mean |
| Competition | Q36 | 30 | 25.6 | 48 | 41 | 23 | 19.7 | 11 | 9.4 | 5 | 4.3 | 2.26 | 1.08 | 2.3103 |
| | Q37 | 26 | 22.2 | 47 | 40.2 | 24 | 20.5 | 16 | 13.7 | 4 | 3.4 | 2.36 | 1.08 | |
| Performance of the banking sector | Q38 | 38 | 32.5 | 42 | 35.9 | 32 | 27.4 | 1 | 0.9 | 4 | 3.4 | 2.07 | .971 | 2.0733 |
| | Q39 | 39 | 33.3 | 42 | 35.9 | 27 | 23.1 | 6 | 5.1 | 3 | 2.6 | 2.08 | 1.00 | |
| Country Economic performance | Q41 | 50 | 42.7 | 36 | 30.8 | 24 | 20.5 | 4 | 3.4 | 3 | 2.6 | 1.92 | 1.00 | 1.8448 |
| | Q41 | 38 | 32.5 | 44 | 37.6 | 28 | 23.9 | 4 | 3.4 | 3 | 2.6 | 2.06 | .967 | |
| | Q42 | 59 | 50.4 | 33 | 28.2 | 19 | 16.2 | 2 | 1.7 | 4 | 3.4 | 1.79 | 1.00 | |
| | Q43 | 64 | 54.7 | 41 | 35 | 9 | 7.7 | 0 | 0 | 3 | 2.6 | 1.61 | .840 | |
| Legal stability | Q44 | 67 | 57.3 | 25 | 21.4 | 22 | 18.8 | 1 | 0.9 | 2 | 1.7 | 1.68 | .925 | 1.6552 |
| | Q45 | 64 | 54.7 | 35 | 29.9 | 16 | 13.7 | 1 | 0.9 | 1 | 0.9 | 1.63 | .816 | |
| Political stability | Q46 | 77 | 65.8 | 22 | 18.8 | 11 | 9.4 | 3 | 2.6 | 4 | 3.4 | 1.59 | 1.00 | 1.5948 |
| | Q47 | 78 | 66.7 | 20 | 17.1 | 11 | 9.4 | 3 | 2.6 | 5 | 4.3 | 1.61 | 1.05 | |

1= Extremely important 2= Important 3= Neutral 4 =Not important 5= Not important at all

**Table 14: Environment related factors frequency and descriptive statistics- Saving services**

| Factor | item | Frequency | | | | | | | | | | Descriptive Statistics | | |
|---|---|---|---|---|---|---|---|---|---|---|---|---|---|---|
| | | 1 | % | 2 | % | 3 | % | 4 | % | 5 | % | Mean | S. D. | Factor mean |
| Competition | Q36 | 52 | 29.4 | 54 | 30.5 | 52 | 29.4 | 10 | 5.6 | 9 | 5.1 | 2.27 | 1.01 | 2.4068 |
| | Q37 | 42 | 23.7 | 42 | 23.7 | 58 | 32.8 | 24 | 13.6 | 11 | 6.2 | 2.55 | 1.17 | |
| Performance of the banking sector | Q38 | 77 | 43.5 | 64 | 36.2 | 34 | 19.2 | 2 | 1.1 | 0 | 0 | 1.78 | .792 | 1.7712 |
| | Q39 | 80 | 45.2 | 64 | 36.2 | 28 | 15.8 | 5 | 2.8 | 0 | 0 | 1.76 | .819 | |
| Country Economic performance | Q41 | 84 | 47.5 | 56 | 31.6 | 32 | 18.1 | 3 | 1.7 | 2 | 1.1 | 1.77 | .882 | 1.7218 |
| | Q41 | 78 | 44.1 | 61 | 34.5 | 35 | 19.8 | 2 | 1.1 | 1 | 0.6 | 1.80 | .835 | |
| | Q42 | 80 | 45.2 | 69 | 39 | 18 | 10.2 | 8 | 4.5 | 2 | 1.1 | 1.77 | .889 | |
| | Q43 | 110 | 62.1 | 46 | 26 | 14 | 7.9 | 6 | 3.4 | 1 | 0.6 | 1.54 | .825 | |
| Legal stability | Q44 | 97 | 55.1 | 51 | 29 | 25 | 14.2 | 2 | 1.1 | 1 | 0.6 | 1.63 | .811 | 1.6222 |
| | Q45 | 94 | 53.1 | 62 | 35 | 17 | 9.6 | 4 | 2.3 | 0 | 0 | 1.61 | .754 | |
| Political stability | Q46 | 124 | 70.1 | 36 | 20.3 | 15 | 8.5 | 2 | 1.1 | 0 | 0 | 1.41 | .694 | 1.4040 |
| | Q47 | 126 | 71.2 | 34 | 19.2 | 14 | 7.9 | 3 | 1.7 | 0 | 0 | 1.40 | .709 | |

1= Extremely important 2= Important 3= Neutral 4 =Not important 5= Not important at all

c) **Environment related factors:** (1) level of competition, (2) overall performance of the banking sector, (3) country Economic performance, (4) legal stability, and (5) political stability.

The test statistic is as follows:

$$t = \frac{\overline{X} - \mu}{S/\sqrt{n}}$$

Where $\overline{X}$ is the sample mean, $\mu$ is the hypothesized mean , $n$ is the sample size, and S is the sample standard deviation

The results of the test as presented in table (15) for both loan and saving services indicate the following:

**New retail banking loan services**

For loan services, all the above mentioned factors proved to be important except market competition with a mean of 2.3 (i.e. significantly >2). This indicates that when considering a new retail banking loan service, customers do not consider available alternatives or substitutes. This could be justified by the sophistication of retail banking services, their special characteristics mentioned earlier, and the multiple factors involved in the decision, and that all combine to make the decision process for each service lengthy and taken on a stand alone basis without regarding what other competing services are offered in the market.

**New retail banking saving services**

For saving services, all the above mentioned factors proved to be important except the availability of technological services with a mean of 2.14 and market competition with a mean of 2.4 (i.e. significantly >2). The lack of importance attributed to the availability of technological services could be justified by their relative novelty in the market and still lower penetration rates. This is particularly true for saving services given the profile of interested customers in new saving services vs. that of interested customers of new loan services who are more likely to be among the early adopters of technological services as they are mainly males with fewer obligations and employed by institutions that are more likely to use advanced technologies. The lack of importance attributed to competition is due to the same reasons mentioned above for new loan services.

**Table 15: One-sample t-test analysis - Testing for the importance attributed to different factors**

| Factors | Loan services | | Saving services | |
|---|---|---|---|---|
| | T-test | p-value | T-test | p-value |
| Uniqueness | -6.58 | 1.000 | -5.89 | 1.000 |
| Sophistication | -6.04 | 1.000 | -5.68 | 1.000 |
| Pricing | -12.48 | 1.000 | -9.11 | 1.000 |
| Tenor | -0.99 | 0.838 | -10.05 | 1.000 |
| Liquidity | -10.22 | 1.000 | -8.70 | 1.000 |
| Risk | -3.01 | 0.998 | -11.79 | 1.000 |
| Documentation | -5.71 | 1.000 | -3.85 | 1.000 |
| Information | -2.43 | 0.992 | -0.99 | 0.839 |
| P. experience | 1.02 | 0.155 | 0.00 | 0.500 |
| **Service related factors** | -9.16 | 1.000 | -10.46 | 1.000 |
| Bank Performance | 0.19 | 0.424 | -4.52 | 1.000 |
| Service quality | -12.78 | 1.000 | -17.62 | 1.000 |
| Convenience | -7.94 | 1.000 | -8.61 | 1.000 |
| Range of services | 0.59 | 0.279 | -1.64 | 0.949 |
| Technological services | -0.54 | 0.705 | 1.63 | 0.052 |
| Performance of previous services | -1.86 | 0.968 | -3.64 | 1.000 |
| Reputation | -6.22 | 1.000 | -14.63 | 1.000 |
| P. experience | -0.76 | 0.776 | -4.51 | 1.000 |
| Ownership/nationality | 1.47 | 0.072 | -1.55 | 0.938 |
| **Bank related factors** | -5.27 | 1.000 | -10.96 | 1.000 |
| Competition | 3.44 | 0.000 | 5.36 | 0.000 |
| Performance of the banking sector | 0.89 | 0.188 | -4.29 | 1.000 |
| Country economic performance | -2.13 | 0.982 | -5.50 | 1.000 |
| Legal stability | -4.49 | 1.000 | -6.95 | 1.000 |
| Political stability | -4.34 | 1.000 | -11.92 | 1.000 |
| **Environment related factors** | -1.80 | 0.963 | -5.40 | 1.000 |

### 4.3.3 Two sample t- test: Difference in importance attributed to different factors between loan and saving Services

In order to examine whether there is a significant difference between the importance attributed to different service, bank, and environment related factors in loan Vs. saving services, a two sample t- test is carried out as a first step before determining the differentiating factors through discriminant analysis. To test the null hypothesis H*0*: $\mu 1 = \mu 2$, the two sample t-test statistic is as follows:

$$t' = (\overline{X}_1 - \overline{X}_2) / \sqrt{\frac{S_1^2}{n_1} + \frac{S_2^2}{n_2}}$$

Where $\overline{X}_1$ and $\overline{X}_2$ are the sample mean of the related factor in loan and saving services, respectively and $S_1^2$ and $S_2^2$ are their sample variances
The results for the two sample t – test are presented in Table (16) and indicate the following:

**a) Service related factors**

Results reveal that there is no significant difference between loan and saving services in the importance attributed to service uniqueness, service sophistication, liquidity, required documentation, availability of information, and previous positive experience with new services.

A significant difference was found between loan and saving services in the importance that customers attribute to pricing with a p-value of 0.006, tenor with a p-value of 0.000, and service risk with a p-value of 0.000. Given the mean importance of these factors presented earlier, these results indicate that the importance attributed to pricing in new loan services is significantly higher than that attributed to pricing in new saving services. They also indicated that the importance attributed to tenor and service risk in new saving services is significantly higher than the importance attributed to the same factors in new loan services.

**b) Bank related factors**

Results reveal that there is no significant difference between loan and saving services in the importance attributed to service quality, convenience, availability of a wide range of other services, availability of technologically advanced services, performance of previous services, and previous positive experience with the bank.

On the other hand, a significant difference between loan and saving services was found in the importance attributed to bank performance with a p-value of 0.006, bank reputation with a p-value of 0.015, and ownership/ nationality of bank with a p-value of 0.036. Given the mean importance of these factors presented earlier, these results indicate that the importance attributed to bank performance, bank reputation, and ownership/nationality of the bank is significantly higher in new saving services than the importance attributed to the same factors in new loan services.

## c) Environment related factors

Results reveal that there is no significant difference between loan and saving services in the importance attributed to competition, country economic performance, legal stability, and political stability

The only environmental factor that was found to have a significant difference between loan and saving services is the performance of the banking sector with a p-value of 0.002. Given the mean importance of this factor presented earlier, this result indicates that the importance attributed to the performance of the banking sector in new saving services is significantly higher than the importance attributed to the same factor in new loan services.

**Table 16: Two-sample t-test results: Difference in importance attributed to different factors in new loan vs. new saving services**

| Factors | t-test | Degrees of freedom | p-value |
|---|---|---|---|
| Uniqueness | -0.64 | 273 | 0.520 |
| Sophistication | -1.08 | 247 | 0.280 |
| Pricing | -2.76 | 271 | 0.006 |
| Tenor | 3.74 | 176 | 0.000 |
| Liquidity | -1.65 | 266 | 0.101 |
| Risk | 4.17 | 216 | 0.000 |
| Documentation | -1.25 | 280 | 0.212 |
| Information | -1.29 | 241 | 0.198 |
| P. Experience | 0.81 | 235 | 0.417 |
| **Service related factors** | **-0.55** | **245** | **0.585** |
| Bank Performance | 2.77 | 222 | 0.006 |
| Service quality | 0.54 | 233 | 0.587 |
| Convenience | -0.63 | 249 | 0.528 |
| Range of services | 1.45 | 230 | 0.149 |
| Technological services | -1.5 | 264 | 0.136 |
| Performance of previous services | 0.74 | 237 | 0.458 |
| Reputation | 2.44 | 201 | 0.015 |
| P. Experience | 1.9 | 215 | 0.059 |
| Ownership/nationality | 2.1 | 233 | 0.036 |
| **Bank related factors** | **1.73** | **211** | **0.085** |
| Competition | -0.82 | 252 | 0.414 |
| Performance of the banking sector | 3.08 | 207 | 0.002 |
| Country Economic performance | 1.39 | 219 | 0.167 |
| Legal stability | 0.35 | 222 | 0.726 |
| Political stability | 1.8 | 180 | 0.073 |
| **Environment related factors** | **1.46** | **210** | **0.146** |

### 4.3.4 Discriminant analysis: Determining differentiating factors between loan and saving services

In order to statistically isolate the differentiating factors between loan and saving services, a canonical discriminant analysis was preformed. Discriminant analysis is a multivariate technique used to investigate observed differences between two or more groups. In this study, this technique is used to define the most important factors in differentiating between new loan and new saving services.

The first step of the discriminant analysis is to test the equality of group means between loan and saving services using the multivariate analysis of variance. Results reveal that using Wilk's Lambada test, there was a significant difference between the group means of loan and saving services with a p-value of 0.000.

The second step is to test the equality of group means for each of the factors separately between loan and saving services. Table (17) presents the Wilk's Lambada and the f-values along with the degrees of freedom and the p-values for testing each factor.

As shown in the table the difference between loan and saving services in pricing, tenor, service risk, bank performance, bank reputation, ownership/ nationality of the bank, and performance of the banking sector was found to be significant while the difference in all other factors was not. The same results were obtained by the two sample t-test earlier in the chapter. Thus, the results obtained were a good validation of the accuracy of the preceding results.

**Table 17: Testing for the equality of factor means between loan and saving services**

| | Wilks' Lambda | F | df1 | df2 | Sig. |
|---|---|---|---|---|---|
| Uniqueness | .999 | .310 | 1 | 287 | .578 |
| Sophistication | .996 | 1.154 | 1 | 287 | .284 |
| Pricing | .977 | 6.827 | 1 | 287 | .009 |
| Tenor | .947 | 15.991 | 1 | 287 | .000 |
| Liquidity | .991 | 2.607 | 1 | 287 | .108 |
| Risk | .938 | 18.852 | 1 | 287 | .000 |
| Documentation | .995 | 1.444 | 1 | 287 | .231 |
| Information | .995 | 1.411 | 1 | 287 | .236 |
| P. Experience | .998 | .641 | 1 | 287 | .424 |
| Bank Performance | .974 | 7.801 | 1 | 287 | .006 |
| Service quality | .999 | .243 | 1 | 287 | .623 |
| Convenience | .999 | .417 | 1 | 287 | .519 |

| | | | | | |
|---|---|---|---|---|---|
| Range of services | .993 | 1.991 | 1 | 287 | .159 |
| Technological services | .992 | 2.249 | 1 | 287 | .135 |
| Performance of previous services | .998 | .551 | 1 | 287 | .459 |
| Reputation | .978 | 6.434 | 1 | 287 | .012 |
| P. Experience | .987 | 3.869 | 1 | 287 | .050 |
| Ownership/nationality | .985 | 4.323 | 1 | 287 | .038 |
| Competition | .997 | .771 | 1 | 287 | .381 |
| Performance of the banking sector | .965 | 10.385 | 1 | 287 | .001 |
| Country Economic performance | .994 | 1.790 | 1 | 287 | .182 |
| Legal stability | 1.000 | .117 | 1 | 287 | .732 |
| Political stability | .987 | 3.672 | 1 | 287 | .056 |

The third step is to test the equality of the covariance matrices in the two groups. According to the p-value of 0.000, the two covariance matrices are significantly different. Therefore, the covariance matrices in the two groups, rather than the pooled covariance matrix (i.e. the common covariance matrix) are used in the analysis.

The fourth step in the analysis is to apply the canonical discriminant analysis to choose the best factors in differentiating between loan and saving services and eliminate those that are not significant differentiators of the two groups. Among all the factors, the canonical discriminant analysis chose, pricing, tenor, liquidity, service risk, documentation, availability of information, and performance of the banking sector to be the significant factors in discriminating between loan and saving services.

Among those chosen factors, the standardized canonical discriminant function was computed. The following table (18) presents the standardized discriminant function coefficients for the chosen factors.

**Table 18: Standardized canonical disciminant function coefficients for the discriminating factors**

| Discriminating factors | Discriminant coefficients |
|---|---|
| Pricing | -.480 |
| Tenor | .464 |
| Liquidity | -.360 |
| Service risk | .825 |
| Documentation | -.310 |
| Availability of information | -.282 |
| Performance of the banking sector | .378 |

Using this discriminate function, the observations were classified, and the result of the overall correctly classified observations was 71.3%. This result indicates an efficient and reliable discriminant function.

The last step of the analysis is to order the factors according to their ability to discriminate between loan and saving services. In order to do that, the correlations between the discriminating factors and the standardized canonical discriminant function were computed. Results are presented in table (19) below:

**Table 19: Correlation coefficients between the discriminating factors and the standardized canonical discriminant function**

| Discriminating factors | Discriminant coefficients |
|---|---|
| Service risk | .472 |
| Tenor | .435 |
| Performance of the banking sector | .350 |
| Pricing | -.284 |
| Liquidity | -.175 |
| Documentation | -.131 |
| Availability of information | -.129 |

As shown in the table, the most important factor in discriminating between responses for loan and saving services was service risk (i.e. it had the highest correlation coefficient with the standardized canonical discriminant function). Following were the factors of tenor, performance of the banking sector, pricing, liquidity, documentation, and availability of information which had the least effect in discriminating between loan and saving services.

**Summary of two sample t-test and discriminant analysis**

Results of the two sample t-test and the discriminant analysis indicate that the most significant factors differentiating between new loan and new saving services in order of significance are service risk, tenor, and performance of the banking sector that are attributed significantly higher importance in new saving services than in new loan services. This is mainly due to the risky nature of saving services that exposes the customers to losing their money if the service risk is high, and that makes them seek trust, not only in the performance of the bank, but also in the performance of the whole sector. Saving services' customers also require anytime withdrawal of their money whether to mitigate unforeseen risks or to meet unforeseen obligations.

### 4.3.5 Analysis of variance (ANOVA): Determining the most important factors affecting customers' decisions to buy new loan and saving services

In order to detect whether there is significant differences in the importance that customers attribute to different factors in each of the two groups (loan and saving), a one way analysis of variance (ANOVA) is performed.

The one way analysis of variance (ANOVA) is a statistical tool that compares 3 or more means by analyzing comparisons of variance estimates. The null hypothesis for this test is H0: $\mu_1 = \mu_2 = \mu_3 = ... = \mu_p$, or that the means for all factors are equal, versus the alternative hypothesis H1: that at least one mean is different than the others.

Results of the one way ANOVA indicate the following:

**First: New loan services**

**a) - Service related factors:**

Results reveal that there are significant differences in the importance attributed to different service related factors in loan services with a p-value of 0.000. Pair wise comparisons conducted to identify those differences reveal the following:

- The importance attributed to pricing is significantly higher than that attributed to uniqueness, sophistication, documentation, service risk, availability of information, tenor and previous positive experience with new services.
- The importance attributed to liquidity is significantly higher than that attributed to documentation, service risk, availability of information, tenor, and previous positive experience with new services.
- The importance attributed to uniqueness is significantly higher than that attributed to tenor and previous positive experience with new services.
- The importance attributed to sophistication is significantly higher than that attributed to tenor and previous positive experience with new services.
- The importance attributed to documentation is significantly higher than that attributed to tenor and previous positive experience with new services.
- The importance attributed to service risk is significantly higher then that attributed to previous positive experience with new services.
- The importance attributed to availability of information is significantly higher than that attributed to previous positive experience with new services.

As per table (20) below, pricing is found to be the most important service related factor affecting customers when taking a decision to buy new retail banking loan service. It is directly followed by liquidity, uniqueness, sophistication, documentation, service risk, availability of information, tenor and finally previous experience with new services as the least important factor.

**Table 20: Order of importance for service related factors - Loan services**

| Factors sorted in order of importance | Average score | Standard deviation |
|---|---|---|
| 1-Pricing | 1.3736 | 0.5405 |
| 2-Liquidity | 1.4397 | 0.5903 |
| 3-Uniqueness | 1.6207 | 0.6207 |
| 4-Sophistication | 1.6250 | 0.6688 |
| 5-Documentation | 1.6422 | 0.6750 |
| 6-Service risk | 1.7888 | 0.7551 |
| 7-Availability of information | 1.8190 | 0.8038 |
| 8-Tenor | 1.9052 | 1.0298 |
| 9- Previous experience with new services | 2.1034 | 1.0905 |

**b) - Bank related factors**

Results reveal that there are significant differences in the importance attributed to different bank related factors in loan services with a p-value of 0.000. Pair wise comparisons conducted to identify those differences reveal the following:

- The importance attributed to service quality is significantly higher than that attributed to convenience, performance of previous services, previous experience with the bank, availability of technological services, bank performance, range of other services, and ownership/ nationality of the bank.
- The importance attributed to bank reputation is significantly higher than that attributed to performance of previous services, previous experience with the bank, availability of technological services, bank performance, range of other services, and ownership/ nationality of the bank.
- The importance attributed to convenience is significantly higher than that attributed to performance of previous services, previous experience with the bank, availability of technological services, bank performance, range of other services, and ownership/ nationality of the bank.
- The importance attributed to performance of previous services is significantly higher than that attributed to ownership/ nationality of the bank.
- The importance attributed to the previous positive experience with the bank is significantly higher than that attributed to ownership/ nationality of the bank

As per table (21) below, service quality is found to be the most important bank related factor affecting customers when taking a decision to buy new retail banking loan service. It is directly followed by bank reputation, convenience, performance of previous services, previous positive experience with the bank, availability of technological services, bank performance, range of services, and ownership/ nationality of the bank as the least important factor.

**Table 21: Order of importance for bank related factors - Loan services**

| Factors sorted in order of importance | Average score | Standard deviation |
|---|---|---|
| 1-Service quality | 1.3420 | 0.5523 |
| 2-Bank reputation | 1.5517 | 0.7757 |
| 3-Convenience | 1.5754 | 0.5760 |
| 4-Performance of previous services | 1.8534 | 0.8470 |
| 5-Previous experience with the bank | 1.9310 | 0.9756 |
| 6-Availability of technological services | 1.9483 | 1.0287 |
| 7-Bank performance | 2.0172 | 0.9649 |
| 8-Range of other services | 2.0517 | 0.9496 |
| 9-Ownership/ nationality of the bank | 2.1638 | 1.2010 |

### c) Environment related factors

Results reveal that there are significant differences in the importance attributed to different environment related factors in loan services with a p-value of 0.000. Pair wise comparisons conducted to identify those differences reveal the following:

- The importance attributed to political stability is significantly higher than that attributed to country economic performance and performance of the banking sector.
- The importance attributed to legal stability is significantly higher than that attributed to the performance of the banking sector

As per table (22) below, political stability is found to be the most important environment related factor affecting customers when taking a decision to buy new retail banking loan service. It is directly followed by legal stability, country economic performance and performance of the banking sector.

**Table 22: Order of importance for environment related factors - Loan services**

| Factors sorted in order of importance | Average score | Standard deviation |
|---|---|---|
| 1-Political stability | 1.5948 | 1.0063 |
| 2-Legal stability | 1.6552 | 0.8273 |
| 3-Country economic performance | 1.8448 | 0.7855 |
| 4-Performance of the banking sector | 2.0733 | 0.8877 |

**Second: New Saving Services**

**a) - Service related factors:**

Results reveal that there are significant differences in the importance attributed to different service related factors in saving services with a p-value of 0.000. Pair wise comparisons conducted to identify those differences reveal the following:

- The importance attributed to service risk is significantly higher than that attributed to uniqueness, sophistication, documentation, availability of information, and previous positive experience with new services.
- The importance attributed to tenor is significantly higher than that attributed to uniqueness, sophistication, documentation, availability of information, and previous positive experience with new services.
- The importance attributed to liquidity is significantly higher than that attributed to documentation, availability of information, and previous positive experience with new services
- The importance attributed to pricing is significantly higher than that attributed to documentation, availability of information, and previous positive experience with new services
- The importance attributed to uniqueness is significantly higher than that attributed to availability of information, and previous positive experience with new services
- The importance attributed to sophistication is significantly higher than that attributed to availability of information, and previous positive experience with new services
- The importance attributed to documentation is significantly higher than that attributed to availability of information, and previous positive experience with new services

As per table (23) below, service risk is found to be the most important service related factor affecting customers when taking a decision to buy new retail banking saving service. It is directly followed by tenor, liquidity, pricing, uniqueness, sophistication, documentation, availability of information, and finally, previous positive experience with new services as the least important factor.

**Table 23: Order of importance for service related factors - Saving services**

| Factors sorted in order of importance | Average score | Standard deviation |
|---|---|---|
| 1-Service risk | 1.4350 | 0.6374 |
| 2-Tenor | 1.5028 | 0.6582 |
| 3-Liquidity | 1.5621 | 0.6692 |
| 4-Pricing | 1.5650 | 0.6354 |

| | | |
|---|---|---|
| 5-Uniqueness | 1.6723 | 0.7404 |
| 6-Sophistication | 1.7119 | 0.6755 |
| 7-Documentation | 1.7542 | 0.8497 |
| 8-Availability of information | 1.9416 | 0.7816 |
| 9-Previous experience with new services | 2.0000 | 1.0280 |

**b) - Bank related factors**

Results reveal that there are significant differences in the importance attributed to different bank related factors in saving services with a p-value of 0.000. Pair wise comparisons conducted to identify those differences reveal the following:

- The importance attributed to service quality is significantly higher than that attributed to convenience, bank performance, previous positive experience with the bank, performance of previous services, ownership/ nationality of the bank, and range of other services.
- The importance attributed to bank reputation is significantly higher than that attributed to convenience, bank performance, previous positive experience with the bank, performance of previous services, ownership/ nationality of the bank, and range of other services.
- The importance attributed to convenience is significantly higher than that attributed to ownership/ nationality of the bank, and range of services.
- The importance attributed to bank performance is significantly higher than that attributed to range of other services.
- The importance attributed to previous positive experience with the bank is significantly higher than that attributed to range of other services.
- The importance attributed to performance of previous services is significantly different from that attributed to service quality, bank reputation, convenience, and range of other services.

As per table (24) below, service quality is found to be the most important bank related factor affecting customers when making their decision to buy new retail banking saving services. It is directly followed by bank reputation, convenience, bank performance, previous positive experience with the bank, performance of previous services, ownership/ nationality of the bank, and finally range of other services as the least important factor.

**Table 24: Order of importance for bank related factors - Saving services**

| Factors sorted in order of importance | Average score | Standard deviation |
|---|---|---|
| 1-Service quality | 1.3068 | 0.5218 |
| 2-Bank reputation | 1.3446 | 0.5958 |
| 3-Convenience | 1.6193 | 0.5867 |
| 4-Bank performance | 1.7137 | 0.8422 |
| 5-Previous positive experience with the | 1.7232 | 0.8169 |

| | | |
|---|---|---|
| bank | | |
| 6-Performance of previous services | 1.7797 | 0.8062 |
| 7-Ownership/ nationality of the bank | 1.8701 | 1.1181 |
| 8-Range of other services | 1.8927 | 0.8692 |

### c) - Environment related factors

Results reveal that there are significant differences in the importance attributed to different environment related factors in saving services with a p-value of 0.000. Pair wise comparisons conducted to detect significant differences between factors reveal the following that the importance attributed to political stability is significantly higher than that attributed to legal stability, country economic performance, and performance of the banking sector.

As per table (25) below, and exactly as in loan services, political stability is found to be the most important environment related factor affecting customers when making their decision to buy new retail banking saving service. It is directly followed by legal stability, country economic performance and performance of the banking sector.

**Table 25: Order of importance for environment related factors - Saving services**

| Factors sorted in order of importance | Average score | Standard deviation |
|---|---|---|
| 1-Political stability | 1.4040 | 0.6652 |
| 2-Legal Stability | 1.6222 | 0.7216 |
| 3-Country Economic Performance | 1.7218 | 0.6736 |
| 4-Performance of the banking sector | 1.7712 | 0.7090 |

### The three sets of factors: New loan and saving services

#### New loan services

Results reveal that there are significant differences in the importance attributed to the three set of factors affecting customers' decision to buy new loan services with a p-value of 0.006. As per table (26) below, service related factors are found to be the most important factors affecting customers when taking a decision to buy new retail banking loan service. They are directly followed by bank related factors, and finally environment related factors. The importance attributed to service related and bank related factors is found to be significantly higher than that than that attributed to environment related factors.

**Table 26: Order of importance for the three sets of factors - Loan services**

| Factors sorted in order of importance | Average score | Standard deviation |
|---|---|---|
| Service Related Factors | 1.6566 | 0.4036 |
| Bank Related Factors | 1.7345 | 0.5406 |
| Environment Related Factors | 1.8872 | 0.6735 |

### New saving services

Results reveal that there are significant differences in the importance attributed to the three set of factors affecting customers' decision to buy new saving services with a p-value of 0.011. As per table (27) below, bank related factors are found to be the most important factors affecting customers when taking a decision to buy new retail banking saving services. They are directly followed by service related factors, and finally environment related factors. The importance attributed to bank related factors is found to be significantly higher than the importance attributed to environment related factors.

**Table 27: Order of importance for the three sets of factors - Saving services**

| Factors sorted in order of importance | Average score | Standard deviation |
|---|---|---|
| Bank Related Factors | 1.6296 | 0.4470 |
| Service Related Factors | 1.6830 | 0.4031 |
| Environment Related Factors | 1.7779 | 0.5452 |

### Summary of one way ANOVA: The most important factors affecting customers' decisions to buy new loan and saving services

Results of one way ANOVA reveal significant differences in the importance attributed to service, bank, and environment related factors affecting customers' decision to buy new loan and saving services. They also reveal significant differences in the importance attributed to different factors within each of these categories as follows:

### New Loan Services

Overall, service related factors are found to dominate customers when taking a decision to buy a new loan service. This result is reasonable in light of the nature of such services that entail taking money from the bank with the maximum risk of having to pay it back before due date and with usually enough guarantees granted by the clients for repayment. Therefore, the conditions of the service itself are considered more important than the offering bank. When considering individual factors, service quality, pricing, liquidity, bank reputation, and convenience were found to be the most important factors affecting customers' decision to buy a new loan service.

**New Saving Services**

Overall, bank related factors are found to dominate customers when taking a decision to buy a new saving service. This result is reasonable in light of the nature of such services that entail giving money to the bank with the risk of losing it and without enough guarantees of the service outcome from the bank. Therefore, the offering bank becomes more important than the conditions of the service in taking the decision to buy a new saving service. When considering individual factors, service quality, bank reputation, political stability, and service risk are found to be the most important factors affecting customers' decision to buy a new saving service.

## 4.4 Influence of demographic variables over importance attributed to different factors: ANOVA

In this section, the influence of each demographic variable (independent variable) on the importance attributed to each factor (dependent variable) is investigated using one way ANOVA. The analysis is conducted for each of the demographic variables on all factors for both loan and saving services. A significant influence of a demographic variable on a certain factor means that the importance that customers attribute to this factor varies according to the different classes of the demographic factor. As presented in tables (28) – (39), results of one way ANOVA for both loan and saving services reveal the following:

**Gender**

➢ **New loan services**

Results of one way ANOVA for loan services as summarized in table (28) reveal that gender has a significant impact on the importance that customers attribute to the following factors:

- Service uniqueness with a p-value of 0.003 where the mean for males is 1.52 compared to 1.89 for females, indicating that males attribute significantly higher importance to service uniqueness than females.
- Service sophistication with a p-value of 0.000 where the mean for males is 1.49 compared to 1.97 for females indicating that males also attribute significantly higher importance to service sophistication than females.

- Documentation with a p-value of 0.003 where the mean for males is 1.53 compared to 1.94 for females indicating that males also attribute significantly higher importance to documentation than females.
- Availability of Information with a p-value of 0.022 where the mean for males is 1.71 compared to 2.09 for females, also indicating that males attribute significantly higher importance to availability of information than females.
- Overall loan service related factors with a p-value of 0.002 where the mean for males is 1.59 compared to 1.84 for females indicating that males attribute significantly higher importance to the attributes of the loan service itself than females.

**Table 28: Summary of gender effect on the importance attributed to different factors - Loan services: One way ANOVA**

| Factors | F-statistic | Df | p-value | Female | Male |
|---|---|---|---|---|---|
| Service uniqueness | 8.93 | (1, 114) | 0.003 | 1.89 | 1.52 |
| Service sophistication | 12.88 | (1, 114) | 0.000 | 1.97 | 1.49 |
| Documentation | 9.05 | (1, 114) | 0.003 | 1.94 | 1.53 |
| Availability of information | 5.36 | (1, 114) | 0.022 | 2.09 | 1.71 |
| **Service related factors** | 9.86 | (1, 114) | 0.002 | 1.84 | 1.59 |

## ➢ New saving services

Results of one way ANOVA for saving services as summerized in table (29) reveal that gender has a significant impact on the importance that customers attribute to the following factors:

- Pricing with a p-value of 0.05 where the mean for males is 1.49 compared to 1.69 for females indicating that males attribute significantly higher importance to pricing than females.
- Documentation with a p-value of 0.010 where the mean for males is 1.63 compared to 1.97 for females indicating that males also attribute significantly higher importance to documentation than females.
- Performance of the banking sector with a p-value of 0.014 where the mean for males is 1.87 compared to 1.60 for females indicating that males attribute significantly lower importance to the performance of the sector than females.

**Table 29: Summary of gender effect on the importance attributed to different factors - Saving services: One way ANOVA**

| Factors | F-statistic | Df | p-value | Female | Male |
|---|---|---|---|---|---|
| Pricing | 3.86 | 1, 175 | 0.05* | 1.69 | 1.49 |
| Documentation | 6.79 | 1, 175 | 0.010* | 1.97 | 1.63 |
| Performance of the banking sector | 6.16 | 1, 175 | 0.014* | 1.60 | 1.87 |

## Age

### ➢ New loan services

Results of one way ANOVA for new loan services as summarized in table (30) reveal that age has a significant impact on the importance that customers attribute to the following factors:

- Bank performance with a p-value of 0.019 where respondents who are above 60 years of age attribute significantly higher importance to bank performance than all other age categories with a mean of 1.17 compared to 2.23 for the age category 21-30, 2.33 for the age category 31-40, 1.74 for the age category 41-50, and 1.79 for the age category 51-60.
- Bank reputation with a p-value of 0.043 where respondents who are above 60 years of age attribute significantly higher importance to bank reputation with a mean of 1.0 than those at the age category of 31-40 with a mean of 1.87.
- Ownership/ nationality of the bank with a p-value of 0.000 where respondents at the age category of 41-50 attribute significantly higher importance to this factor with a mean of 1.53 than respondents at the age categories of 21-30 and 31-40 with means of 2.33, and 2.83 respectively.
- Performance of the banking sector with a p-value of 0.001 where respondents at the age categories of 31-40 attribute significantly lower importance to this factor with a mean of 2.55 than respondents at the age categories of 41-50 and 51-60 with means of 1.65 and 1.88 respectively
- Political stability with a p-value of 0.013 where respondents at the age category of 31-40 attribute significantly lower importance to this factor with a mean of 2.06 than respondents at the age categories of 41-50 and above 60 with means of 1.22 and 1.25 respectively.
- Overall environment related factors with a p-value of 0.009 where respondents at the age categories of 21-30 and 31-40 attribute significantly lower importance to environmental factors, with means of 2.00 and 2.18 respectively, than respondents at the age categories of 41-50, 51-60, and above 60 with means of 1.62, 1.73, and 1.63 respectively.

**Table 30: Summary of age effect on the importance attributed to different factors - Loan services: One way ANOVA**

| Factors | F-Statistic | Df | p-value | 1<br>21-30 | 2<br>31-40 | 3<br>41-50 | 4<br>51-60 | 5<br>60- |
|---|---|---|---|---|---|---|---|---|
| Bank Performance<br>*(Pair wise comparison)* | 3.07 | 4, 111 | 0.019 | 2.23<br>(1,5) | 2.33<br>(2,5) | 1.74<br>(3,5) | 1.79<br>(4, 5) | 1.17 |
| Bank Reputation<br>*(Pair wise comparison)* | 2.56 | 4, 111 | 0.043 | 1.53 | 1.87<br>(2,5) | 1.33 | 1.52 | 1.00 |
| Bank Ownership/ Nationality<br>*(Pair wise comparison)* | 5.88 | 4, 111 | 0.000 | 2.333<br>(1,3) | 2.84<br>(2,3) | 1.533 | 1.857 | 2.00 |
| Performance of The Banking Sector<br>*(Pair wise comparison)* | 4.67 | 4, 111 | 0.001 | 2.13 | 2.55<br>(2,3)<br>(2,4) | 1.65 | 1.88 | 2.13 |
| Political Stability<br>*(Pair wise comparison)* | 3.34 | 4, 111 | 0.013 | 1.67 | 2.06<br>(2,3)<br>(2,5) | 1.22 | 1.41 | 1.25 |
| **Environment Related Factors**<br>*(Pair wise comparison)* | 3.55 | 4, 111 | 0.009 | 2.00<br>(1,3)<br>(1,4)<br>(1,5) | 2.18<br>(2,3)<br>(2,4)<br>(2,5) | 1.62 | 1.73 | 1.63 |

➢ **New saving services**

Results of one way ANOVA for new saving services as summarized in table (31) reveal that age has a significant impact on the importance that customers attribute to the following factors:

- Service sophistication with a p-value of 0.006 where respondents at the age of 60 and above attribute significantly higher importance to this factor with a mean of 1.36 than respondents at the age categories of 21-30, 31-40, and 51-60 with means of 1.99, 1.73, and 1.76 respectively.
- Documentation with a p-value of 0.010 where respondents at the age categories of 21-30 and 31- 40 attribute significantly lower importance to this factor with means of 1.99 and 2.03 respectively than respondents at the age categories of 51-60 and above 60 with means of 1.47 and 1.50 respectively.
- Ownership/ nationality of the bank with a p-value of 0.000 where respondents at the age category of 21-30 attribute significantly lower importance to this factor with a mean of 2.57 than all other age categories with means of 1.919 for the age category 31-40, 1.66 for the age cate-

gory 41-50, 1.72 for the age category 51-60, and 1.42 for the age category 60 and above.

**Table 31: Summary of age effect on the importance attributed to different factors - Saving services: One way ANOVA**

| Factors | F-Statistic | Df | P-Value | 1<br>21-30 | 2<br>31-40 | 3<br>41-50 | 4<br>51-60 | 5<br>60- |
|---|---|---|---|---|---|---|---|---|
| Service Sophistication<br>*(Pair wise comparison)* | 3.71 | 4,172 | 0.006 | 1.99<br>(1,5) | 1.73<br>(2,5) | 1.66 | 1.76<br>(4,5) | 1.36 |
| Documentation<br>*(Pair wise comparison)* | 3.40 | 4,172 | 0.010 | 1.99<br>(1,4)<br>(1,5) | 2.03<br>(2,4)<br>(2,5) | 1.73 | 1.47 | 1.50 |
| Bank Ownership/ Nationality<br>*(Pair wise comparison)* | 5.61 | 4,172 | 0.000 | 2.571<br>(1,2)<br>(1,3)<br>(1,4)<br>(1,5) | 1.919<br>(2,5) | 1.659 | 1.722 | 1.429 |

### Level of education

- **New loan services**

Results of one way ANOVA for new loan services reveal that level of education has no significant impact on the importance that customers attribute to any of the different factors.

- **New saving services**

Results of one way ANOVA for new saving services as summarized in table (32) reveal that level of education has a significant impact on the importance that customers attribute to the following factors:

- Availability of information with a p-value of 0.041 where respondents with high school education attribute significantly higher importance to this factor with a mean of 1.73 than respondents with MA/ PhDs with a mean of 2.24.
- Bank performance with a p-value of 0.021 where respondents with high school education attribute significantly higher importance to this factor with a mean of 1.13 than respondents with bachelor degrees and MA/PhDs with means of 1.70 and 1.96 respectively.
- Convenience with a p-value of 0.043 where respondents with high school education attribute significantly higher importance to this factor with a mean of 1.28 than respondents with MA/PhDs with a mean of 1.79.

- Range of other services with a p-value of 0.000 where respondents with MA/PhDs attribute significantly lower importance to this factor with a mean of 2.42 than respondents with high school education and bachelor degrees with means of 1.70 and 1.78 respectively.
- Performance of previous services with a p-value of 0.009 where respondents with high school education attribute significantly higher importance to this factor with a mean of 1.20 than respondents with bachelor degrees with a mean of 1.75, who in turn attribute significantly higher importance to this factor than respondents with MA/PhDs with a mean of 2.06.
- Overall service related factors with a p-value of 0.005 where respondents with high school education attribute significantly higher importance to the attributes of the service itself with a mean value of 1.26 than respondents with bachelor degrees and MA/PhDs with means of 1.62 and 1.78 respectively.

**Table 32: Summary of level of education effect on the importance attributed to different factors - Saving services: One way ANOVA**

| **Factors** | **F-Statistic** | **Df** | **p-value** | **2 H.School** | **3 BA** | **4 MA/PhD** |
|---|---|---|---|---|---|---|
| Availability Of Information *(Pair wise comparison)* | 3.26 | (2,174) | 0.041 | 1.73 (2,4) | 1.88 | 2.24 |
| Bank Performance *(Pair wise comparison)* | 3.94 | (2,174) | 0.021 | 1.13 (2,3) (2,4) | 1.70 | 1.96 |
| Convenience *(Pair wise comparison)* | 3.21 | (2,174) | 0.043 | 1.28 (2,4) | 1.60 | 1.79 |
| Range Of Other Services *(Pair wise comparison)* | 8.25 | (2,174) | 0.000 | 1.70 (2,4) | 1.78 (3,4) | 2.42 |
| Performance Of Previous Services *(Pair wise comparison)* | 4.86 | (2,174) | 0.009 | 1.200 (2,4) (2,3) | 1.754 (3,4) | 2.061 |
| **Bank Related Factors** *(Pair wise comparison)* | 5.53 | (2,174) | 0.005 | 1.26 (2,3) (2,4) | 1.62 | 1.78 |

**Marital status**

➢ **New loan services**

Results of one way ANOVA for new loan services as summarized in table (33) reveal that marital status has a significant impact on the importance that customers attribute to tenor with a p-value of 0.05 where married respondents attribute significantly higher importance to this factor with a mean of 1.81 than single respondents with a mean of 2.26.

**Table 33: Summary of marital status effect on the importance attributed to different factors - Loan services: One way ANOVA**

| Factors | F-Statistic | Df | P-Value | Single Mean | Married Mean |
|---|---|---|---|---|---|
| Tenor | 3.93 | (1,111) | 0.05 | 2.269 | 1.816 |

➢ **New saving services**

Results of one way ANOVA for new saving services as summarized in table (34) reveal that marital status has a significant impact on the importance that customers attribute to the ownership/ nationality of the bank with a p-value of 0.002 where married respondents attribute significantly higher importance to this factor with a mean of 1.75 than single respondents with a mean of 2.46.

**Table 34: Summary of marital status effect on the importance attributed to different factors - Saving services: One way ANOVA**

| Factors | F-Statistic | Df | P-Value | Single Mean | Married Mean |
|---|---|---|---|---|---|
| Bank Ownership/ Nationality | 10.13 | (1,160) | 0.002 | 2.467 | 1.750 |

**Number of children**

➢ **New loan services**

Results of one way ANOVA for new loan services reveal that number of children has no significant impact on the importance that customers attribute to any of the different factors.

➢ **New saving services**

Results of one way ANOVA for new saving services as summarized in table (35) reveal that number of children has a significant impact on the importance that customers attribute to the ownership/ nationality of the bank with a p-value of 0.036 where respondents with no children and 1 child attributed significantly lower importance to this factor, with means of 2.23 and 2.13 than respondents with 2 children, 3 children, and more than 3 children with means of 1.84, 1.54, and 1.55 respectively.

**Table 35: Summary of number of children effect on the importance attributed to different factors - Saving services: One way ANOVA**

| Factors | F-statistic | Df | p-value | Child 0 | Child 1 | Child 2 | Child 3 | Child 3- |
|---|---|---|---|---|---|---|---|---|
| Bank Ownership/ Nationality *(Pair wise comparison)* | 2.63 | (4,171) | 0.036 | 2.237 (0,3) (0,4) | 2.136 (1,3) | 1.847 | 1.541 | 1.550 |

**Employment status**

➢ **New loan services**

Results of one way ANOVA for new loan services as summarized in table (36) reveal that employment status has a significant impact on the importance that customers attribute to the following factors:

- Documentation with a p-value of 0.029 where unemployed respondents attributed significantly lower importance to this factor with a mean of 2.22 than all other types of employment with means of 1.71 for private sector employees, 1.6 for public sector employees, 1.5 for private business owners, and 1.35 for other types of employment.
- Previous positive experience with new services with a p-value of 0.009 where unemployed respondents attributed significantly lower importance to this factor with a mean of 3.33 than all other types of employment with means of 1.91 for private sector employees, 2.08 for public sector employees, 2.13 for private business owners, and 1.92 for other types of employment.

➢ **New saving services**

Results of one way ANOVA for new saving services as summarized in table (37) reveal that employment status has a significant impact on the importance that customers attribute to the following factors:

- Pricing with a p-value of 0.035 where privately employed respondents attribute a significantly higher importance to this factor with a mean of 1.37 than public sector employees and business owners with means of 1.73 and 1.69 respectively.
- Tenor with a p-value of 0.11 where privately employed respondents attribute significantly lower importance to this factor with a mean of 1.73

than private business owners, unemployed respondents and other types of employment with means of 1.30, 1.37 and 1.30 respectively.

- Ownership/ nationality of the bank where private sector employees attribute significantly lower importance to this factor with a mean of 2.33 than public sector employees, unemployed respondents and respondents with other employment status with means of 1.72, 1.44, and 1.69 respectively.
- Performance of the banking sector with a p-value of 0.039 where private sector employees and business owners attribute significantly lower importance to this factor with means of 1.96 and 1.89 respectively than unemployed respondents with a mean of 1.48.
- Political stability with a p-value of 0.033 where private sector employees attribute significantly lower importance to this factor with a mean of 1.65 than public sector employees, unemployed respondents, and respondents with other employment status with means of 1.31, 1.29, and 1.22 respectively.

**Income level**

➢ **New loan services**

Results of one way ANOVA for new loan services reveal that income level has no significant impact on the importance that customers attribute to any of the different factors.

➢ **New Saving Services**

Results of one way ANOVA for new saving services as presented in table (38) reveal that income level has a significant impact on the importance that customers attribute to the availability of information with a p-value of 0.021 where respondents with monthly income above LE 10000 attribute significantly lower importance to this factor with a mean of 2.40 than respondents with monthly income of less than 2000 with a mean of 1.78 and respondents with monthly income in the range of 2000-5000 with a mean of 1.95

**Table 36: Summary of employment status effect on the importance attributed to different factors - Loan services: One way ANOVA**

| Factors | F-statistic | Df | p-value | 1 Private empl. | 2 Public empl. | 3 Business owners | 4 Unem-ployed | 5 Other |
|---|---|---|---|---|---|---|---|---|
| Documentation *(Pair wise comparison)* | 2.81 | (4, 110) | 0.029 | 1.71 (1,4) | 1.60 (2,4) | 1.50 (3,4) | 2.22 (4,5) | 1.35 |
| Previous Experience With New Services*(Pair wise comparison)* | 3.57 | (4, 110) | 0.009 | 1.91 (1,4) | 2.08 (2,4) | 2.13 (3,4) | 3.33 (4,5) | 1.92 |

**Table 37: Summary of employment status effect on the importance attributed to different factors - Saving services: One way ANOVA**

| Factors | F-statistic | Df | p-value | 1 Private empl. | 2 Public empl. | 3 Business owners | 4 Unem-ployed | 5 Other |
|---|---|---|---|---|---|---|---|---|
| Pricing *(Pair wise comparison)* | 2.65 | (4,172) | 0.035 | 1.37 (1,2) (1,3) | 1.73 | 1.69 | 1.45 | 1.65 |
| Tenor *(Pair wise comparison)* | 3.39 | (4,172) | 0.011 | 1.73 1 With 3, 4, And 5 | 1.58 | 1.30 | 1.3793 | 1.30 |
| Bank Ownership/ National-ity *(Pair wise comparison)* | 3.61 | (4,172) | 0.008 | 2.32 (1 With 2, 4, 5) | 1.72 | 1.87 | 1.448 | 1.69 |
| Performance Of The Banking Sector*(Pair wise comparison)* | 2.58 | (4,172) | 0.039 | 1.96 (1,4) | 1.70 | 1.89 (3,4) | 1.48 | 1.70 |
| Political Stability *(Pair wise comparison)* | 2.68 | (4,172) | 0.033 | 1.65 (1 With 2, 4, 5) | 1.31 | 1.38 | 1.29 | 1.22 |

**Table 38: Summary of level of income effect on the importance attributed to different factors - Saving services: One way ANOVA**

| Factors | F-statistic | Df | p-value | 1 Less 2000 | 2 2000-5000 | 3 5000-10000 | 4 More 10000 |
|---|---|---|---|---|---|---|---|
| Availability Of Information<br>*(Pair wise comparison)* | 3.34 | (3,167) | 0.021 | 1.78<br>(1,4) | 1.95<br>(2,4) | 2.05 | 2.40 |

## Summary of One Way ANOVA

Results of one way ANOVA conducted to examine the effect of different demographic variables on the importance attributed to different factors reveal the following:

➢ **New loan services**

- For loan services, males attribute significantly higher importance to service uniqueness, service sophistication, documentation, and availability of information, and overall loan service related factors than females.
- Younger respondents (at the age categories of 21- 30 and 31- 40) generally attribute lower importance to bank related factors, specifically bank performance and ownership/ nationality; and environment related factors, specifically political stability and performance of the banking sector than older respondents.
- Married respondents attribute significantly higher importance to tenor than single respondents
- Unemployed respondents attribute significantly lower importance to documentation and previous positive experience with new services.

➢ **New saving services**

- For saving services, males attribute significantly higher importance to pricing and documentation than females who in turn attribute significantly higher importance to the performance of the banking sector than males.
- Younger respondents (at the age categories of 21- 30 and 31- 40) generally attribute lower importance to service sophistication, documentation and bank ownership/ nationality than older categories.

- Respondents with high school certificates attribute generally higher importance to availability of information, bank performance, convenience, range of other services, performance of previous services, and overall bank related factors than BA holders who in turn attribute higher importance to range of other services and performance of previous services than MA/ PhD holders.

- Married respondents attribute significantly higher importance to bank nationality/ownership than single respondents

- Respondents with two or more children generally attribute higher importance to bank ownership/ nationality than respondents with no or one child.

- While privately employed respondents attribute higher importance to pricing, they attribute lower impotence to tenor, bank ownership/nationality, and political stability. On the other hand, unemployed respondents attribute higher importance to the performance of the banking sector.

- The higher the income, the less the importance attribute to the availability of information.

## 4.5 Factors relationships and subsets: Factors analysis

The objective of this section is to apply factor analysis on different service, bank and environment related factors for both loan and saving services to describe the structure of each group of factors, that is, to examine the relationship between different factors in order to find out subsets of the factors that compose together more general factors. The procedure of factor analysis is as follows:

1. Choosing the number of factors that represent together one subset. The number of chosen subsets is equal to the number of eigenvalues for the correlation matrix of the factors which are greater than or equal to one.

2. Testing the adequacy of the chosen subsets using the Kaiser-Meyer-Olkin (KMO) measure of sampling adequacy. A value of 0.7 or more is considered to be a good indicator for the adequacy of the subsets chosen (Lomax, 2001).

3. Extracting the factors using the Principal Component Analysis and calculating the initial loadings. The loadings are the correlation coefficients between the factors and the new subsets.

4. Rotating the initial loadings using the varimax rotation method

**New loan services**

**a) Service related factors**

Factor analysis was conducted to the 9 items representing service related dimensions in new loan services. Three factors had eigenvalues greater than or equal to one. The Kaiser-Meyer-Olkin (KMO) measure of sampling adequacy is 0.77 which indicates a good model. The rotated loadings are presented in table (40) below.

**Table 39: Rotated factor loadings for the service related factors - loan services**

| | Component | | |
|---|---|---|---|
| | 1* | 2 | 3 |
| Service Uniqueness | .308 | .171 | .628 |
| Service Sophistication | .090 | .798 | .069 |
| Pricing | .493 | .552 | .028 |
| Tenor | .473 | .379 | -.133 |
| Liquidity | .740 | -.036 | .197 |
| Service Risk | .759 | .141 | -.004 |
| Documentation | .634 | .080 | .408 |
| Availability Of Information | -.072 | .645 | .498 |
| Previous Experience With New Services | -.002 | .006 | .755 |

* Service conditions

As shown in the table, tenor, liquidity, service risk, and documentation all load on the first subset of factors. The analysis was not very decisive about pricing which almost equally loads on the first and the second subset of factors. Service sophistication and availability of information load on the second factor, and finally, service uniqueness and previous experience with new services load on the third subset of factor.

The percent of variance of the first subset of factors is approximately 32% which is more than double that of the second subset of factors that accounted for 13.4% of the variance. Thus, we can claim that there is a strong relationship between the group of factors (pricing, tenor, liquidity, service risk, and documentation) which represent together service conditions and that they compose together the most correlated subset of service related factors that customers consider when taking a decision to buy a new loan service.

**b) - Bank related factors**

Factor analysis was conducted to the 9 items representing bank related dimensions in new loan services. 2 factors had eigenvalues greater than or equal to one. The Kaiser-Meyer-Olkin (KMO) measure of sampling adequacy is 0.85

which indicates a good model. The rotated loadings are presented in table (41) below.

**Table 40: Rotated factor loadings for the bank related factors - loan services**

| | Component | |
|---|---|---|
| | 1* | 2** |
| Bank Performance | .841 | .163 |
| Service Quality | .625 | .433 |
| Convenience | .237 | .675 |
| Range Of Other Services | .187 | .679 |
| Technologically Advanced Services | .043 | .793 |
| Performance Of Previous Services | .630 | .383 |
| Bank Reputation | .868 | .169 |
| Previous Experience With The Bank | .486 | .352 |
| Bank Ownership/ Nationality | .752 | .008 |

* Bank risk
** Relationship convenience

As shown in the table, bank performance, service quality, performance of previous services, bank reputation, previous positive experience with the bank and bank ownership/ nationality all load on the first subset of factors. Although the loading for service quality is more into the first subset, it also considerably contributes to the second subset. Convenience, the availability of other services, and the availability of technologically advanced services load on the second subset of factors.

The percent of variance of the first subset of factors is approximately 44% which is almost triple that of the second factor that accounted for 13.3% of the variance. Thus, we can claim that there is a strong relationship between the group of factors that describe the bank's risk and that they together compose the most correlated bank related factors that customers consider when taking a decision to buy a new loan service. The factors that load to the second subset are all related to relationship convenience.

**c) - Environment related factors**

Factor analysis was conducted to the 5 items representing environment related dimensions in new loan services. 1 factor had an eigenvalue greater than one. The Kaiser-Meyer-Olkin (KMO) measure of sampling adequacy is 0.77 which indicates a good model. This subset includes all environmental factors (competition, performance of the banking sector, country economic performance, legal stability, and political stability) and accounts for 58.6% of total variance.

**New saving services**

**a) -Service related factors**

The factor analysis that was conducted to the 9 items representing service related dimensions in new saving services reveal that 2 factors had eigenvalues greater than or equal to one. The Kaiser-Meyer-Olkin (KMO) measure of sampling adequacy is 0.75 which indicates a good model. The rotated loadings are presented in table (42) below.

**Table 41: Rotated factor loadings for the service related factors - Saving services**

| | Component | |
|---|---|---|
| | 1 | 2 |
| Service Uniqueness | .077 | .587 |
| Service Sophistication | .256 | .578 |
| Pricing | .724 | -.004 |
| Tenor | .073 | .542 |
| Liquidity | .607 | .195 |
| Service Risk | .752 | .212 |
| Documentation | .575 | .211 |
| Availability Of Information | .151 | .670 |
| Previous Experience With New Services | .140 | .533 |

As shown in the table, pricing, liquidity, service risk, and documentation all load on the first subset of factors. Service uniqueness, service sophistication, tenor, availability of information, and previous experience with new services all load on the second subset of factors.

The percent of variance that both factors account to is only 41% indicating a weak correlation between factors. The first subset of factors that includes all service conditions (except for tenor) accounts for approximately 28% of the variance.

**b) - Bank related factors**

The factor analysis that was conducted to the 9 items representing bank related dimensions in new saving services reveal that 3 factors had eigenvalues greater than or equal to one. The Kaiser-Meyer-Olkin (KMO) measure of sampling adequacy is 0.79 which indicates a good model. The rotated loadings are presented in table (43) below.

**Table 42: Rotated factor loadings for the bank related factors - saving services**

| | Component | | |
|---|---|---|---|
| | 1* | 2 | 3 |
| Bank Performance | .114 | .639 | .478 |
| Service Quality | .451 | .000 | .525 |
| Convenience | .698 | .226 | .328 |
| Range Of Other Services | .801 | .143 | .086 |
| Technologically Advanced Services | .799 | .097 | -.055 |
| Performance Of Previous Services | .292 | .677 | -.072 |
| Bank Reputation | -.042 | .727 | .362 |
| Previous Experience with the Bank | .136 | .717 | -.080 |
| Bank Ownership/ Nationality | .026 | .070 | .799 |

* Relationship convenience

As shown in the table, convenience, range of other services, and the availability of technologically advanced services all load on the first subset of factors. Bank performance, performance of previous services, bank reputation, and previous positive experience with the bank all load on the second subset of factors. Finally, ownership/ nationality of the bank and service quality load on the third subset with no significant difference in the loading of service quality between the first and the third subset of factors.

The percent of variance of the first subset of factors is approximately 34% which is more than double that of the second factor that accounted for 15% of the variance. Thus, we can claim that there is a strong relationship between the group of factors that are related to relationship convenience and that they compose together the most correlated bank related factors that customers consider when taking a decision to buy a new saving service.

**c) - Environment related factors**

The factor analysis that was conducted to the 5 items representing environment related dimensions in new loan services reveal that only 1 factor had an eigenvalue greater than one. The Kaiser-Meyer-Olkin (KMO) measure of sampling adequacy is 0.79 which indicates a good model. This subset includes all environmental factors (competition, performance of the banking sector, country economic performance, legal stability, and political stability) and accounts for 54% of total variance.

**Summary of factor analysis**

For loan services, the group of factors representing service conditions (pricing, tenor, liquidity, service risk, and documentation) has the strongest relationship among all service related factors, those representing bank's risk (bank performance, service quality, performance of previous services, bank reputation, previous positive experience with the bank and bank ownership/ nationality ) has the strongest relationship among all bank related factors.

For saving services, no strong relationship is evident between service related factors, while the group of factors representing relationship convenience (convenience, range of other services, the availability of technologically advanced services, and service quality) has the strongest relationship among bank related factors.

For both loan and saving services all environmental factors proved to have a strong relationship that they together compose one subset.

## 4.6 Summary of statistical analysis results

The following table (43) contains a summary of the research hypothesis examined, the statistical analysis carried out to examine each of them, and the results reached for each hypothesis:

| Hypothesis | Test | New Loan Services | | New Saving Services | |
|---|---|---|---|---|---|
| | | Decision | Result | Decision | Result |
| Null Hypothesis 1:<br><br>The following demo-graphic variables don't affect customers' interest in new retail banking services: | ▪ Chi- square<br>▪ Logistic regression | | | | |
| (a) gender | | Reject | Males are 3.3 times more interested in new loan services than females | Fail to reject | No effect |
| (b) age | | Fail to reject | No effect | Fail to reject | No effect |
| (c) level of education | | Fail to reject | No effect | Fail to reject | No effect |
| (d) marital status | | Fail to reject | No effect | Fail to reject | No effect |
| (E) number of children | | Reject | Customers with no children are more interested in new loan services than customers with 3 children or more | Fail to reject | No effect |
| (F) employment status | | Reject | Private sector employees and business owners are more interested in new loan services than public sector employees & unemployed customers | Fail to reject | No effect |
| (G) level of income | | Fail to reject | No effect | Fail to reject | No effect |

| Hypothesis | Test | New Loan Services | | New Saving Services | |
|---|---|---|---|---|---|
| | | Decision | Result | Decision | Result |
| **Null Hypothesis 2:**<br><br>The following sets of factors are not important for customers when taking the decision to buy new retail services. | One Sample T-test | | | | |
| **A - Service related factors:** | | | | | |
| (1) Service uniqueness | | Reject | Important | Reject | Important |
| (2) Service sophistication | | Reject | Important | Reject | Important |
| (3) Pricing | | Reject | Important | Reject | Important |
| (4) Tenor | | Reject | Important | Reject | Important |
| (5) Liquidity | | Reject | Important | Reject | Important |
| (6) Service risk | | Reject | Important | Reject | Important |
| (7) Documentation required | | Reject | Important | Reject | Important |
| (8) Availability of information | | Reject | Important | Reject | Important |
| (9) Previous positive experience with new retail banking services | | Reject | Important | Reject | Important |
| **B- Bank related factors:** | | | | | |
| (1) Bank performance | | Reject | Important | Reject | Important |
| (2) Service quality | | Reject | Important | Reject | Important |
| (3) Convenience | | Reject | Important | Reject | Important |
| (4) Availability of a wide range of other services | | Reject | Important | Reject | Important |
| (5) Availability of technologically advanced services | | Reject | Important | Fail to Reject | Not Important |
| (6) Performance of previous new services | | Reject | Important | Reject | Important |

| Hypothesis | Test | New Loan Services | | New Saving Services | |
|---|---|---|---|---|---|
| | | Decision | Result | Decision | Result |
| (7) Bank reputation | | Reject | Important | Reject | Important |
| (8) Previous positive experience with the bank | | Reject | Important | Reject | Important |
| (9) Ownership/ Nationality of bank. | | Reject | Important | Reject | Important |
| **C- Environmental related factors:** | | | | | |
| (1) Level of competition | | Fail to Reject | Not Important | Fail to Reject | Not Important |
| (2) Overall performance of the banking sector | | Reject | Important | Reject | Important |
| (3) Country Economic performance | | Reject | Important | Reject | Important |
| (4) Legal stability | | Reject | Important | Reject | Important |
| (5) Political stability | | Reject | Important | Reject | Important |
| **Null Hypothesis 3:**<br>No factors are considered more important for customers when taking the decision to buy new retail banking loan and saving services than others.<br><br>**Null Hypothesis 4:**<br>Most important factors affecting customers' decisions to buy new retail banking loan services are not different from those affecting their decision to buy new retail banking saving services. | -ANOVA<br>-Two sample t- test<br>-Discriminant analysis | Reject | New Service related factors are attributed significantly higher importance<br>**Most important factors in order**<br>1-Service quality<br>2-Pricing (discriminating factor)<br>3-Liquidity (Discriminating factor)<br>4-Bank reputation<br>5-Convenience | Reject | Bank related factors are significantly attributed higher importance<br><br>**Most important factors in order**<br>1-Service quality<br>2-Bank reputation<br>3-Political stability<br>4-Service risk (discriminating factor)<br>5-Tenor (discriminating factor) |

| Hypothesis | Test | New Loan Services | | New Saving Services | |
|---|---|---|---|---|---|
| | | **Decision** | **Result** | **Deci-sion** | **Result** |
| **Null Hypothesis 5:**<br>The following Demographic variables do not affect the importance that customers attribute to different factors when taking their decision to buy new retail banking services: | ANOVA | | | | |
| (a) Gender | | Reject | Significantly affects:<br>▪ Service uniqueness<br>▪ Service sophistication<br>▪ Documentation<br>▪ Availability of information<br>▪ Overall service related factors | Reject | Significantly affects:<br>▪ Pricing<br>▪ Documentation<br>▪ Performance of the banking sector |
| (b)Age | | Reject | Significantly affects:<br>▪ Bank performance<br>▪ Ownership/ nationality<br>▪ Overall bank related factors<br>▪ Political stability<br>▪ Performance of the banking sector<br>▪ Overall environment related factors | Reject | Significantly affects:<br>▪ Service sophistication<br>▪ Documentation<br>▪ Bank ownership/ nationality |

| Hypothesis | Test | New Loan Services | | New Saving Services | |
|---|---|---|---|---|---|
| | | Decision | Result | Decision | Result |
| (c) Level of education | | Fail to reject | No effect | Reject | Significantly affects:<br>▪ Availability of information<br>▪ Bank performance<br>▪ Convenience<br>▪ Range of other services<br>▪ Performance of previous services<br>▪ Overall bank related factors<br>▪ Range of other services<br>▪ Performance of previous services |
| (d) Marital status | | Reject | Significantly affects:<br>▪ Tenor | Reject | Significantly affects:<br>▪ Bank nationality/ ownership |
| (e) Number of children | | Fail to reject | No effect | Reject | Significantly affects:<br>▪ Bank ownership / nationality |
| (f) Employment status | | Reject | Significantly affects<br>▪ Documentation<br>▪ Previous positive experience with new services. | Reject | Significantly affects<br>▪ Pricing,<br>▪ Tenor<br>▪ Bank ownership/ nationality, and<br>▪ Political stability<br>▪ Performance of the banking sector. |
| (g) Level of income | | Fail to reject | No effect | Reject | ▪ Availability of information |

# Chapter 5- Discussion

This chapter starts by discussing the results of the statistical analysis presented in chapter four which demonstrate the most important findings of the empirical research. These results serve to achieve the first objective of our research, that is, to identify the most important factors affecting customer's decision to buy new retail banking loan and saving services. The chapter then proceeds to discuss the second objective of the research which is how to incorporate those factors into the new service development process discussed in chapter two in order to introduce new services that are valued and demanded by customers

## 5.1 Customers' interest in buying new retail banking loan and saving services

Results of the statistical analysis as presented in the previous chapter reveal that Egyptian customers' interest in buying new retail banking services could be considered generally high if compared to other markets. This is evidenced by the fact that 79% of respondents showed interest in buying new retail banking services vs. only 62% in the survey conducted by the American Banker/Gallup in 1999 (Garmhausen, 1999). However, their interest in buying new saving services is much higher than that in buying new loan services. This is not only reflected in their response to how interested they are in both services and that reveals that 88% of customers are interested in new saving services vs. only 68% interested in new loan services, but also in the response rate to the questionnaires of both services that reached 80% for saving services as compared to only 68% for loan services. This is mainly due to the fact that loan services are considered relatively new in the market with many customers not accustomed to the idea of borrowing for personal use. This is especially true in light of the risk averse nature of the Egyptian culture. In addition, being an Islamic country with more than 85% Muslim populations, many Muslims hold the belief that interest is usury which is forbidden by Islam, especially if the loan is used for personal not business purposes.

As for the demographic variables affecting customers' interest in new services; out of the general typical retail banking customers' profile as mainly males, at the age of 31-50, holding a bachelor degree, married with two children, employed by the private sector, and earning monthly income of LE 2000-LE 5000, none of these demographic variables proved to have an effect over customers' interest in new saving services. For loan services, however, gender, number of children and employment status affect customers' interest in buying new services. Males are 3.3 times more interested in buying new loan service than females as they are usually responsible for the family financial planning and bank relationships, especially when it comes to borrowing obligations. They typically have two children or less and are employed by the private sector or have their own private business, thus they are accustomed to the idea of borrowing not necessarily out of a need, but even out of leveraging one's financial position.

The above results partially support hypothesis 1 which states that "the demographic variables of (a) gender, (b) age, (c) level of education (d) marital status, (e) number of children, (f) employment status, and (g) level of income affect customers' interest in buying new retail banking loan and saving services". For saving services, none of the examined demographic variables proved to have an effect over customers' interest in buying new services. For loan services, gender, number of children, and employment status proved to affect customers' interest in buying new services.

## 5.2 Factors affecting customers' decisions to buy new retail banking loan and saving services

The results of the analysis indicate that all the three sets of service, bank, and environment related factors proved to be important for customers when taking the decision to buy new retail banking loan and saving services. This supports the argument of El Khodeiry (1999) who divides determinants of demand for new retail banking services into factors related to the service itself, factors related to the offering bank and factors related to the market. However, the order of importance attributed to these sets of factors proved to be different in loan services than in saving services as illustrated by the following diagram:

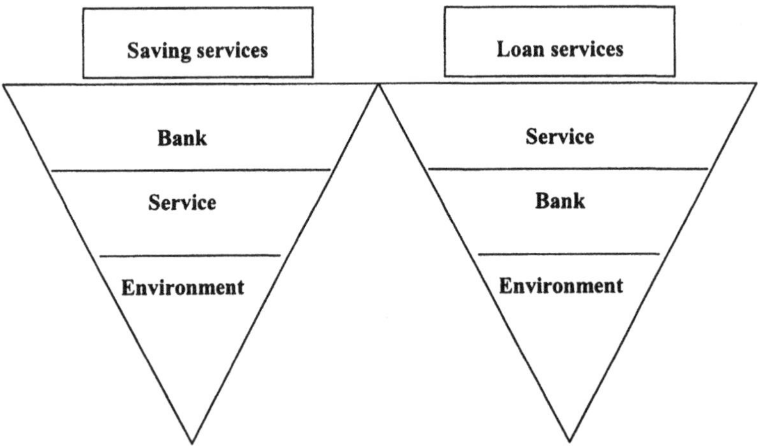


**Figure 7: Order of importance of different sets of factors for new loan and saving services**

As illustrated in the diagram, Bank related factors dominate customers' decision to buy new retail banking saving services followed by service related and then environment related factors. On the other hand, service related factors dominate customers' decision to buy new retail banking loan services followed by bank related and then environment related factors. This is due to the difference in the nature of both loan and saving services and customers' perception of risk for both of them. For new loan services, customers are granted a loan amount with a fixed ceiling from the bank for a specific purpose and with certain conditions, pricing, guarantees, and tenor. The maximum risk that clients face is losing their guarantees or having to pay back the loan before maturity, therefore, they primarily care about the service conditions. As for new saving services, customers deposit their money with the bank with almost no guarantees that they will receive it back except for the level of trust that they have in this bank, and therefore, they primarily care about the bank attributes even before considering the service conditions.

In terms of the order of importance attributed to individual factors affecting customers' decisions to buy new retail banking loan and saving services, the top five most important factors that customers consider in the evaluation and decision making stage of the buying process for new loan and saving services are presented in table (44). Out of those identified factors, service quality, bank reputation, pricing, and convenience were also identified by most of the researches who explored the factors affecting bank choice. These include Lasheen (1992), Boyd et al (1994), Kinnington, Hill &Rakwaska, (1996), Devlin (1998), El Khodeiry (1999), Ta & Har (2000), Dick (2002), Devlin & Gerrard (2004), and Tank & Tyler (2005).

**Table 44: Most important factors affecting customers' decisions to buy loan and saving services sorted in order of importance**

| Order of importance | Saving services | Loan services |
|---|---|---|
| 1 | Service quality | Service quality |
| 2 | Bank reputation | Pricing |
| 3 | Political stability | Liquidity |
| 4 | Service risk | Bank reputation |
| 5 | Tenor | Convenience |

For both loan and saving services, service quality of the offering bank proved to be the most important factor affecting customers when they make the decision to buy a new service. The tested dimensions of service quality are staff friendliness and helpfulness, efficiency and accuracy in completing transactions, and prompt and speedy service. This signals that customers' behavior changed in accordance with the accelerating rhythm of life towards valuing speedy, reliable, and friendly services. It also indicates that service quality has become an important competitive advantage that can differentiate one bank from another.

For saving services, bank reputation follows as the second most important factor for customers when taking the decision to buy a new service. This can be attributed to the fact that a solid reputation, strong brand name, and market continuity are usually translated by customers as signals of trust that we explained is most needed in saving services. Political stability then appears as the third most important factor affecting customers when taking the decision to buy new saving services. This reflects customers' concerns about having a stable political environment before taking the risk of trying a new saving service, as a stable political environment would reflect positively on having a stable legal and economic environment. Customers worry that any political turmoil could lead to the loss of their money when they most need it. This is particularly important in a country like Egypt where the external political threat could be a foreign invasion while the internal political threat could be a complete turn around in the whole political, legal, and economic system by the Islamic fundamentalists.

Service risk, in terms of the expected size of loss in case of service failure, appears in the fourth rank as some service such as equity mutual funds may involve high risk that some customers may consider too high to accept. Finally, in the fifth rank appears the flexibility of deciding on service tenor which implies ability to withdraw the deposited amount at any time without restrictions. The fact that those factors are considered more important than pricing reflects that, when evaluating new saving services, customers give a higher weight to minimal risk than competitive expected return.

For loan services, and after service quality, pricing comes in the second rank. As mentioned before, loan customers generally care about the service itself more than the offering bank, and the most important service related factor that they care about is the loan pricing. This means that customers' most important evaluation criteria of the new loan service is the interest and commission rates charged on the loan relative to market average, as well as, the stability of this rate over the life time of the loan facility. Liquidity, or the ability to withdraw or pre -pay any amount within the loan ceiling without restrictions or extra cost appears as the third most important factor considered by customers. Customers particularly care about having the freedom to prepay part of or even the entire loan amount without extra fees as banks sometimes impose prepayment fees on loans. Bank reputation in terms of brand name and market stability then comes in the fourth rank as customers don't want to be surprised that the bank is closing or downsizing its operations and calling back all of its loans. Finally, convenience in terms of extended opening hours and a widespread network of branches and ATMs appears in the fifth rank.

Demographic variables are found to affect the degree of importance that customers attribute to different factors. Although it may vary in some factors as will be explained later, the general trend is that young males that are either single or married with two children or less and who are highly educated and employed by the private sector or have their own business tend to have more tolerance to risk. This is indicated by the fact that they attribute less importance to the factors related to environment or bank risk, and more importance to the factors related to bank relationship convenience and service features.

Although the above mentioned factors are considered to be the most important determinants of customers' decision to buy new retail banking services, other factors related to the service, bank, and environment are also considered to be important as discussed in the following section.

### 5.2.1 Environment related factors

The environment related factors presented in table (45) proved to be important for customers when taking the decision to buy new retail banking loan and saving services. Competition is the only examined environmental factor that was identified by El Khodeiry (1999) as an important determinant of demand for retail financial services, but was found not to be considered as important by customers in our research. The explanation for this might be that competition drives banks to introduce better new retail banking services that increase demand. Thus, the relationship between competition and customers' demand is indirect. However, due to the complexity of decision and involvement of several factors, new retail banking services are usually considered on a stand alone basis when they are offered and not compared to already existing services in the market. Economic, legal, and banking sector related factors were already identified as important by Abdel Naby (1999) and El Khodeiry (1999). Political stability, however, was not previously identified as an important determinant of demand for new retail banking services. This might be attributed to the high sense of political instability and high rate of political changes currently witnessed in Egypt.

**Table 45: Important environment related factors sorted in order of importance**

| Order of importance | Saving services | Loan services |
|---|---|---|
| 1 | Political stability | Political stability |
| 2 | Legal stability | Legal stability |
| 3 | Country economic performance | Country economic performance |
| 4 | Performance of the banking sector | Performance of the banking sector |

In terms of order of importance, the set of environment related factors comes in the third position after service related and bank related factors for both loan and saving services. However, the importance attributed to environment related factors in saving services is higher than that in loan services. This is due to the difference in the nature of both services mentioned above that makes saving customers seek to trust both the bank and the environment in which the bank operates in terms of the stability of the legal, political and economic system of the country. This is also the reason why the performance of the banking sector is attributed significantly higher importance in saving services than in loan services that it became the third differentiating factor between both. As for the order of importance attributed to the different environmental factors, it is found to be the same for both loan and saving services. Political stability is considered to be the most important factor followed by legal stability then country economic performance and finally performance of the banking sector. This order reflects the fact that political stability is the most influential environmental factor that affects all of the others.

As for the effect of demographic variables over the importance that customers attribute to different environment related factors for both loan and saving services; for saving services, males, private sector employees, and business owners are found to attribute lower importance to the performance of the banking sector than females, public sector employees and unemployed customers. This might be attributed to the fact that the former usually have more tolerance to risk than the later. Political stability was also attributed lower importance by private sector employees than all other employment categories including business owners who are usually among the first to be affected by any political turbulence. As for loan services, age is found to have an impact over the importance that customers attribute to the performance of the banking sector, the political stability, and the overall environment related factors where younger customers at the age category of 21-40 attribute lower importance to those factors than customers above 40 year of age. This could also be attributed to the fact that younger generations usually have more tolerance to risk than older ones.

### 5.2.2 Bank related factors

Results reveal that the bank related factors presented in table (46) are considered important for customers when taking the decision to buy new retail banking loan services. They are all considered important when taking the decision to buy new retail banking saving services except for the availability of technologically advanced services such as internet and mobile bank. This is due to the fact that such services are still new to the market and are still in the early adoption phase with low market penetration rates. The fact that those services are considered important by loan customers could be attributed to their demographic profile mentioned above that makes them more likely to be among the early adopters of technological services. As already mentioned, the first three factors of service quality, bank reputation and convenience were already mentioned as bank selection criteria by most of the researchers who explored this area such as Lasheen (1992), Boyd et al (1994), Kinnington, Hill &Rakwaska, (1996), Devlin (1998), El Khodeiry (1999), Ta & Har (2000), Dick (2002), Devlin & Gerrard (2004), and Tank & Tyler (2005). Bank performance, performance of previous new services and variety of services offered were identified by few researchers including EL Khodeiry (1999).

**Table 46: Important bank related factors sorted in order of importance**

| Order of importance | Saving services | Loan services |
|---|---|---|
| 1 | Service quality | Service quality |
| 2 | Bank reputation | Bank reputation |
| 3 | Convenience | Convenience |
| 4 | Bank performance | Performance of previous services |
| 5 | Previous positive experience with the bank | Previous positive experience with the bank |
| 6 | Performance of previous services | Availability of technologically advanced services |
| 7 | Ownership/ nationality of the bank. | Bank performance |
| 8 | Availability of a wide range of other services | Availability of a wide range of other services |
| 9 | | Ownership/ nationality of the bank |

The above mentioned factors could be grouped into two subsets of bank risk and relationship convenience. Bank risk would include the factors of bank performance, performance of previous services, bank reputation, previous experience with the bank, and bank ownership/nationality, while relationship convenience would include the factors of service quality, convenience, range of other services, and the availability of technologically advanced services.

Bank related factors are found to dominate customers when taking the decision to buy new retail banking saving services followed by service related factors. This is due to the risky nature of saving services explained above that makes customers consider trust in the depositing institution as even more important than the service itself. When considering individual factors, service quality is found to be the most important bank related factor affecting customers' decision to buy both new retail banking loan and saving services followed by bank reputation and then convenience. Although the order of importance of the first three factors is the same for both services, the importance attributed to bank reputation is higher in saving services while the importance attributed to convenience is higher in loan services for the reasons mentioned before.

As for the effect of demographic variables over the importance that customers attribute to different bank related factors; For saving services, younger customers especially those at the age category of 21-30, singles, and respondents with no or one child attribute lower importance to bank's ownership/ nationality than older married customers with two children or more. This might be attributed to the formers' more acceptance of the idea of globalization and transnational companies than the later who still think that government owned banks are safer to deposit their money with. In addition, the higher the education level, the lower the importance that customers attribute to bank related factors in general and to bank performance, performance of previous services, convenience, and range of other services in particular. This might be the result of the fact that highly educated customers usually have more financial education that would allow them to take decisions regarding the service directly without having to seek trust through the bank.

For loan services, younger respondents at the age category of 21-40 generally attribute lower importance to bank related factors, especially bank performance, bank reputation, and bank ownership/ nationality. This might be attributed to their high tolerance to risk especially in a loan service where the bank's risk is not as important as the service conditions.

### 5.2.3 Service related factors

All the examined service related factors as presented in table (47) proved to be important for customers when taking the decision to buy both new retail banking loan and saving services. Out of those factors, pricing is the most widely identified selection criterion by most of the researchers who conducted previous research on the subject such as Lasheen (1992), Boyd et al (1994), Kinnington, Hill & Rakwaska, (1996), Ta & Har (2000), El Khodeiry (1999), Dick (2002), Devlin & Gerrard (2004), and Devlin (1998). Service sophistication, service uniqueness, and availability of information were also identified as important determinants of demand for new services by several researchers such as El Khodairy (1999).

As for the level and order of importance attributed to different factors, it was found to be different between the two types of loan and saving services due to their different natures as explained before. The order of importance attributed to different factors is as follows:

**Table 47: Important service related factors sorted in order of importance**

| Order of importance | Saving services | Loan services |
|---|---|---|
| 1 | Service Risk ** | Pricing ** |
| 2 | Tenor ** | Liquidity ** |
| 3 | Liquidity ** | Service Uniqueness |
| 4 | Pricing ** | Service sophistication |
| 5 | Service uniqueness | Documentation |
| 6 | Service sophistication | Service risk ** |
| 7 | Documentation | Availability of Information |
| 8 | Availability of information | Tenor ** |
| 9 | Previous positive experience with new services | Previous positive experience with new services |

**** Discriminating factors**

As mentioned before, service related factors dominate customers when taking the decision to buy a new loan service. Of those factors, the factors representing the service conditions of pricing, tenor, liquidity, risk, and documentation proved to have the strongest relationship among all. Competitive stable interest and commission rates proved to be the most important service related factor that customers consider when buying a new loan service, followed by the ability to withdraw or prepay part of or the entire loan amount without restrictions or extra cost. In the third rank appears service uniqueness in terms of the service offering of new advantages or fulfillment of a specific need that no other available services offer. This is especially important for loans as most of them are offered for a specific purpose such as education loans or installment loans from some big shops, and therefore, customers care that the loan would be offered for new purposes or offering new advantages.

As for saving services, the set of service related factors ranks second after bank related factors in the most important factors that customers consider when taking the decision to buy new saving services. Service risk or the expected loss of interest or principal in case of the service's poor performance appears as the most important service related factor affecting customers when buying new saving services. This could be attributed to the risky nature of saving services mentioned before. In addition, the risk of some services such as equity mutual funds may be too high for customers to accept. The flexibility of deciding on service tenor then appears in the second rank as customers would like to have the freedom to tailor make the saving tenor according to their needs. Liquidity or the ability to increase or withdraw from the saving amount without restriction or loss of interest, which is too much related to the service tenor, appears in the third rank followed by the competitiveness and stability of the earned return which surprisingly customers do not consider as important as the minimal service risk or as the flexibility to get their money back any time

As for the effect of demographic variables over the importance that customers attribute to different service related factors; for loan services, service uniqueness, service sophistication, availability of information, and documentation are attributed higher importance by males than females. This conforms to the finding that males are more interested in new loan services and consequently in the details of those services than females. Tenor is considered more important for married customers who have many obligations and care more about their financial planning then single respondents. Unemployed customers do not attribute much importance to documentation or previous experience with new loan services as most probably they do not have such experience since most loan services require either full cash cover or direct salary transfer to the bank.

As for saving services, competitive pricing and documentation are found to be significantly more important to males than females. Private sector employees also attribute higher importance to pricing than public sector employees and business owners who care more about having the flexibility to decide on the service tenor. Younger respondents at the age category of 21-40 attribute significantly lower importance to documentation then older ones due to their tolerance to risk. In addition, the lower the education, the higher the importance attributed to the availability of information about the service through advertising, brochures and direct selling as customers with lower education who are also probably not financially educated seek to know more information about the service before buying it. Finally, the higher the income, the lower the importance attributed to the availability of information as wealthy customers are usually familiar with different types of saving services and have the luxury not to care much about the details.

The above discussed results partially support hypothesis 2 which states that "The following sets of factors are important for customers when taking the decision to buy new retail banking loan and saving services.

a. **Service related factors:** (1) service uniqueness (2) service sophistication, (3) pricing, (4) tenor, (5) liquidity, (6) service risk (7) documentation required, (8) availability of information and (9) previous positive experience with new retail banking services.

b. **Bank related factors:** (1) bank performance, (2) service quality, (3) convenience, (4) availability of a wide range of other services, (5) availability of technologically advanced services, (6) performance of previous new services, (7) bank reputation, (8) previous positive experience with the bank, and (9) ownership/ nationality of the bank.

c. **Environmental related factors:** (1) level of competition, (2) overall performance of the banking sector, (3) country's economic performance, (4) legal stability, and (5) political stability."

For saving services, the availability of technologically advanced services and the level of competition were not found to be important for customers when buying new saving services. On the other hands, for loan services, competition was the only factor that was not found to be important for customers when buying new services.

As also indicated by the above discussed results, some factors such as service quality were found to be more important to customers than others. This supports hypothesis 3 which states that "some factors are considered more important for customers when taking the decision to buy new retail banking loan and saving services than others." Results also indicate that the importance attributed to different factors in new loan services is different than that in new saving services. Thus, hypothesis 4 which states that "most important factors affecting customers' decisions to buy new retail banking loan services are different from those affecting their decision to buy new retail banking saving services" is also supported.

Finally, results also partially support hypothesis 5 which state that "the demographic variables of (a) gender, (b) age, (c) level of education, (d) marital status, (e) number of children, (f) employment status, and (g) income affect the importance that customers attribute to different factors when taking their decision to buy new retail banking loan and saving services". Level of education, number of children, and level of income were not found to affect the importance attributed to any of the above mentioned factors in loan services.

## 5.3 Incorporating the most important factors affecting customers' decisions to buy new retail banking services into the new service development process

After identifying the most important factors that affect customers' decision to buy new retail banking loan and saving services, the last objective of our research is to incorporate those factors into the new service development process in order to come up with successful new services that customers value and desire. As explained before, the new service development process could be divided into predevelopment activities of setting a new service strategy, idea generation, idea screening, concept development, and business analysis; development activities of service development and market testing, and finally the launch activity. Researchers such as Papastathopoulou, Avlonitis & Indounas (2001) argue that it is the proper implementation of the predevelopment activities that maximizes the chances of the new service success. This is due to the facts that the proper implementation of those activities leads to accurately defined service specifications that would reduce the time to market. In addition, through those activities, failures could be identified early enough so as to save the organization the efforts and resources that would be wasted if the idea is further developed. Many researchers also argue that customers' involvement in the different stages of the new service development process would increase the potentials of success (Alam & Perry, 2002, Martin & Horne, 1994, Johne & Storey, 1998, Edvardson & Olsson, 1996, Meidan, 1996, Lasheen, 1992, and Costanzo, Keasey & Short, 2003). We build up on those arguments and add that if the factors that affect customers decision to buy new services are directly integrated and considered in the implementing of the predevelopment activities, the potentials of customers' acceptance of the new service would be maximized and the market testing stage could be minimized. This is particularly true for radical new services that customers perceive as entailing higher risk and that usually require extensive market testing. Therefore, by incorporating those factors into the predevelopment activities of the NSD process, the potentials of market success would be increased and the testing costs, time and money, and threats, of competitors' copying the new service would be minimized. As such, the identified environment, bank, service and demographic factors should directly affect the implementation of the predevelopment activities which would indirectly impact the following development and launch activities as illustrated by figure 8.

### 5.3.1 Pre development activities

The most important factors that affect customers' decisions to buy new retail banking services should directly affect the predevelopment activities of the new service development process as those activities establish the detailed concept and features of the new service that determine the final success of the whole process. However, not all sets of factors affect each and every stage of the predevelopment phase. As illustrated by figure 9, while idea generation and screening are affected by all sets of factors, setting the new service strategy would only be affected by environment and bank related factors, concept development by bank, service and demographic related factors, and finally, business analysis by demographic variables. The general trend that can be noticed is that, the more we go from general to specific, i.e. from environment to bank to service to demographic, the earlier the stages that are affected by those factors.

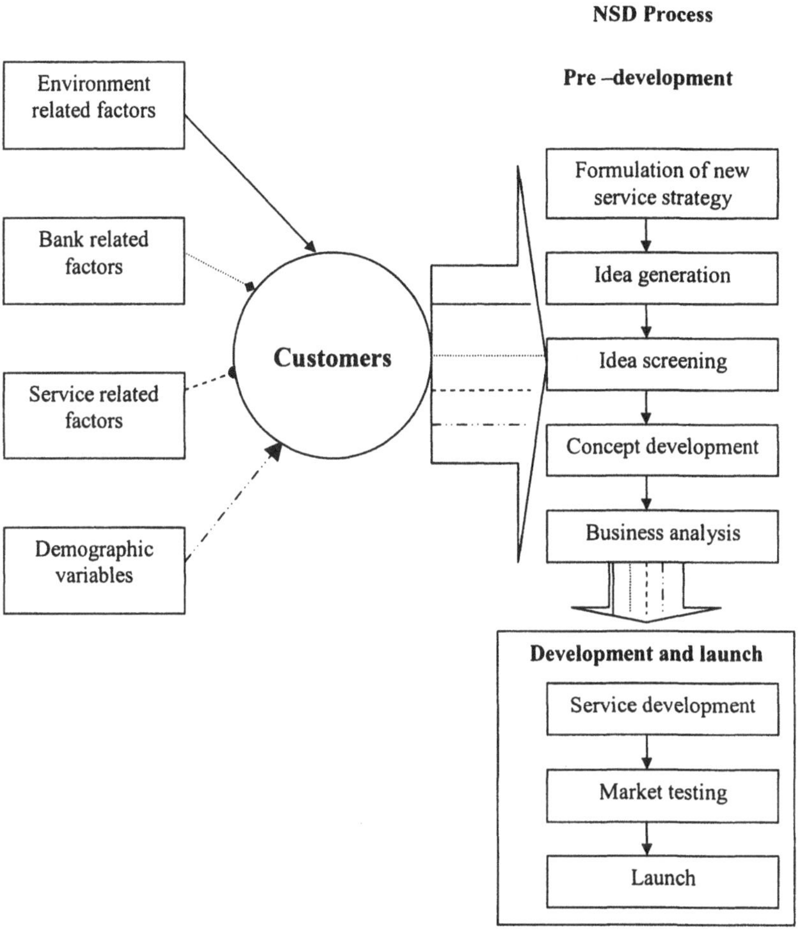


**Figure 8: Framework for incorporating the factors affecting customers' decisions to buy new retail banking services into the NSD process**

### 5.3.1.1 Formulation of new service strategy

As mentioned before, the continuous introduction of new services has become a fact of life for those banks that want to maintain and improve their market position (Pete Naude & Dengler, 1998). However, as per the results of our research, uncertain environmental conditions such as political and legal instability or poor performance of the economy or the banking sector may result in customers' refraining from taking the risk of trying a new service. To solve this dilemma, banks that want to be proactive to those conditions should adopt an innovation strategy that responds to those important environmental factors that customers consider when making the decision to buy a new retail banking service.

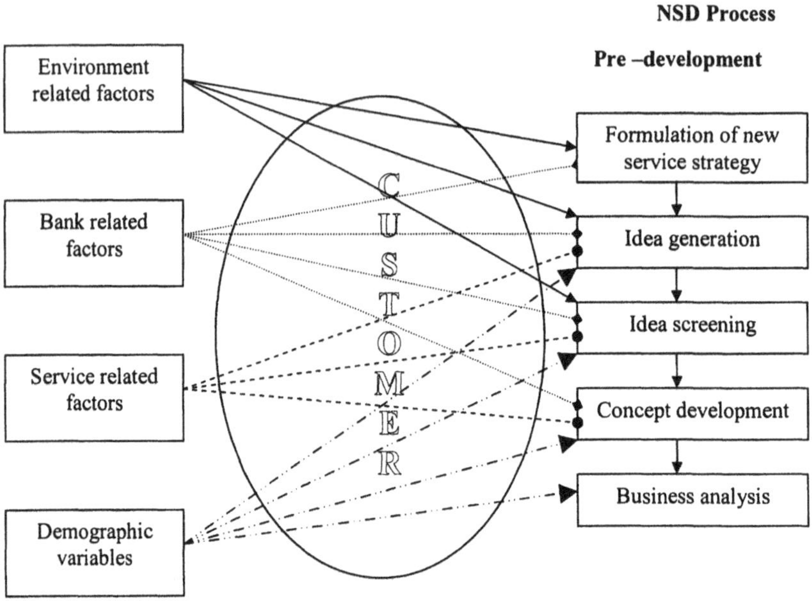


**Figure 9: Factors Affecting different stages of NSD predevelopment phase**

As such, whenever there is a great uncertainty in the political, legal, economic, or banking sector conditions of the country, it is not advisable for banks to explore new markets or new types of services through the satellite product strategy that would be perceived by customers as bearing greater risk. It would be more advisable to exploit current successful service or client base through the expansion strategy or the differentiation strategy. When selecting the innovation type, and although radical innovation represents the greatest potential for success (Costanzo, Keasey & Short, 2003), it also represents the highest risk for both the bank and the customer. Therefore, at the time of environmental turbulence, banks should focus on incremental continuous innovations that would not lead to major changes in either the product types or the customers' behavior patterns. However, it should be noted that a satellite product or a radical innovation that would be proactively designed to mitigate those environmental risks may prove to be very successful at the time of environmental turbulence.

Important bank related factors would also to a great extent affect the strategy that the bank adopts when introducing a new service. Given that customers value quality service, solid reputation and convenience, banks that enjoy those competencies would be able to capitalize on them to explore new markets by introducing satellite product or radical new services. Those services are more likely to succeed as customers already trust the bank and favor dealing with it even if the new service conditions are not as favorable as services offered by weaker banks. This is especially true for saving services for which customers attribute greater importance to the offering bank than the service itself. Weaker banks, however, may be obliged to depend on exploiting their current customer base through cross selling until they build up those strategic competencies.

#### 5.3.1.2 Idea generation

The purpose of idea generation is to identify high potential new ideas. Those new ideas could be generated through internal or external sources among which customers are considered to be the most important source leading to the most successful ideas (Meidan, 1996, Scheuing & Johnson, 1989). Therefore, the results of our research could serve as a guide that directs idea generation efforts towards the highest potential ideas that are more likely to be accepted by customers. This could be realized either through focusing on generating ideas that would emphasize and capitalize on the most important factors that affect customers' decision to buy new services or through disregarding ideas that would contradict with those factors.

As such, important environment related factors could affect the type of new service to be offered, i.e. loan or saving, and at the same time could serve as a source of successful new ideas. Knowing that customers of new saving services attribute great importance to political stability, offering a new saving service in times of political turbulence would not be a successful idea except if this service is designed to mitigate this political risk. Important bank related factors, especially those related to bank risk, could also affect the type of service offered as higher risk banks would not be advised to introduce new retail banking saving services for which customers require a high level of trust in the bank. As for the bank related factors associated with relationship convenience, they may serve as a source of new ideas for services that would be specifically tailored to satisfy customers' aspiration for the highest level of quality and convenience.

The most important service related factors would serve to guide banks on the important service features that customers value and look for when buying a new service so that they would give them the highest priority during idea generation. Those important features are minimal service risk, flexible tenor and high liquidity for saving services, and competitive fixed pricing, high liquidity and uniqueness for loan services. Finally, the demographic variables and how they affect customers' interest to buy new service and the importance they attribute to different factors could also serve as a source of successful ideas. For example, knowing that males are three times more interested in buying new loan services than females, a new loan service targeting male customers and satisfying their particular needs is likely to be more successful than a new loan service targeting both genders.

#### 5.3.1.3 Idea screening

The fact that idea generation efforts are directed to respond to the important factors affecting customers' decisions to buy a new service would to a great extent simplify the idea screening process that serves to rank ideas according to a pre set criteria in order to determine whether they justify the time and expense of further study (Cowell, 1988). This is especially true when applying consumer screens that are suggested by Papastathopoulou, Avlonitis & Indounas (2001) to check whether the new idea would be accepted by customers. Despite this fact, whenever new ideas are screened for their customer acceptance, banks should set their screening criteria to reflect the most important factors that affect customers' decision to buy a new service which are service quality, bank reputation, political stability, service risk, and tenor for saving services; and service quality, pricing, liquidity, bank reputation and convenience for loan services. Services that satisfy customers' most valued criteria should be given the highest rank. Numerical weighting models would be the most suitable screening technique to be used as it provides an appropriate method to set different weights to the varying importance that customers attribute to different factors.

#### 5.3.1.4 Concept development

After screening generated ideas for those that have the highest potential for success, a detailed description of the new service should be prepared including its benefits and how they satisfy customer needs, as well as, both of its core and supporting features (Papastathopoulou, Avlonitis & Indounas, 2001). At this stage, customers' preferences regarding factors related to bank relationship as well as service features should be considered for different types of services. For example, as loan customers care about convenience more than saving customers, the supporting features of a new loan service should cater for easier access. On the other hand, when developing the concept of a new saving service, a minimal service risk should be given a priority even if it may negatively reflect on pricing for which customers do not attribute the same degree of importance. However, the effect of demographic variables over the importance attributed to different factors should also be considered as it also affects the design of the supporting service features according to the market segment that the new service is targeting. For example, in developing the concept of a new saving service that would target private sector employees as part of their payroll service package, competitive pricing should be given the highest priority even over service risk as it is more valued for this segment of customers.

#### 5.3.1.5 Business analysis

This stage mainly involves assessing the business attractiveness of the idea in terms of profitability and cost benefit analysis (Cowell, 1988, Meidan, 1996). Martin & Horne (1994) associate the use of customers' information at this stage with the success of the new service innovation. Therefore, at this stage, the demographic variables that affect customers' interest in different types of new services, as well as, the importance that different demographic segments attribute to different factors would help in the assessment of the size of the potential market and consequently in the sales forecasts. By the end of this stage, a clear concept of a customer oriented new service is developed along with its features, expected benefits, and feasibility.

### 5.3.2 Development and launch activities

The last three stages of the NSD process serve to translate the concept generated trough predevelopment activities into a real service, test it, and then commercialize it. As the factors affecting customers decisions to buy new services are already rooted in the design of the new service concept, those last activities of the NSD process would be indirectly affected by those factors as follows:

#### 5.3.2.1 Development

Development involves making the investments necessary to translate the concept generated from predevelopment activities into an actual service (Meidan, 1996). This might involve preparing a prototype of the service, deciding on the brand name, designing the advertising and promotion material and so on. All of these steps are carried out to represent, reflect, and emphasize the previously designed service features and target market.

#### 5.3.2.2 Market testing

This stage involves testing the new service on a limited sample of the target market to check market acceptance of the service and identify potential implementation problems (Meidan, 1996). Given that the design of the new service has already responded to the factors that affect customers' decisions to buy new services, the timing and scope of this stage could be reduced into a short limited trial run that would be mainly carried out to check the functionality of the service and the quality of implementation. Thus, the time and money cost associated with this stage could be reduced. In addition, the risk of competitors' copying the new service before its launch would be largely mitigated.

#### 5.3.2.3 Launch

This stage involves market introduction and full scale commercialization of the service. The quality of launch greatly affects the success of the new service especially in a market where customers attribute the highest importance to quality. Communication, advertising, and distribution efforts should be tailored to target the right segments and should emphasize the most desired features by those segments such as quality service and valued service conditions. Enough time and financial resources should be devoted to this stage as it is the stage responsible of communicating the service image to the target customer. This image, that has been developed specifically to satisfy this target market, must be properly communicated to them in order to grasp their attention and motivate them to take the decision to buy.

Finally, it should be noted that, over the long run, banks, that would like to have the flexibility to respond to any environmental changes with different types of services targeting any market segment, must reset their strategic priorities so as to equip themselves with the most important competencies that customers look for in any bank offering a new type of service. Those competencies could be summarized, as per the results of our research, in providing quality service, enjoying a solid reputation, and providing the highest level of convenience. Given the special nature of financial services that makes customers attribute great importance to the offering bank, those banks that could be identified by customers as reputable banks providing top quality convenient services are more likely to introduce successful new services that customers desire than other banks that could be even providing better service features. In addition, those banks that could also add to those competencies the capability to respond to the factors affecting customers' decision to buy new services with the right type of new service, in the most suitable timing, targeting the most lucrative potential segment with the most appropriate features, will most likely have the highest potentials of success.

### 5.4 Summary

This chapter illustrated the findings of the statistical analysis presented in chapter Four. It explains that, when making a decision to buy a new saving service, customers primarily care about the bank risk and relationship convenience of offering bank even before considering the service conditions. They attribute the highest importance to service quality followed by bank reputation, political stability, service risk, and finally tenor. Conversely, when buying new loan services, customers primarily care about the service condition. They attribute the highest importance to service quality followed by pricing, liquidity, bank reputation and finally convenience. Those factors for which customers attribute the highest importance should be directly integrated into the predevelopment activities of the new service development process which are setting the new service strategy, idea generation, idea screening, concept development and business analysis. Thus, they will have an indirect impact on the implementation of the last development, testing, and commercialization activities.

# Chapter 6 – Summary and Conclusion

## 6.1 Summary of research

The retail banking business has been witnessing tremendous change and growth since the beginning of the 1980s. Banks that used to give little attention to the personal sector now realize that it has unlimited potentials for growth with the minimal possible risk. Therefore, the industry structure, technology, delivery systems, offered services, and marketing tools all developed, not only to take advantage of the opportunities that the retail business offers, but also to respond to the rapidly changing environment in terms of intensifying competition, changing technology, deregulation and consolidation, and most importantly, changing customers behavior and needs. The result is a very dynamic market where continuous innovation has become the rule, not the exception, especially when new innovations are rapidly imitated due to the lack of patenting.

In such a market where the services offered are usually sophisticated and entail a considerable amount of risk while the target market is the mass population of usually financially uneducated customers, banks must strive to balance the functional with the market success of their new services. In order to do that, they must not base the development of their new services on what competitors offer or what internal resources and capabilities they have, but most importantly, they must incorporate the customers' needs, logic, and assessment criteria into the design of their new services. Banks must carefully study the factors that affect customers when taking the decision to buy new retail financial services. Those factors, due the risky and complex nature of retail financial services, are not only limited to the customers' evaluation of the service itself, but also include their assessment of the offering bank and the environmental conditions. They are also likely to be different from one type of service to another given the wide range and different risk nature of different types of new retail financial services. In order to come up with new services that customer's value and desire, those factors must be considered and incorporated into the new service development (NSD) process.

The objectives of this research are first, to find out the most important demographic, service, bank, and environment related factors that affect customers' interest and decisions to buy the most two prevalent types of new core retail banking services, loan and saving service. And second, to incorporate those factors into the NSD process in order to come up with customer oriented new services. Thus, banks could gain a sustainable competitive advantage by repositioning themselves as innovative customer centric institutions. At the same time, they could save themselves the time, efforts, money, and reputation costs associated with introducing services that fail to satisfy customers.

To achieve the first objective, an empirical research was conducted in one of the growing markets for retail banking services, Egypt, which witnesses the same trends of growth, competition, rapid innovation, and deregulation taking place in other international retail banking markets. To identify the factors to be examined, multiple exploratory methods were employed. These included literature reviews of the available published academic literature related to the factors affecting customers' choice with regard to retail banking, reviews of articles and features addressing new financial services, reviews of marketing material for new services, a series of semi structured interviews with retail banking managers, and a series of semi structured in depth interviews with a limited sample of the population. The importance of frequently mentioned factors from the exploratory research along with their measures was further investigated through pilot testing. The following factors were identified to be further examined through the survey questionnaires:

d. **Service related factors:** (1) service uniqueness (2) service sophistication, (3) pricing, (4) tenor, (5) liquidity, (6) service risk (7) documentation required, (8) availability of information and (9) previous positive experience with new retail banking services.

e. **Bank related factors:** (1) bank performance, (2) service quality, (3) convenience, (4) availability of a wide range of other services, (5) availability of technologically advanced services, (6) performance of previous new services, (7) bank reputation, (8) previous positive experience with the bank, and (9) ownership/ nationality of the bank.

f. **Environmental related factors:** (1) level of competition, (2) overall performance of the banking sector, (3) country Economic performance, (4) legal stability, and (5) political stability.

In Addition, customers' demographic variables of (a) gender, (b) age, (c) level of education, (d) marital status, (e) number of children, (f) employment status, and (g) level of income were also obtained to test whether it has an impact over their interest in buying new retail banking services or over the importance that they attribute to different factors.

The content and construct validity of the questionnaires were evaluated by three professional judges from the banking sector. Pilot testing was conducted on selected members of the population in order to clear any ambiguities in the questions and make them at the technical level understood by the general public. And finally, a test- retest procedure was carried out to measure the reliability of the instrument. A sample of 500 customers out of the population of 7-8 million accounts already existing retail banking market in Egypt was accidentally selected and asked to participate in the survey while waiting for their service to be delivered in bank branches. 250 questionnaires were administered for loan services and 250 questionnaires for saving services. Data was collected from nine branches of three banks each representing one of the three types of banks operating in Egypt and the sample was distributed prorate to their market share. These were the National Bank of Egypt representing public sector banks, National Societe Generale Bank representing joint venture and private sector banks, and American Express Bank representing branches of foreign banks.

The overall response rate was 74.6% representing 80.4% response rate for saving questionnaires and 68.8% response rate for loan questionnaires. Data was first edited, coded and entered to the SPSS version 11 statistical analysis software. It was then analyzed using different statistical analysis techniques to reach the desired results. These are frequency distribution analysis that was conducted to describe the demographic characteristics of the sample, the demographic characteristics of uninterested customers in new retail banking loan and saving services, and interested customers' response to different questionnaire items in terms of frequencies, mean and variability; chi Square analysis that was performed to test the significance of the impact of demographic variables on customers' interest in new retail banking loan and saving services; and logistic regression analysis that was performed in an attempt to predict customers' interest in new services from their demographic variables. Also conducted is one sample t- test to determine whether the different factors mentioned are considered important for customers when taking a decision to buy new loan and saving services, as well as, two sample t -test to determine the difference between importance attributed to different factors for both loan and saving services. It was followed by discriminant analysis that was performed to isolate the discriminating factors between loan and saving services. Analysis of variance (ANOVA) was used to determine the most important factors that customers consider when taking the decision to buy new retail banking loan and saving services. It was also used to investigate the effect of demographic variables over customers' response to different factors for both loan and saving services. Finally, factor analysis was used to examine the relationship between factors in an attempt to redefine them into fewer numbers of subsets for both loan and saving services

Results reveal that customers consider all of the above mentioned factors as important when taking the decision to buy new retail banking services except for the level of competition and availability of technologically advanced services for saving services, and the level of competition for loan services. They also reveal that, when taking a decision to buy a new saving service, customers primarily care about the offering bank's risk and relationship convenience even before considering the service conditions. They attribute the highest importance to service quality followed by bank reputation, political stability, service risk, and finally tenor. On the other hand, when buying new loan services, customers primarily care about the service condition. Although they still attribute the highest importance to service quality, it is followed by pricing, liquidity, bank reputation and finally convenience.

Demographic variables are found to affect customers' interest in new loan services as males are 3.3 times more interested in buying new loan services than females. They typically have two children or less and are employed by the private sector or have their own private business. Demographic variables also affect the degree of importance that customers attribute to different factors. Although it may vary in some factors as explained before, the general trend is that young males that are either single or married with two children or less and who are highly educated and employed by the private sector or have their own business tend to attribute less importance to the factors related to environment or bank risk, and more importance to the factors related to bank relationship convenience and service features. This is a strong signal that they generally have more tolerance to risk.

The second objective of the research is to incorporate the results of the empirical research into the new service development process in order to introduce customer oriented new services that customers value and desire. In order to achieve this objective, literature related to forces, types, strategies, and processes of developing new financial services, as well as, this related to customer orientation in new service development was reviewed. A sequence of new service development steps is proposed to be used as it consists of the most important and most comprehensive steps that have to be systematically, completely, and proficiently carried out in order to ensure the success of any new service effort. These steps could be divided into the predevelopment activities that consist of setting the new service strategy, idea generation, idea screening, concept development, and business analysis; and the development and launch activities that consist of service development, market testing, and finally launch.

The most important factors affecting customers' decisions to buy new services should be directly incorporated into the predevelopment activities of the NSD process. This could be accomplished by choosing the innovation type, whether radical or incremental, as well as, the innovation strategy that most suits the political, legal, economic, and banking sector environmental conditions. The innovation strategy in terms of exploring new markets or services via satellite products or exploiting current markets or services via expansion or differentiation should also reflect the extent to which the bank enjoys the most important bank related factors of service quality, reputation, and convenience. Idea generation should be directed towards choosing the service type, such as loan or saving services, which would most suit the bank's risk and environmental factors. It should also be guided to respond and capitalize on customers' most important environment, bank, and service related factors.

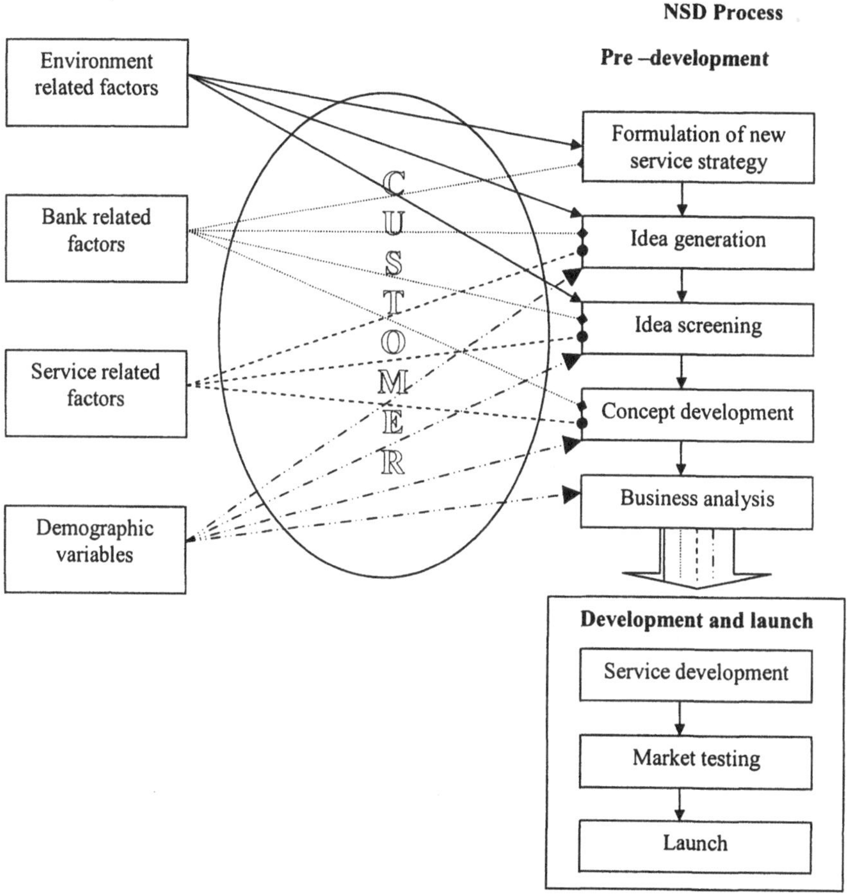


**Figure 10: Incorporating the factors affecting customers' decisions to buy new retail banking services into the NSD process**

When applying consumer screens in the idea screening phase, ideas should be ranked according to how much they respond and fit with the most important factors that customers care about for different types of services which are service quality, bank reputation, political stability, service risk, and tenor for saving services; and service quality, pricing, liquidity, bank reputation and convenience for loan services. In developing the service concept, customers' most important bank relationship and service related factors should be considered for different types of services. The relationship between the service type, the target segments and the features valued and desired by those segments should also be regarded. Finally, in conducting the business analysis, an accurate estimation of the size of the target market would be made possible given how valuable the offered features are for different segments. In carrying out the development and launch activities, the customer oriented new service concept is translated into an actual service. Thus, the costs and risks associated with market testing could be minimized and launching could be appropriately executed. As such, the identified factors indirectly affect those activities.

In addition, banks, that would like to establish a solid base on which they can build up a stream of continuously successful innovations, must reset their strategic priorities in order to build up the competencies that customers look for in any bank offering any type of new service. Those competencies could be summarized, according to the results of our research, in providing quality service, establishing a solid reputation, and offering the highest level of convenience.

## 6.2 Conclusion

In such a dynamic growing market as retail banking where each day new services are introduced, new technologies emerge, and new structures originate, change has become the only constant for those banks that want to lead the market. Within this change, banks that seek to surpass their competitors must engage in an endless race of service innovation in order to maintain their current market share and attract new customers. However, given this high rhythm of competition and change, new service failures may prove to have enormous money, time and reputation costs. Therefore, whenever introducing new retail banking services, banks must strive to achieve both the functional and the market success of the new service. This could be one of the bank's most challenging tasks given the sophisticated risky nature of those new services, especially radical higher risk ones, in contrast to the simple usually risk averse nature of the target market.

In order to achieve this balance, banks must incorporate the factors that affect customers' interest and decisions to buy new retail banking services into the new service development process in order to come up with new services that, in addition to achieving the functional success, are considered valued and desired by customers. Those factors are not only concerned with the new service itself, but given the risky nature of financial services, they also concern the offering bank and the surrounding environment, and are affected to a great extent by the demographic variables of customers. Due to the different risk nature of different types of services, they may also change from one type of service to another.

In attempting to identify those factors in the Egyptian retail banking market for two of the most prevalent core services, loan and saving services, customers are found to consider all the three sets of environment, bank, and service related factors as important whenever they take the decision to buy new retail banking loan and saving services. Important environment related factors that are considered when buying new loan services are political stability, legal stability, country economic performance, and performance of the banking sector. These all proved to be also important when taking the decision to buy new saving services. As for the bank related factors that proved to be important when buying new loan services, they could be divided into factors related to bank risk including bank performance, performance of previous services, bank reputation, previous experience with the bank, and bank ownership/nationality, and factors related to relationship convenience including the factors of service quality, convenience, range of other services, and the availability of technologically advanced services. The same factors are found to be considered important for customers of new saving services except for the availability of technologically advanced services. Finally, important service related factors for both new loan and saving services' customers include the service conditions of pricing, tenor, liquidity, risk, and documentation, as well as other factors such as service risk, uniqueness, sophistication, availability of information and previous positive experience with new services.

Although customers of both types of services consider all the three sets of factors as important, the degree of importance that they attribute to different sets and to different factors proved to be different from one type of service to another. For new saving services, customers primarily care about the offering bank's risk and relationship convenience even before considering the service conditions. They attribute the highest importance to service quality followed by bank reputation, political stability, service risk, and finally tenor. On the other hand, for new loan services, customers primarily care about the service condition. Although they still attribute the highest importance to service quality, it is followed by pricing, liquidity, bank reputation and finally convenience. While males, customers with two children or less, private sector employees, and business owners are more likely to be interested in buying new retail banking loan services, neither of the demographic variables of gender, age, education, marital status, number of children, employment status, and level of income proved to affect customers' interest in new saving services. However, they are found to affect the degree of importance that customers attribute to different factors. The general trend is that young males that are either single or married with two children or less and who are highly educated and employed by the private sector or have their own business tend to attribute less importance to the factors related to environment or bank risk, and more importance to the factors related to bank relationship convenience and service features. This constitutes a strong indication of their higher tolerance to risk.

The above mentioned factors should be taken into consideration when developing new retail banking loan and saving services in order to introduce new services that customers are willing to buy. They should be directly incorporated into the predevelopment activities of the NSD process which establish the service concept and set the stage for the development and launch activities. The first of these activities is setting the new service strategy that includes determining the innovation type, whether radical or incremental, and the innovation strategy, whether satellite, expansion or differentiation, to be used. These should be determined according to how stable are the environmental political, legal, and economic conditions and how competent is the bank in terms of service quality, reputation, and convenience. Radical innovations specifically require a higher degree of environmental stability as they are usually perceived as entailing higher risk. During idea generation, the new service type should be selected according to the level of bank and environmental risks. These, as well as, all other factors should also guide idea generation as they represent sources of new ideas. When applying consumer screens in the idea screening phase, ideas should be ranked according to how much they respond and fit with the most important factors that customers care about for different types of services. Customers' most important bank relationship and service related factors should be imbedded in the developed service concept that should also reflect the relationship between the service type, the target segments and the features valued and desired by those segments. Finally, the effect of demographic variables over customers' interest in different types of services and over the importance they attribute to different factors within each type, would enable the bank to conduce an accurate business analysis as it would allow for a more accurate estimation of the size of the target market. In carrying out the development and launch activities where the idea is translated into an actual service, having a solid customer oriented new service concept would minimize the costs and risks associated with lengthy market testing and would allow for the appropriate execution of the launch activities. As such, the identified factors indirectly affect those activities. In addition, banks that would like to have a solid base on which they can build up a stream of continuously successful innovations must also incorporate those factors that customers look for in any bank offering a new service into the bank's corporate strategy. Thus Egyptian banks must redirect their strategic priorities towards improving service quality, establishing a solid brand name, and providing conveniently accessible services.

If banks succeed to appropriately integrate the different demographic, service, bank, and environment related factors into a comprehensive high quality new service development process, they would be able to introduce new services that are perceived by customers as differentiated valuable services, and would be able to achieve the balance between both the operational and the market success of their new services. In addition, if banks also integrate those factors into their control tools, they would be able to reinforce their importance and ensure their integration into the NSD model. This could be achieved by including them in the customer perspective part of the balanced scorecard or basing the management incentive system on how successful managers are in introducing customer oriented new service. It is those customer oriented services that promise the greatest success in terms of ensuring customer retention, attracting new customers, achieving highest customer satisfaction, reflecting positively on the company's image and realizing the highest profits, in other words, putting the company on the right track to market leadership.

## 6.3 Managerial Implications

Identifying the factors that affect customers' decisions to buy new retail banking loan and saving services and how they could be integrated into the new service development process has very important long term and short implications for bank managers, not only in Egypt, but in other countries as well. This is due to the fact that, although the importance attributed to different factors may vary, the general framework identifying the set of factors affecting customers and how they can be incorporated into the NSD process will remain the same across markets.

Over the long run, bank managers must reset their strategic priorities towards building up the most important factors that customers look for in any bank offering a new service. Being identified by Egyptian customers as a reputable bank providing high quality convenient services will give the bank the flexibility to respond to any environmental changes or arising market needs, as well as, will enable it to easily market any new service. Banks also must build up the capabilities required to integrate customers' voice as represented in the factors identified through our research into the pre development stages of the NSD process. These include how to the analyze the different external environmental factors and internal bank competencies and respond to them with successful new services that take into consideration the target customers' desired service features given their particular demographic characteristics.

Over the short run, whenever the bank is introducing a new loan or saving service, it must implement a comprehensive well planned NSD process while taking the following factors into consideration;

- In setting the new service strategy the environmental factors of political stability, legal stability, and economic performance must be assessed along with the bank's service quality, strength of brand name, and convenience. If those factors do not provide the necessary support for a radical new service or a satellite product that targets new market segments, incremental innovations, and services offered using the differentiation and expansion strategies may prove to be more successful.

- During idea generation, proposed new service types should be directed towards those types that most suit the level of environmental and bank risk at the time of launch. If these are considered high, services that need customers trust in the bank and confidence in the environment, such as saving services, could be difficult to market. On the other hand, those risks could also serve as a source of new ideas to mitigate their negative effect on customers. Customers' proven aspiration for high service quality and convenience, as well as, their search for particular service features for different types of services may also serve to guide idea generation towards generating new ideas that satisfy those aspirations and disregarding those that do not. The most desired service features for saving services are minimal risk, flexible tenor and high liquidity, while the most desired service features for loan services are competitive fixed pricing, high liquidity, and uniqueness.

- In applying customer screens, a numerical weighting model should be used to rank ideas according to how much they satisfy the most important factors that customers care about for different types of services which are service quality, bank reputation, political stability, service risk, and tenor for saving services; and service quality, pricing, liquidity, bank reputation and convenience for loan services.

- During concept development, banks should strive to achieve customers' preferences regarding relationship convenience and service features for different types of services and for different target markets. As an example, when introducing a new saving service, banks must strive to facilitate higher level of service quality and convenience and at the same time to reduce the service risk and increase its tenor flexibility even if this is translate into higher pricing. However, if the service is targeting employees of corporate clients as part of a payroll package, pricing is to be given higher priority over risk.

- During business analysis, banks must estimate the size of their target market based on the customers' demographic variables and how they relate, whether negatively or positively, to the developed concept features.

- ➢ Given that the outcome of the predevelopment phase is a clear feasible customer oriented business concept, development is made easier and testing could be limited to a short trial run to check the functionality of the new service. Launch must be of the top quality and must make sure to emphasize the desired features of various segments. it must also be able to properly communicate the customer centric image of the bank. Thus, banks would not only improve the new service's chances of market success, but would also create an image of being customer oriented which would improve their reputation and lead to more success.

## 6.4 Research limitations and future research areas

The limitations of this research mostly stem from the wide scope and the relative novelty of the topic that combine to impose some limitations on this research and necessitate and open up new topics for additional research. The first of these limitations is that the research is carried out in one market, Egypt. Although the general framework of the research and how the different sets of factors can be integrated into the NSD process will remain the same across different markets, the specific factors under each set and the degree of importance attributed to each of them may differ from one market to another according to the level of competition, needs of customers, and the degree of market development. Other types of banks such as Islamic banking might also prove to have different criteria that might, for example, involve religious considerations. Further Research on the area in other markets in recommended.

The fact that the research is examining the factors affecting customers' decisions to buy new loan and saving services only represents another limitation. This is due to the wide range of retail banking services that, although mainly fall under those two broad types, may include services affected by different factors such as insurance, pensions, mortgages, etc.

The last limitation of the research is that it only examines how to integrate the customer voice into the NSD process while disregarding customers' internal psychological factors and banks' internal resources, and capabilities. Customers' psychological factors include their attitudes and perceptions towards banks and new services. Banks' internal factors include strategic factors such as a dynamic strategy and flexible resources, a clearly defined, credible, and shared vision supporting innovation, a strong corporate culture tolerating risk and promoting innovation, and a learning organizational mentality that adapts quickly to environmental changes. Supportive knowledgeable leaders and managers who demonstrate a strong and visible support and commitment to innovation are also a necessity for any innovation effort to succeed. Internal factors also include a strong, appropriate, and supportive organizational structure that depends on high levels on inter-functional coordination, decentralized decision making, and very effective communication. Last but not least, employees must be encouraged and motivated to think creatively and must be rewarded for their innovative ideas. All these factors, among others, should also be considered if we want to come up with a comprehensive methodology that banks can immediately apply when introducing new successful retail banking services. Therefore, they must be integrated into the previously developed model to ensure a higher probability of success. After integrating those factors, the model should be tested for empirical success.

These limitations all open up new areas to widen the scope of this research to include other markets, other services, and the internal factors affecting the bank when introducing new services.

## Bibliography


Abdel Naby, Mohamed Ahmed (1999). *Athar al Motagheirat al Beiaea ala Istrategiet Takhteet al Khadamat al Masrefia*. Unpublished Doctoral Thesis, Zakazik University. Egypt (in Arabic).

Abou Seada, Safaa Abdel Aziz (1995). *Athar Istekhdam al Asaleeb al Ebtikaria Ala Tarweeg al Khadamat al Masrefia* . Unpublished Master Thesis. Banha University. Egypt (in Arabic).

Aboul Enin, Amr & Hanna, Amir (2004). *Egypt Banking Sector Report*. HC Brokerage, Cairo.

Alam, Ian & Perry, Chad (2002). A Customer Oriented New Service Development Process. *Journal of Services Marketing*, Vol. 16, 515-534.

Albro, Walt (2000). The Future of Banks: It is the customer, stupid. *Bank Marketing* Vol. 32, 8.

Amato -McCoy, Deena M. (2005). One Stop Banking. *Bank Systems and Technology*, Vo. 42, Issue 11, 43- 47.

Andrew, Kenneth (1986). *The Bank Marketing Handbook*. Woodhead- Faulkner Ltd. England.

Angur, Madhukar G., Natataajan,Rajan & Jahera jr., John S. (1999). Service Quality in the Banking Industry: An Assessment in a Developing Economy. *International Journal of Bank Marketing*. 17/3, 116-123.

Attia, Taher Morsi (1990). Measuring Bank Service Quality. *Journal of Management*, Vol. 23.

Avlonitis, George J. & Papastathopoulou, Paulina (2000). Marketing Communication and Product Performance: Innovative vs. non Innovative New Retail Financial Products. *International Journal of Bank Marketing*, 18/1, 27-41.

Avlonitis, George J. & Papastathopoulou, Paulina (2001). The Development Activities of Innovative and Non Innovative New Retail Financial Products: Implications for Success. *Journal of Marketing Management*. Vol. 17: 705-738.

Bahaa Eldin, M. & Mohie Elddin, M. (1998). *Financial Development in Emerging Markets: The Egyptian Experience*. The Egyptian Center for Economic Studies, Cairo.

BAI, UNISYS & Wharton Financial Institutions Center (2001). Competition, Innovation and Strategy in the Financial Services Industry. http// www.ai.org/competition (2004).

Banking on the Right Image (2003, 28 August). *Marketing Week*, 28-29.

Bainbridge, Alex & Meere, Daniel (2001, April). An e-dog eat e-dog world. *The Banker*. 122-123.

Balling, Mortan, Lierman, Frank & Mullineux, Andy (2003). *Technology and Finance: Challenges for Financial Markets, Business Strategies, and Policy Makers*. Routledge , London.

Baumann, Chris, Burton, Suzan & Elliott, Greg (2005). Determinants of Customer Loyalty and Share of Wallet in Retail Banking. *Journal of Financial Services Marketing*, Vol. 9, No. 3, 231-248.

Baveja, Sarabjit Singh, Gilbert, Jim & Ledingham, Dianne (2004). From Products to Services: Why It Is Not So Simple. *Harvard Management Update*. April 2004.

Beckett, Antony, Hewer, Paul & Howcroft, Berry (2000). An Exposition to the Consumer Behavior in the Financial Services Industry. *International Journal of Bank Marketing*, 18/1, 15-26.

Birnbaum, David (2004). *How to Invent a Service Product*. Retrieved from www.pacifichorizon.net (2005).

Booz, Allan & Hamilton (1982). *New Product Development for the 1980s*. New York: Booz, Allen & Hamilton.

Bortree, William H (1991). Consumer Input: The Key to New Product Success. *Bankers Magazine*. Vol. 174, Issue 2, 14-20.

Botin, Ana Patricia (2006). Banking's Technology Revolution. *Global Agenda*, Vol. 4, Issue 1, 120-121.

Bowers, Michael R. (1989). Developing New Services: Improving the Process Makes it Better. *The Journal of Service Marketing*. Vol. 3, No. 1: 15-20.

Boyd, William L., Leonard, Myron & White, Charles (1994). Customer Preference for Financial Services: An Analysis. *International Journal of Bank Marketing*. Vol. 12 No. 1, pp.9-15.

Brady, Micheal K. & Cronin Jr., J. Joseph (2001). Customer Orientation. Effects on Customer Service Perceptions and Outcome Behaviors. *Journal of Service Research*, Vol. 3, No. 3, 241-251.

Bryson J.R., Daniels, P.W. & Warf, B. (2004) *Service Worlds: People, Organizations, Technologies*, Routledge, 286 pages.

Burr, Wolfgang & Stephan, Michael (2006). *Dienstleistungs-management. Innovative Werstschopfungskonzepte fur Dienstleistungsunternehmen.* W. Kohlhammer, Stuttgart.

Campbell, Marry & Collins, Andrew (2001). In Search of Innovation. *The CPA Journal*. April 2001: 27 -35.

Central Bank of Egypt (2002/2003). Annual Report. Cairo.

Central Bank of Egypt (2003/2004). Annual Report. Cairo.

Central Bank of Egypt (2005/2006). Annual Report. Cairo.

Cetorelli, Nicola (2001). Competition Among Banks: Good or Bad? *Economic Perspectives*, Vol. 25, Issue 2, 38-49.

Chakravorti, Sujit & Jankowski, Carrie (2005). *Innovations, Incentives, and Regulation: Forces Shaping the Payments Environment* (No. 218 a). Chicago: The Federal Reserve Bank of Chicago.

Charofas, Dimitris N. (1999). *The Commercial Banking Handbook: Strategic Planning for Growth and Survival in the New Decade*. London: MAC Millan Press.

*Competition, Innovation, and Strategy in the Financial Service Industry* (2001). www.ai.org/competition

Cook, Peter (1998). The Creativity Advantage- Is your Organization the leader of the pack? *Industrial and Commercial Training*, Vol. 30, No. 5, 179-184.

Cooper, Robert G. & Edgett, Scott J. (1996). Critical Success Factors for New Financial Services. *Marketing Management*. Fall 1996 : 26-37.

Costanzo L.A., Keasey, K. & Short, H. (2003). A Strategic Approach to the Study of Innovation in the Financial Services industry: The case of Telephone Banking. *Journal of Marketing Management*. Vol. 19: 259-281.

Cowell, Donald W (1988). New Service Development. *Journal of Marketing Management*. Vol. 3, No. 3: 296-312.

Crosby, Lawrence A, Johnson, Sheree L. & Winslow, Karen D. (2003). Innovation –Not for the Fainthearted. *Marketing Management*. Mar/Apr. 2003, Vol. 12 Issue 2, P 10.

Davis, S.M. (1997) "Bringing Innovation to Life" *Journal of Consumer Marketing* Vol. 14, No. 5 P.P. 38-361.

Debackere, K., Van Looy, B. and Papastathopoulou, P. Managing Innovation in a Service Environment. In: *Services Management: An integrated approach*, Van Dierdonck, R., Van Looy B. and Gemmel, P. (eds.), London: Pitman Publishing, 1998, pp. 387-405.

Demoranville, Carol W., Kaminski, Peter, Ridnour, Rick E. & Young, Tom (1999). How Sandwich State Bank Took a Market Orientation to Face the Changes in Traditional Community Banking. *Journal of Retail Banking Services*. Vol. 21 Issue 2.

De Paula, Matthew (2003, September). Jumping the Gap: Marketing to Multiple Generations, *USBanker*, Vol. 113, Issue 9, 38-40.

Der Hovanesian, Mara (2006, March). Coffee, Tea, or Mortgage? *Business Week*, Issue 3978, 48-49.

Devlin, James F. (1995). Technology and Innovation in Retail Banking Distribution. *International Journal of Bank Marketing*. Vol. 13 issue 4, 19-26.

Devlin, James F. (1998). Adding Value to Service Offerings: The Case of Financial Services. *European Journal of Marketing*, Vol.32, 11,12, pp.1091-1109.

Devlin, James F. (2000). Adding Value to Retail Financial Services. *International Journal of Bank Marketing*, 18/5, 222-232.

Devlin, James F. (2002). Customer Knowledge and Choice Criteria in Retail Banking. *Journal of Strategic Marketing* 10, 273-290.

Devlin, James F. & Gerrard, Philip (2004). Choice Criteria in Retail Banking: An Analysis of Trends. *Journal of Strategic Marketing*. Vol. 12 issue 1, 13-15.

Devlin, James F. & Yeung, Matthew (2003). Insights Into Customer Motivations for Switching to Internet Banking. *International Review of Retail, Distribution & Consumer Research*, Vol. 13, Issue 4, p.1.

Dick, Astrid A. (2002). Demand estimation and consumer welfare in the banking industry www.federalreserve.gov/pubs/feds/2002/200258/ 20025abs.html

DIN Deutsches Institut für Normung e.V. (Hrsg., 1998). *Service Engineering – Entwicklungsbegleitende Normung (EBN) für Dienstleistungen*, Berlin [u.a.]: Beuth.

Dobni, Brooke (2002). A Model for Implementing Service Excellence in the Financial Services Industry. *Journal of Financial Services Marketing*, Vol. 7, No. 1, 42-53.

Drew, Stephen A.W. (1995). Strategic Benchmarking: Innovation Practices in Financial Institutions. *International Journal of Bank Marketing*, Vol. 13, No. 1, 4-16.

Easingwood, Christopher J. & Storey, Christopher D. (1993). Marketplace Success Factors for New Financial Services. *Journal of Services Marketing*, Vol. 7 No. 1: 41-54.

Economist Intelligence Unit (2005). Financial Industry Forecast: Egypt. www.eiu.com Retrieved 2006.

Edgett, Scott (1994). The Traits of Successful New Service Development. *Journal of Service Marketing*, Vol. 8 No. 3: 40-49.

Edgett, Scott & Parkison, Steven (1994). The Development of New Financial Services: Identifying Determinants of Success and Failure. *International Journal of Service Industry Management*. Vol. 5 No. 4: 24-38.

Edgett, Scott & Snow, Kim (1997). Benchmarking Measures of Customer Satisfaction, Quality and Performance for New Financial Service Products. *Journal of Product and Brand Management*, Vol. 6, No. 4, 250-259.

Edvardsson, Bo & Olsson, Jan (1996). Key Concept for New Service Development. *The Service Industries Journal*. Vol. 16, No. 2, pp. 140-164.

EFG- Hermes. American Express Bank Mutual Fund No. 1 First Quarter Report 2002. www.efg-hermes.com/business_lines/research (2003)

Egan, Colin & Shipley, David (1995). Dimensions of Customer Orientation: An Empirical Investigation of the UK Financial Services Sector. *Journal of Marketing Management*, No. 11, 807-816.

El Bossat, Hesham (1988). *New Trends in Bank Marketing*. Beirut, Arab Banks Association.

El Ganady, Mansour (2000). Moving Towards Adolescence. *Business Today* http://www.arabia.com/BusinessToday (2003)

El Khodeiry, Mohsen Ahmed (1999). *El Tasweek al Masrafy*. Cairo: Itrac Publishing and Distribution Company (in Arabic).

El Maiouf, Salah Ibn Moaz (2001). Al Awamel al Mohadeda Lekhtiar al Omalaa Al Seaudeen Lel Benook fi Madinat Al Riad Bel Mamlaka Al Saudia . *Al Idara al Ama*. Vol. 40, No. 4, 611-641 (in Arabic).

Esteban, Agueda, Millan, Angel, Molina, Arturo& Martin-Consuegra, David (2002). Market Orientation in Service. *European Journal of Marketing*, Vol. 36, No. 9/10, 1003-1021.

Euromoney Instiutional Investor PLC (2001). *Egypt: Regional Leader and Global Player: A Market for the 21st Century*. London: Nestor House.

Facing New Challenges (2003, October). *Middle East*, Issue 338, P.33.

Finch, J. Howard & Helms, Marilyn M. (1996). The Changing Face of Retail Banking. *Bank Marketing*, Vol. 28, Issue 6, 49-52.

Fisher, Caroline & Schutta, James T. (2003). *Developing New Services, Incorporating the Voice of the Customer into Strategic Service Development*. Milawaukee, Wisconsin; American Society for Quality Press.

Fitzsimmons, James A. & Fitzsimmons, Mona J. (1994) Service Management for Competitive Advantage. New York: McGraw Hill Inc.

Foust, Dean & Natarajan, Anand (2003, October). Bofa Heads Back to Main Street. *Business Week*, Issue 3857, P.41.

Frame, W. Scott & White, Lawrance J. (2002). Empirical Studies of Financial Innovation: Lots of Talks, Little Action? Federal Reserve Bank of Atlanta. Working Paper 2002-12.

Frei, Frances X., Harket, Patrick T. & Hunter, Larry W. (1998). Innovation in Retail Banking. http// fic.wharton.upenn.edu/fic/forumpapers.html

Gadallah, Gamal El Din Mohamed El Morsi (1979). *Tasweek Khadamat al Eidaa Belbeonnk al Togaria al Masria*. Unpublished MBA Thesis. Faculty of Commerce, Cairo University (in Arabic).

Gardner, Edward, Howcroft, Barry & Williams, Jonathan (1999). The New Retail Banking Revolution. *The Service Industries Journal*, Vol. 19, No. 2, 83-100.

Garland, Ron (2005). Segmenting Retail Banking Customers. *Journal of Financial Services Marketing*, Vol. 10, No. 2, 179-191.

Garmhausen, Stephen (1999). Consumers Show Interest in New Products but are Buying Fewer of them. *American Banker*, Vol. 164, Issue 151. P.17.

Guirdham, M. (1987). How to Market Unit Trusts: a consumer Behavior Model. *Marketing Intelligence and Planning*, 2, 15- 19.

Gupta, Anil K., Smith, Ken G.& Shalley, Christina E (2006). The Interplay between Exploration and Exploitation. *Academy of Management Journal*, vol. 49, no. 4, 693-706.

Han, Jin K., Kim, Namwoon & Srivastava, Rajendra K. (1998). Market Orientation and Organizational Performance: Is Innovation a Missing Link? *Journal of Marketing*. Vol. 62, 30-45.

Harborne, Paul & Johne, Axel (2002). Many Leaders make Light Work in Banking Innovation Projects. *Journal of Financial Services Marketing*. Vol. 6 issue 3: 267-280.

Harisson, Tina (2003). Understanding the behavior of Financial Services Consumers: A Research Agenda. *Journal of Financial Services Marketing*. Vol. 8, 6-9.

Harris, Creg (2002). Brand Strategy in the Retail Banking Sector: Adapting to the Financial Services Revolution. *Brand Management*. Vol. 9, no. 6, 430 – 436.

Hassan, El Sayed Metwally (1990). Towards a Comprehensive Marketing Model to Identify the changes that affect the Arab citizens in dealing with banks. *Trade and Finance*. Vol. 2, 179-228.

HC Brokerage (2004). Egypt Banking Sector Report 2004. WWW.hc-si.com (2005).

Hedley, Kimberly, White, John, Petit dit de la Roche, Cormac & Banerjea, Sunny (2005). The Paradox of Banking 2015: Achieving More by Doing Less.http://www935.ibm.com/services/us/index.wss/ibvstudy/imc/a1022912 ? cntxt=a1000043

Hill, P (1990), From Dairy Deserts to debit cards – new product research in consumer and financial markets. *How to market financial services in an increasingly competitive environment*, ESOMAR, Amersterdam, 71-85.

Holliday, Karen (1999). Knowing your Customer' Can be Lost on Some Banks. *Mississippi Business Journal*. Vol. 21, Issue 49, p.30.

Homann, Ulrich, Rill, Michael & Wimmer, Andreas (2004). Flexible Value Structures in Banking. *Communication of the AC*, Vol. 47, No. 5, 34-36.

Hope, Christine & Muhlemann, Alan ( 1997). *Service Operations Management: Strategy Design and Delivery*. Pearson Education Limited. England.

Horne, David Andrew (1982). *Consumer Reaction to a Financial Service Innovation: Electronic Funds Transfer Point of Sale Devices*. Unpublished PhD. Thesis, The University of Michigan.

Howcroft, Barry, Hewer, Paul & Hamilton, Robert (2003). Consumer Decision Making Styles and the Purchase of Financial Services. *The Service Industries Journal*, Vol. 23, No. 3, 63-81.

Howcroft, J.W. & Lavis, J. (1986). Retail Banking, *The New Revolution In Structure and Strategy*. UK: Basil Blackwell Inc.

Hubband, Mark (1999). *Egypt Leading the Way. Institution Building and Stability in the Financial System*. London: Euromoney Institutional Investor Publications PLC.

Hulshoff, H.E., Westhof, F.M.J., Kirchhoff, J.J., Kirchhoff, B.A. & Walsh, S.T. (1998). *New Services. Strategic exploratory Survey of a Dynamic Phenomenon*. EIM: Zoetermeer.

In Motion (2001, August 1). *Business Today*, 2-4.

ING, Cap Gemini Ernst & Young & European Financial Management and Marketing Association (2004). *World Retail Banking Report 2004*. Cap Gemini Ernst & Young.

Javalgi, Rai. G., Martin, Charles L. & Young, Robert B. (2006). Marketing Research, Market Orientation, and Customer Relationship Management: A Framework and Implications for Service Providers. *Journal of Services Marketing*, 20/1, 12-23.

Jamal, Ahmed (2004). Retail Banking and Customer Behavior: A Study of Self Concept, Satisfaction and Technology Usage. *International Review of Retail, Distribution and Consumer Research*, Vol. 14, No.3, 357-379.

Jamal, Ahmed & Naser, Kamal (2002). Customer satisfaction and retail Banking: An assessment of Some of the key antecedents of customer satisfaction in retail banking . *International Journal of Bank Marketing*, Vol. 20, 146-160.

Johne, Axel & Storey, Chris (1998). New Service Development: a review of the Literature and Annotated Bibliography. *European Journal of Marketing*. Vol. 32, No. 3/4, 184-251.

Johannsen, Rolland D. (1992). The Changing Course of Retail Banking. *Bankers Magazine*. Vol. 175 Issue 2, 12-19.

Johnson, Eugene M., Scheuing, Eberhard E. & Gaida, Kathleen A. (1986). *Profitable Service Marketing*. Homewood, III: Dow Jones – Irwin.

Johnston, Robert (1997). Identifying the Critical determinants of Service Quality in Retail Banking: Importance and Effect. *International Journal of Bank Marketing* 15/4, 111-116.

Jordan, Jerry L. The Functions and Future of Retail Banking. (1996) http//www.clev.frb.org/ccca/jj100196.htm (Nov. 2003)

Joydeep, Sengupta & Renny, Thomas (1996). What Indian Consumers Want from Banks. http://moneytoday.in/html/banking-story3.html (2006)

Kandampully, Jay & Duddy, Ria (2005). Competitive Advantage through Anticipation, Innovation, and Relationships. *Management Decision*, vol. 37, issue 1.

Kennington, Carolyn, Hill, Jeanne & Rakowska, Anna (1996). Consumer selection Criteria for Banks in Poland. *International Journal of Bank Marketing*. 14/4, 12-21.

Kotler, P. (1994). *Marketing Management: Analysis, Planning, Implementation, and Control.* London: Prentice Hall International.

Kourouian, Rafy (1998). Redemptions Trigger Market Tumble. *Middle East Times*. http// www.metimes.com/ issue98-29/bus/redemptions_trigger_ market.htm (2004).

Kyriakopoulos, Kyriakos & Moorman, Christine (2004). Tradeoffs in marketing exploitation strategies: The overlooked role of market orientation. *International Journal of Research in Marketing*, Vol. 21, 219-240.

Lasheen, Abdel Aaty (1992). *Tasweek al Khadamat al Masrefia.* Unpublished Masters Thesis. Cairo University. Egypt (in Arabic).

Laurino, John A (1993). Developing Your Own Nich. *Bank Marketing*. Vol. 25, Issue 7.

Levesque, Terrence & McDougall, Gordon H.G. (1996). Determinants of Customer Satisfaction in Retail Banking. *International Journal of Bank Marketing*. 14/7, 12-20.

Lewis, Barbara R. & Soureli, Magdalini (2006). The Antecedents of Consumer Loyalty in Retail Banking. *Journal of Consumer Behavior*, Vol. 5, Issue 1, 15 -32.

Lian, Tanja (1995). The New Definition of Retail Banking. *International Journal of Bank Marketing*_ Vol. 27 issue 4, p.5.

Lievens, Annoul, Moenaert, Rudy K. & S'Jegers, Rosette (1999). Linking Communication to Innovation Success in the Financial Service Industry: A Case Study Analysis. *International Journal of Service Industry Management*. Vol. 10, No.1: 23-47.

Lomax, R.G. (2001). *An Introduction to Statistical Concepts for Education and Behavioral Science.* NJ: Laurance Erlbaum Associates Inc.

Machauer, Achim & Morgner, Sebastian (2001). Segmentation of bank customers by expected benefits and attitudes. *International Journal of Bank Marketing*, Vol. 19, 6-18.

Mahoney, Lisa (1994). Surveys Help Determine Opinions. *Bank Marketing*. Vol. 26, issue 6, 61-63.

Managing Change in Your Organization (2000). *International Trade Forum*, Issue 2, p 26.

March, James J. (1991). Exploration and Exploitation in Organizational Learning. *Organizational Science*, Vol. 2, No. 1, 71-87.

Marcus, Amy Dockser. Rising Sphinx. http// www.sis.gov.eg/ eginfnew/ economy/ ireco/ html/ sphinx.htm

Martin JR, Claude R & Horne, David A. (1995). Level of Success Inputs for Service Innovation in the Same Firm. *International Journal of Service Industry Management*, Vol. 6, No. 4: 40-56.

McGoldrick, Peter J. & Greenland, S.J. (1994). *Retailing of financial services*. London: McGraw Hill book Co.

McKechnie, S (1992), Consumer buying behavior in financial services: an overview, *International Journal of Bank Marketing*, Vol. 19 No.5, 4-12.

Meala, Nagy (1994). *Mabadeaa al Tasweek al Masrafy*. Oman: El Safwa Printing Press (in Arabic).

Meidan, Arthur (1996). *Marketing financial services*. Great Britain: Antony Rowe Ltd.

Meinhardt, Ron (2006, April). Retail Banking is here to Stay. *USBanker*, p. 56.

Menor, Lawrance Jon. (2000). An Empirical Study of New Service development Competence and Performance. http:// wwwlib.umi.com/ dissertations/ preview-all/ 9993348 (2003).

Miller, Kent D., Zhao, Meng & Calantone, Roger J. (2006). Adding Interpersonal Learning and Tacit Knowledge to March's Exploration-Exploitation Model. *Academy of Management Journal*, Vol. 49, No. 4, 709-722.

Mohie Eldin, Mahmoud (2001). On Bank Market Structure and Competition in Egypt. *Arab Economic Journal*, Vol. 10, No. 25, 3-35.

Moschis, George, Bellenger, Danny & Curasi, Carolyn Folkman (2003). Financial service preferences and patronage motives of older consumers. *Journal of Financial Services Marketing*, Vol. 7, 331-340.

Moskowitz, Howard R. & Krieger, Bert (2001). Financial Products: Rapid, Iterative and Segmented Development by Conjoint Measurement and Self-authoring Iterative Procedures. *Journal of Financial Services Marketing*, Vol. 5, 343-355.

Mylonakis, John, Malliaris, Peter G. & Siomkos, George J. (1998). Marketing Driven Factors Influencing Savers in The Hellenic Bank Market. *Journal of Applied Business Research*, Vol. 14, issue 2, 109-117.

Naude, Pete, Blackman, Ian & Dengler, Steve (1998). The Managerial Implications of Real Time New Product Development in Financial Services. *Creativity and Innovation Management*, Vol. 7, No. 2, 54-61.

Normann, Richard (2002). *Service Management: Strategy and Leadership in Service Business.* . UK: John Wiley & Sons Ltd.

Oldenboom, Nicola & Abratt, Russell (2000). Success and Failure Factors in Developing new Banking and Insurance Services in South Africa. *International Journal of Bank Marketing*, 18/5, 233-245.

Oteify, Rania (2003, May). Risky Business. *Business Today* http://www.businesstodayegypt.com/issues/0305/681B/0305681B.asp (Oct. 2003).

Papastathopoulou, Paulina; Avlonitis, George & Indounas, Kostis (2001). The Initial Stages of New Service Development: A Case Study from the Greek Banking Sector. *Journal of Financial Services Marketing*. Vol. 6, 147-161.

Pennings, Joost M.E., Wetzels, Martin G.M. & Meulenberg, Matthew T.G. (1999). The Marketing – Finance Interface towards Financial Services with Special Reference to the New Service Provided by Futures Exchanges. *European Journal of Marketing*, Vol. 33, No. 5/6, 531- 547.

Purcell, Philip J. (1982). Separating the Winners from the Losers. Speech delivered at the International Conference, Financial Executives Institute, Michigan.

Raddon, Gary H. (1998). What Customers Want in Investment Services. *Journal of Retail Banking Services*, Vol. 20, Issue 3, 39-44.

Reidenbach, R. Erich & Pitts, Robert E. (1986). *Bank Marketing: A Guide to Strategic Planning*. Prentice Hall. USA.

Reidenback, E. & Moak, D. (1986). Exploring Retail Bank Performance and New Product Development: A Profile of Industry Practices. *Journal of Product Innovation Management*, Vol. 3, No. 3, 187- 194.

Retail Banking Dictionary. http/ www.Investopedia.com. (2004)

Roberts, Peter W. & Amit, Raphael (2003). The Dynamics of Innovative Activity and Competitive Advantage: The Case of Austrian Retail Banking , 1981 to 1995. *Organization Science: A Journal of the Institute of Management Sciences*, Vol. 14, Issue 2, 107-123.

Roscoe, David (2001). The Customer Knowledge Journey. *Journal of Financial Services Marketing*, Vo. 5, No. 4, 314-318.

Roushdy, Ahmed Samir (1998). *Athat el Istrategia al Tasweekia ala Aladaa Beltatbeek ala el Ketaa al Masrafy fi Gomhoriat Masr al Arabia*. Unpublished MBA Thesis. Faculty of Commerce, Cairo University (in Arabic).

Scarbrough, Harry & Lannon, Ronnie (1989). The Management of Innovation in the Financial Service Sector: A Case Study. *Journal of Marketing Management*. Vol. 5, No. 1, 51-62.

Scheuing, E.E. & Johnson, E.M. (1989) "New product development and Management in Financial Institutions" *International Journal of Bank Marketing*, Vol. 7 No. 2, P 17-21.

Scheuing, Eberhard E. & Johnson, Eugene M (1989). A Proposed Model for New Service Development. *The Journal of Services Marketing*. Vol. 3, No. 2: 25-34.

Schneider, Ivan (2005). Don't Apologize – Anthropologize. *Bank Systems and Technology*, Vol. 42, Issue 1, P. 38.

Sciulli, Lisa M. (1998). How Organizational Structure Influences Success in Various Types of Innovation. *Journal of Retail Banking Services*. Vol. 20 Issue 1.

Sengupta, Joydeep & Thomas, Renny (2005). What Indian Consumers Want from Banks. *McKinsey Quarterly*, 2005 Special Edition, 12- 16.

Service Excellence: Lessons from the Banking Industry (1996). *The Journal of Service Marketing*. Vol. 10, no. 5, 54-56.

Serviceinnovationen (2005). http/www.economics.phil.uni-erlangen.de/ bwl/ lehrbuch/ kapr/ servinno/ servinno.pdf. (2006)

Sobhi, Yasser (2003). Pushing Personal Loans. *Al Ahram Weekly*, Issue 620, Jan. 2003.

Song, M. & Montoya – Weiss, M. (1998)."Critical Development Activities for Really new versus Incremental Products" *Journal of Product Innovation Management*, Vol.15, pp. 124-135.

Spitler, Rick (2005). The New Survival Skills. *ABA Banking Journal*, Vol. 97, Issue 2, 58-61.

Stanton, Anthony (2002, April). Getting to Know You. *The Banker*, 19-22.

Storey, Chris & Kelly, David (2001). Measuring the Performance of New Service Development. http//130.195.95.71:8081/www/ANZMAC1998/cd-rom/ Storey175.pdf-supplemental result.

Storey, Christopher & Easingwood, Christopher (1993). The Impact of the New Product Development Project on the success of Financial Services. *The Service Industries Journal*. Vol. 13, No. 3, 40-54.

Storey, Christopher & Easingwood, Christopher (1996). Determinants of New Product Performance, A Study in The Financial Services Sector. *International Journal of Service Industry Management*. Vol. 7 no. 1: 32-55.

Stuart, F. Ian (1998). The Influence of Organizational Culture and Internal Politics on New service Design and Introduction. *International Journal of Service Industry Management*. Vol. 9 No. 5: 469-489.

Suoranta, Mari & Mattila, Minna (2004). Mobile Banking and Consumer Behavior: New Insights into the Diffusion Pattern. *Journal of Financial Services Marketing*, Vol. 8, No. 4, 354-366.

Ta, Huu Phuong & Har, Kar Yin (2000). A study of bank selection decisions in Singapore using the analytical hierarchical process. *International Journal of Bank Marketing*, Vol. 18, 170-180.

Tank, Janki & Tyler, Katherine (2005). UK Student Banking Revisited: Influences and the Decision Making Process. *Journal of Financial Services Marketing*. Vol. 10, No.2, 152-64.

Thomke, Stefan (2003). R&D Comes to Services: Bank of America's Pathbreaking Experiments. *Harvard Business Review*. April 2003: 71-79.

Tidd, Joe, Bessant, Jihn & Pavitt, Keith (2001). *Managing Innovation*. John Wiley & Sons Ltd. England.

Ulengin, Burc (1998). Using Hierarchical Information Integration to Examine Customers' Preferences in Banking. *International Journal of Bank Marketing*. 16/5, 202-210.

Veryzer, R.W. (1998). "Discontinuous Innovation and the new product Development Process". *Journal of Product Innovation Management*, Vol. 15, pp. 304-321.

Warren, William E., Abercrombie, C.L. & Berl, Robert L. (1989). Adoption of Service innovation: A Case Study with Managerial Implications. *The Journal of Service Marketing*. Vo. 3, No. 1, 21 -33.

Winnie, Yuk-Lan Wong & Kanji, Gopal K. (2001). Measuring Customer Satisfaction: Evidence from Hong Kong Retail Banking Industry. *Total Quality Management*, Vol. 12, No. 7 &8, 939- 948.

Yavas, Ugur & Shemwell, Donald J. (1997). Analyzing a Bank's Competitive Position and Appropriate Strategy. *Journal of Retail Banking Services*, Vol. 19, Issue 4, 43-52.

Zahn, Erich (2003), Customer Related Service Engineering. http:// www.corse-projekt.de (2003).

Zahn, E, Foschiani, F. Lienhard, P. & Meyer, S. (2003). Kundenorientierte Servicestrategien für hybride Produkte. in: Kersten, W. (Hrsgj: E-Collaboration — Prozessoptimierung in der WertschUpfungs kette, Wiesbaden, 2003, S. 133-157.

Zahn, Erich, Stanik, Martin (2002): Wachstumspotenziale kleiner und mittlerer Dienstleister. *Mit Dienstleistungswerken zu Full-Service-Leistungen*, Stuttgart. 2002.

Zahn, Erich, Spath, Dieter, Scheer, August-Wilhelm (Hrsg. 2004). *Vom Kunden zu Dienstleistungsmethoden, Instrumente und Strategien zum Customer related Service Engineering*, Stuttgart 2004.

Zahn, Erich, Stanik, Martin (2006). *Integrierte Entwicklung von Dienstleistungen und Netzwerken - Dienstleistungskooperationen als strategischer Erfolgsfaktor, in: Bullinger, Hans-Jörg; Scheer, Wilhelm-August (Hrsg.): Service Engineering*, Berlin, Heidelberg 2006, p. 299-319.

# Appendixes

## A- Questionnaire Items Measuring Different Factors

| Factor | Questionnaire Items |
|---|---|
| **1) Service Related Factors** | |
| • Service uniqueness | (Q1, Q2) |
| • Service sophistication | (Q3, Q4) |
| • Pricing | (Q5, Q6, Q7) |
| • Tenor | (Q8) |
| • Liquidity | (Q9, Q10) |
| • Service Risk degree | ( Q11, Q12) |
| • Documentation required | (Q13, Q14) |
| • Availability of information | (Q15, Q16, Q17) |
| • Previous positive experience with new retail banking services | (Q18) |
| **2) Bank Related Factors** | |
| • Bank performance | (Q19, Q20, Q21) |
| • Service quality | (Q22, Q23, Q24) |
| • Convenience | (Q25, Q26, Q27, Q28) |
| • Availability of a wide range of other services | (Q 29) |
| • Availability of Technologically advanced services | (Q30)<br>(Q31) |
| • Performance of previous new services | |
| • Bank's reputation | (Q32, Q33) |
| • Previous positive experience with the bank either directly or through trusted acquaintances | (Q34)<br>(Q35) |
| • Ownership/ Nationality of bank | |
| **3) Environmental Related Factors** | |
| • Level of competition | (Q36, Q37) |
| • Overall performance of the banking sector | (Q38, Q39) |
| • Country Economic performance | (Q40, Q41, Q42, Q43) |
| • Legal stability | (Q44, Q45) |
| • Political stability | (Q46, Q47) |

## B- Cover Page and Questionnaire for Loan Services

**Dear Survey Respondents,**

The attached questionnaire solicits your opinion on the most important factors that you consider when taking a decision to buy a retail banking loan service that is **offered by a bank for the first time**. The service might be completely new to the Egyptian market such as Internet Cards, Speed loans, etc…, or might be already offered by other banks such as Credit cards or car financing programs, etc…

The questionnaire is part of a study conducted to find out the factors that customers base their decision to buy new retail banking loan services on. The aim of the research is to help retail banks develop customer oriented services that would meet customers' requirements and satisfy their needs.

We are asking for your kind help in completing the attached questionnaire which is conducted as part of the requirements of a PhD in Management.

Data collected will be anonymous and highly confidential. It will only be used for the purpose of research.

Thank you for your kind cooperation,

**Hadia Hamdy, PhD Candidate** **Prof. Dr. Erich Zahn, Supervisor**

**Part I**

**1- Have you ever tried a retail banking loan service offered by a bank for the first time?**

Yes ☐ No ☐

**2- What is the degree of interest that you would have if you knew that one of the banks is offering a new retail banking loan service?**

| (1) Interested | (2) Neutral | (3) Not interested |
|---|---|---|
| | | |

**If your answer to Question no. 1 is "No", and your answer to question no. 2 is "not interested", please go directly to Part III.**

**If your answer is otherwise, please go on to the next part.**

**Part II**

Please place a "v" mark inside the cell that presents the degree of importance that each of the following factors represents to you in making your decision to buy a new retail banking **loan** service offered by a bank for the first time.

**A- Factors related to the offered service**

| | | (1) Extremely important | (2) Import-ant | (3) Neutral | (4) Not import-ant | (5) Not impor-tant at all |
|---|---|---|---|---|---|---|
| 1 | Service offering of new benefits that were not offered before. | | | | | |
| 2 | Service fulfillment of a need that no other services in the market fulfils | | | | | |
| 3 | Easily understood service features and operating mechanism | | | | | |
| 4 | Familiarity of service type (for example, most clients are familiar with car financing programs, but less familiar with internet cards) | | | | | |
| 5 | Lower debit interest rate relative to market | | | | | |
| 6 | Lower service fees and commissions relative to market | | | | | |
| 7 | Fixed debit interest rate for the life time of the loan | | | | | |
| 8 | Flexible repayment tenors | | | | | |

| | | (1) Extremely important | (2) Important | (3) Neutral | (4) Not important | (5) Not important at all |
|---|---|---|---|---|---|---|
| 9 | Possibility of drawing additional amounts within the approved limit any time and without any restrictions | | | | | |
| 10 | Possibility of repayment before due date (prepayment) without paying extra fees or commissions. | | | | | |
| 11 | Expected consequences in case of default (consequences might be limited to loss of guarantees or extended to reach prison) | | | | | |
| 12 | Limited required guarantees | | | | | |
| 13 | limited required documentation | | | | | |
| 14 | Minor legal responsibility of loan documentation to be signed (e.g. some banks require checks with the total amount of principal + interest (usually not dated)) | | | | | |
| 15 | Informative Advertising for the product through newspapers and media | | | | | |
| 16 | The availability of printed brochures providing product details | | | | | |
| 17 | Direct selling efforts through direct mail or personal calls | | | | | |
| 18 | Previous positive experience with other newly introduced loan services either directly or through trusted acquaintances | | | | | |

## B- Factors related to the offering bank

| | | (1) Extremely important | (2) Important | (3) Neutral | (4) Not important | (5) Not important at all |
|---|---|---|---|---|---|---|
| 19 | Bank's market share | | | | | |
| 20 | Strength of the bank's financial position. | | | | | |
| 21 | Growth of the bank's profitability | | | | | |
| 22 | Bank's reputation in terms of staff friendliness and helpfulness | | | | | |
| 23 | Bank's reputation in terms of efficiency and accuracy in completing transactions | | | | | |
| 24 | Bank's reputation in terms of prompt and speedy services | | | | | |
| 25 | extended operating hours (the official working hours of some banks are extended to 5 pm instead of 2 pm) | | | | | |
| 26 | Widespread network of branches | | | | | |

| | | (1) Extremely important | (2) Import-ant | (3) Neutral | (4) Not import-ant | (5) Not impor-tant at all |
|---|---|---|---|---|---|---|
| 27 | Conveniently located branches | | | | | |
| 28 | Widespread network of Automatic Teller Machines (ATMs) | | | | | |
| 29 | Availability of a wide range of other services | | | | | |
| 30 | Availability of technologically ad-vanced services like home banking and internet banking | | | | | |
| 31 | Success of previous new products introduced by the same bank | | | | | |
| 32 | Bank's name and market reputation | | | | | |
| 33 | Bank's stability and continuity in the market | | | | | |
| 34 | Previous positive experience with the bank either directly or through trusted acquaintances | | | | | |
| 35 | Ownership and nationality of the bank (whether local, multinational, or Joint venture) | | | | | |

In case your answer to the previous question (No. 35) is "important" or "extremely im-portant", please specify which type of the following three you prefer to deal with

| Egyptian public sec-tor Banks | Private sector or Joint venture Banks | Branches of foreign Banks |
|---|---|---|
| | | |

**C- Environmental Factors (factors related to the performance of the banking sector and the economic, political, and legal conditions prevailing at the time of launching the new service**

| | | (1) Extremely important | (2) Import-ant | (3) Neutral | (4) Not import-ant | (5) Not impor-tant at all |
|---|---|---|---|---|---|---|
| 36 | Availability of successful competi-tive products offered by other banks | | | | | |
| 37 | Availability of successful substitute products offered by other sectors (such as installment programs offered by some companies or labor unions) | | | | | |
| 38 | Growth of the banking sector and its related investments | | | | | |
| 39 | Performance of the banking sector in terms of size of doubtful debts (and the subsequent profitability growth) | | | | | |
| 40 | Overall Economic condition (reces-sion/boom) | | | | | |
| 41 | Favorable economic forecasts | | | | | |
| 42 | Stability of foreign exchange rates | | | | | |

| | | (1) Extremely important | (2) Important | (3) Neutral | (4) Not important | (5) Not important at all |
|---|---|---|---|---|---|---|
| 43 | Stability of interest rates | | | | | |
| 44 | Stability of economic legislations (such as tax and investment legislations) | | | | | |
| 45 | Stability of banking policies (such as credit and monetary policies set by the central bank of Egypt) | | | | | |
| 46 | Absence of external political pressures or threats | | | | | |
| 47 | Absence of internal political turmoil | | | | | |

**Part III**

**1- Gender**
Female ☐ Male ☐

**2- Age**
21- 30 ☐ 31-40 ☐ 41-50 ☐ 51-60 ☐ above 60 ☐

**3- Education**
Basic education ☐ High School or equiv. ☐ BA or equivalent ☐ Master / PhD ☐

**4- Marital Status**
Single ☐ Married ☐ Widowed ☐ Divorced ☐

**5- Number of Children**
Non ☐ 1 ☐ 2 ☐ 3 ☐ More than 3 ☐

**6- Field of Work**
Employed by a private organization ☐ Employed by a Government organization ☐ Private Business ☐ Unemployed ☐ others ☐

**7- Monthly income in Egyptian Pounds (Monthly salary + Income from property and investments)**
Less than 2000 ☐ 2000-5000 ☐ 5000-10000 ☐ more than 10000 ☐

*Thank you for completing the questionnaire, your kind cooperation is highly appreciated.*

**أعزائى المشاركين فى الرد على قائمة الاستقصاء**

ان الهدف من قائمة الاستقصاء المرفقة هو معرفة رأيكم فى أهم العوامل التى تـاخذونها فى الأعتبار عند شراء خدمة اقتراض شخصى **يقدمها أحد البنوك لاول مرة**، سواء كانت هذة الخدمة جديدة تماما على السوق المصرى مثل كروت الانترنت، و القروض السريعة ، أو سبق تقديمها من قبل بعض البنوك الاخرى مثل قروض تمويل شراء السيارات و السلع المعمرة أو كروت الائتمان.

هذة القائمة هى جزء من دراسة يتم اعدادها لمعرفة أهم العوامل التى يتخذ العملاء على أساسها قراراتهم بشراء خدمات الاقتراض الشخصي **الجديدة** لكى تؤخذ هذة العوامل فى الأعتبار عند تصميم هذة الخدمات.

و لهذا فبرجاء التكرم بمساعدتنا باستيفاء قائمة الاستقصاء المرفقة و التى هى جزء من رسالة دكتوراة فى العلوم الادارية بالجامعة الالمانية بالقاهرة.

هذا و نؤكد لسيادتكم أن المعلومات التى سوف يتم جمعها ستكون على درجة عالية من السرية و لن يتم أستخدامها الا لأغراض البحث العلمى فقط لا غير.

و اذ نشكركم على حسن تعاونكم، تفضلوا بقبول فائق الاحترام،

**هادية حمدى**
**مدرس مساعد و طالبة دكتوراة**
**الجامعة الألمانية بالقاهرة**

**الأستاذ الدكتور/ أيريك سان**
**العميد المؤسس لكلية الادارة**
**الجامعة الألمانية بالقاهرة**

**الجزء الأول**

1- هل سبق لك تجربة خدمة اقتراض شخصي يقدمها احد البنوك لاول مرة ؟

نعم ☐ لا ☐

2- ما هى درجة الأهتمام التى تتكون لديك عند علمك أن احد البنوك يقدم خدمة اقتراض شخصي جديدة ؟

| مهتم | محايد | غير مهتم |
|---|---|---|
| | | |

اذا كانت اجابتك على السؤال الأول هى "لا" و اجابتك على السؤال الثانى هى "غير مهتم"، فبرجاء الاجابة على الجزء الثالث مباشرة. أما اذا كانت الاجابه بغير ذلك فبرجاء الاجابه على الجزء التالى.

**الجزء الثانى**

برجاء تقييم العوامل الاتيه من حيث درجة اهميتها بالنسبة لك عند اتخاذك قرار شراء خدمة اقتراض شخصي يقدمها احد البنوك لاول مرة و ذلك بوضع علامة (√ ) أمام الخانة التى تمثل درجة أهمية العامل بالنسبة لك.

**أ: عوامل تتعلق بالخدمة المعروضة**

| | | (1) هام جدا | (2) هام | (3) محايد | (4) غير هام | (5) غير هام على الاطلاق |
|---|---|---|---|---|---|---|
| 1 | تقديم الخدمة لمزايا اضافية جديدة لم يسبق تقديمها من قبل | | | | | |
| 2 | تلبية الخدمة لاحتياجات لا تلبيها اى من الخدمات الاخرى المعروضة فى السوق | | | | | |
| 3 | سهولة فهم خصائص و أليات عمل الخدمة | | | | | |
| 4 | المعرفة السابقة بنوعية الخدمة المقدمة (مثال على ذلك ان قروض تمويل شراء السيارات تعتبر من خدمات الاقتراض المعروفة لعدد كبير من العملاء بعكس كروت تميمة او كروت الانترنت) | | | | | |
| 5 | انخفاض معدل الفائدة المدينة مقارنة بالسوق | | | | | |
| 6 | انخفاض العمولات البنكية مقارنة بالسوق | | | | | |
| 7 | ثبات معدل الفائدة المدينه طوال المدة الزمنية لسداد القرض | | | | | |
| 8 | مرونة تحديد مدة السداد | | | | | |
| 9 | امكانية السحب من الحد المسموح بة فى اى وقت و بدون اية قيود | | | | | |
| 10 | امكانية السداد قبل ميعاد الاستحقاق بدون تحمل عمولات اضافية | | | | | |
| 11 | حجم العواقب المتوقعة فى حالة عدم السداد (قد تمتد العواقب الى السجن أو تكون مقصورة على خسارة الضمانات المقدمة) | | | | | |
| 12 | قلة الضمانات المطلوبة | | | | | |
| 13 | قلة المستندات المطلوبة | | | | | |

| | | (1) هام جدا | (2) هام | (3) محايد | (4) غير هام | (5) غير هام على الاطلاق |
|---|---|---|---|---|---|---|
| 14 | عدم جثامة المسئولية القانونية للمستندات التى سوف يتم التوقيع عليها(مثال على ذلك أن بعض البنوك تطالب بتوقيع شيك غير مؤرخ باجمالى مبلغ القرض + الفوائد) | | | | | |
| 15 | توفر معلومات تفصيلية عن الخدمة فى الجرائد و وسائل الاعلام | | | | | |
| 16 | توافر المطبوعات التى تشرح خصائص و مزايا الخدمة | | | | | |
| 17 | قيام البنك بالتسويق مباشرة لك عن طريق المراسلات او المقابلات الشخصية | | | | | |
| 18 | وجود تجربة ايجابيه سابقه لخدمات اقتراض شخصي جديدة سواء شخصيا او عن طريق اشخاص موثوق بهم | | | | | |

**ب: عوامل تتعلق بالبنك المقدم للخدمة**

| | | (1) هام جدا | (2) هام | (3) محايد | (4) غير هام | (5) غير هام على الاطلاق |
|---|---|---|---|---|---|---|
| 19 | حصة البنك من السوق | | | | | |
| 20 | قوة المركز المالى للبنك | | | | | |
| 21 | معدل نمو ارباح البنك | | | | | |
| 22 | حسن سمعة موظفى البنك من حيث تعاونهم و مساعدتهم للعملاء | | | | | |
| 23 | حسن سمعة البنك من حيث المهارة والدقة فى تنفيذ المعاملات البنكية | | | | | |
| 24 | حسن سمعة البنك من حيث السرعة فى اداء مختلف الخدمات البنكية | | | | | |
| 25 | طول مدة ساعات العمل (تمتد ساعات العمل فى بعض البنوك حتى الساعة الخامسة عصرا بدلا من الثانية ظهرا) | | | | | |
| 26 | الانتشار الجغرافى الواسع للفروع | | | | | |
| 27 | ملائمة مواقع الفروع لاحتياجاتك | | | | | |
| 28 | الانتشار الجغرافى الواسع لماكينات السحب الالى ATM | | | | | |
| 29 | توافر مجموعة كبيرة من الخدمات الاخرى | | | | | |
| 30 | توافر الخدمات المتقدمة تكنولوجيا مثل أجراء المعاملات البنكية من المنزل Home Banking أو عن طريق الانترنت Internet Banking | | | | | |
| 31 | نجاح الخدمات الجديدة التى سبق لهذا البنك تقديمها | | | | | |
| 32 | أسم و سمعة البنك فى السوق | | | | | |
| 33 | ثبات و استمرارية البنك فى السوق | | | | | |
| 34 | وجود تجربة ايجابيه سابقة فى التعامل مع البنك المقدم للخدمة سواء شخصيا او عن طريق اشخاص موثوق بهم | | | | | |
| 35 | ملكية و جنسية البنك (قطاع عام مصرى، ملكية مصرية اجنبية مشتركة، أو فرع لبنك أجنبى) | | | | | |

اذا كانت اجابتك عن السؤال السابق (رقم 35) هى"هام جدا" أو "هام"، برجاء تحديد أى من الفئات الثلاثة تفضل التعامل معه

بنوك القطاع العام المصرية ☐ بنوك القطاع الخاص و البنوك المشتركة ☐ فروع البنوك الأجنبية ☐

**ج : عوامل بيئية (عوامل تتعلق بظروف السوق المصرفى و كذلك الظروف الاقتصادية و السياسية و القانونية السائدة عند تقديم البنك للخدمة الجديدة).**

| | | (1) هام جدا | (2) هام | (3) محايد | (4) غير هام | (5) غير هام على الاطلاق |
|---|---|---|---|---|---|---|
| 36 | توافر خدمات مماثلة ناجحة مقدمة من بنوك اخرى | | | | | |
| 37 | توافر خدمات بديلة ناجحة مقدمة من خارج القطاع المصرفى ( مثال على ذلك برامج تقسيط السلع أو السيارات الى تقدمها بعض الشركات او النقابات) | | | | | |
| 38 | نمو القطاع المصرفى وزيادة استثماراتة | | | | | |
| 39 | أداء القطاع المصرفى من حيث قلة الديون المشكوك فى تحصيلها (و ما يترتب عليها من نمو الارباح) | | | | | |
| 40 | الحالة الأقتصادية العامة للبلاد من انتعاش أو ركود أقتصادى | | | | | |
| 41 | التوقعات الأقتصادية الايجابية | | | | | |
| 42 | استقرار اسعار صرف العملات الاجنبية | | | | | |
| 43 | استقرار معدلات الفائدة | | | | | |
| 44 | استقرار القوانين الاقتصادية (مثل القوانين الضريبية و قوانين الاستثمار) | | | | | |
| 45 | استقرار السياسات البنكية (مثل السياسات النقدية و الائتمانية التى يحددها البنك المركزى) | | | | | |
| 46 | عدم وجود تهديدات او تدخلات سياسية خارجية | | | | | |
| 47 | عدم وجود اضطرابات سياسية داخلية | | | | | |

**الجزء الثالث (بيانات شخصية)**

**1- النوع**

انثى ☐ ذكر ☐

**2- العمر**

30-21 ☐ 40-31 ☐ 50-41 ☐ 60-51 ☐ اكبر من 60 ☐

**3- التعليم**

تعليم أساسى ☐ ثانوية عامة أو ما يعادلها ☐ بكالوريوس أو ما يعادله ☐ ماجستير/ دكتوراة ☐

**4- الحالة الاجتماعية**

اعزب ☐ متزوج ☐ أرمل ☐ مطلق ☐

**5- عدد الاطفال**

لا يوجد ☐ 1 ☐ 2 ☐ 3 ☐ اكثر من 3 ☐

**6- مجال العمل**

موظف بالقطاع الخاص ☐ موظف بالقطاع العام ☐ عمل حر ☐ لا أعمل ☐ مجالات اخرى ☐

**7- الدخل الشهرى بالجنية المصرى (يشمل الراتب الشهرى+ العائد الشهرى من الاملاك و الاستثمارات)**

اقل من 2000 جم ☐ من 2000-5000 جم ☐ من 5000-10000 جم ☐ أكثر من 10000 جم ☐

**نشكركم على استكمال قائمة الاستقصاء و لكم منا خالص التقدير و التحية**

## C- Cover Page and Questionnaire for Saving Services

**Dear Survey Respondents,**

The attached questionnaire solicits your opinion on the most important factors that you consider when taking a decision to buy a retail banking saving or investment service that is **offered by a bank for the first time**. The service might be completely new to the Egyptian market such as Millionaire Certificates, Daily income funds certificates, etc…, or might be already offered by other banks such as Certificates of deposits, etc…

The questionnaire is part of a study conducted to find out the factors that customers base their decision to buy new retail banking saving and investment services on. The aim of the research is to help retail banks develop customer oriented services that would meet customers' requirements and satisfy their needs.

We are asking for your kind help in completing the attached questionnaire which is conducted as part of the requirements of a PhD in Management.

Data collected will be anonymous and highly confidential. It will only be used for the purpose of research.

Thank you for your kind cooperation,

**Hadia Hamdy, PhD Candidate** **Prof. Dr. Erich Zahn, Supervisor**

**Part I**

**1- Have you ever tried a retail banking saving or investment service offered by a bank for the first time?**

Yes ☐ No ☐

**2- What is the degree of interest that you would have if you knew that one of the banks is offering a new retail banking saving or investment service?**

| (1) Interested | (2) Neutral | (3) Not interested |
|---|---|---|
| | | |

**If your answer to Question no. 1 is "No", and your answer to question no. 2 is "not interested", please go directly to Part III.**

**If your answer is otherwise, please go on to the next part.**

**Part II**

Please place a "v" mark inside the cell that presents the degree of importance that each of the following factors represents to you in making your decision to buy a new retail banking **saving or investment** service offered by a bank for the first time.

**A- Factors related to the offered service**

| | | (1) Extremely important | (2) Important | (3) Neutral | (4) Not important | (5) Not important at all |
|---|---|---|---|---|---|---|
| 1 | Service offering of new benefits that were not offered before. | | | | | |
| 2 | Service fulfillment of a need that no other services in the market fulfils | | | | | |
| 3 | Easily understood service features and operating mechanism | | | | | |
| 4 | Familiarity of service type (for example, most clients are familiar with certificates of deposits, but less familiar with daily income funds certificates) | | | | | |
| 5 | Higher expected return relative to market | | | | | |
| 6 | Lower service fees and commissions relative to market | | | | | |
| 7 | Fixed expected return for the life time of the service | | | | | |
| 8 | Possibility of adjusting saving or investment tenor according to your personal needs (i.e. one month, three months, etc-) service tenor | | | | | |

| | | (1) Extremely important | (2) Import-ant | (3) Neu-tral | (4) Not import-ant | (5) Not impor-tant at all |
|---|---|---|---|---|---|---|
| 9 | Possibility of saving or investing additional amounts any time and without any restrictions | | | | | |
| 10 | Possibility of early redemption without deductions | | | | | |
| 11 | Size of expected loss out of return or principal in case of product failure | | | | | |
| 12 | Strong guarantees provided from the bank for paying back principal and return | | | | | |
| 13 | limited required documentation | | | | | |
| 14 | Bank commitments are explicitly stated in service documentation | | | | | |
| 15 | Informative Advertising for the product through newspapers and media | | | | | |
| 16 | The availability of printed brochures providing product details | | | | | |
| 17 | Direct selling efforts through direct mail or personal calls | | | | | |
| 18 | Previous positive experience with other newly introduced saving services either directly or through trusted acquaintances | | | | | |

**B- Factors related to the offering bank**

| | | (1) Extremely important | (2) Import-ant | (3) Neu-tral | (4) Not import-ant | (5) Not impor-tant at all |
|---|---|---|---|---|---|---|
| 19 | Bank's market share | | | | | |
| 20 | Strength of the bank's financial position. . | | | | | |
| 21 | Growth of the bank's profitability | | | | | |
| 22 | Bank's reputation in terms of staff friendliness and helpfulness | | | | | |
| 23 | Bank's reputation in terms of efficiency and accuracy in completing transactions | | | | | |
| 24 | Bank's reputation in terms of prompt and speedy services | | | | | |
| 25 | extended operating hours (the official working hours of some banks are extended to 5 pm instead of 2 pm) | | | | | |
| 26 | Widespread network of branches | | | | | |
| 27 | Conveniently located branches | | | | | |
| 28 | Widespread network of Automatic Teller Machines (ATMs) | | | | | |
| 29 | Availability of a wide range of other services | | | | | |

| | | (1) Extremely important | (2) Import-ant | (3) Neu-tral | (4) Not import-ant | (5) Not impor-tant at all |
|---|---|---|---|---|---|---|
| 30 | Availability of technologically advanced services like home banking and internet banking | | | | | |
| 31 | Success of previous new products introduced by the same bank | | | | | |
| 32 | Bank's name and market reputation | | | | | |
| 33 | Bank's stability and continuity in the market | | | | | |
| 34 | Previous positive experience with the bank either directly or through trusted acquaintances | | | | | |
| 35 | Ownership and nationality of the bank (whether local, multinational, or Joint venture) | | | | | |

In case your answer to the previous question (No. 35) is "important" or "extremely important", please specify which type of the following three you prefer to deal with

| Egyptian public sector Banks | Private sector or Joint venture Banks | Branches of foreign Banks |
|---|---|---|
| | | |

**C- Environmental Factors (factors related to the performance of the banking sector and the economic, political, and legal conditions prevailing at the time of launching the new service**

| | | (1) Extremely important | (2) Import-ant | (3) Neutral | (4) Not import-ant | (5) Not impor-tant at all |
|---|---|---|---|---|---|---|
| 36 | Availability of successful competitive products offered by other banks | | | | | |
| 37 | Availability of successful substitute products offered by other sectors (such direct investment in the stock market) | | | | | |
| 38 | Growth of the banking sector and its related investments | | | | | |
| 39 | Performance of the banking sector in terms of size of doubtful debts (and the subsequent profitability growth) | | | | | |
| 40 | Overall Economic condition (recession/boom) | | | | | |
| 41 | Favorable economic forecasts | | | | | |
| 42 | Stability of foreign exchange rates | | | | | |
| 43 | Stability of interest rates | | | | | |
| 44 | Stability of economic legislations (such as tax and investment legislations) | | | | | |
| 45 | Stability of banking policies (such as credit and monetary policies set by the central bank of Egypt) | | | | | |

| | | (1) Extremely important | (2) Import-ant | (3) Neutral | (4) Not import-ant | (5) Not impor-tant at all |
|---|---|---|---|---|---|---|
| 46 | Absence of external political pres-sures or threats | | | | | |
| 47 | Absence of internal political turmoil | | | | | |

**Part III**

**1- Gender**
Female ☐ Male ☐

**2- Age**
21- 30 ☐ 31-40 ☐ 41-50 ☐ 51-60 ☐ above 60 ☐

**3- Education**
Basic edu-cation ☐ High School or equiv. ☐ BA or equivalent ☐ Master / PhD ☐

**4- Marital Status**
Single ☐ Married ☐ Widowed ☐ Divorced ☐

**5- Number of Children**
Non ☐ 1 ☐ 2 ☐ 3 ☐ More than 3 ☐

**6- Field of Work**
Employed by a private or-ganization ☐ Employed by a Government organization ☐ Private Business ☐ Unem-ployed ☐ others ☐

**7- Monthly income in Egyptian Pounds (Monthly salary + Income from property and investments)**
Less than 2000 ☐ 2000-5000 ☐ 5000-10000 ☐ more than 10000 ☐

*Thank you for completing the questionnaire, your kind cooperation is highly appreciated.*

**أعزائى المشاركين فى الرد على قائمة الاستقصاء**

ان الهدف من قائمة الاستقصاء المرفقة هو معرفة رأيكم فى أهم العوامل التى تـاخذونـها فى الأعتبار عند شراء خدمة ادخار أو استثمار شخصي **يقدمها أحد البنوك لاول مرة**، سواء كانت هذة الخدمة جديدة تماما على السوق المصرى مثل شهادة المليونير و وثائق صناديق الاستثمار ذات العائد اليومى، أو سبق تقديمها من قبل بعض البنوك الاخرى مثل شهادات الاستثمار و الادخار.

هذة القائمة هى جزء من دراسة يتم اعدادها لمعرفة أهم العوامل التى يتخذ العملاء على أساسها قراراتهم بشراء خدمات الادخار و الاستثمار الشخصي **الجديدة** لكى تؤخذ هذة العوامل فى الأعتبار عند تصميم هذة الخدمات.

و لهذا فبرجاء التكرم بمساعدتنا باستيفاء قائمة الاستقصاء المرفقة و التى هى جزء من رسالة دكتوراة فى العلوم الادارية بالجامعة الالمانية بالقاهرة.

هذا و نؤكد لسيادتكم أن المعلومات التى سوف يتم جمعها ستكون على درجة عالية من السرية و لن يتم أستخدامها الا لأغراض البحث العلمى فقط لا غير.

و اذ نشكركم على حسن تعاونكم، تفضلوا بقبول فائق الاحترام،

**هادية حمدى**
**مدرس مساعد و طالبة دكتوراة**
**الجامعة الألمانية بالقاهرة**

**الأستاذ الدكتور/ أيريك سان**
**العميد المؤسس لكلية الادارة**
**الجامعة الألمانية بالقاهرة**

**الجزء الأول**

1- هل سبق لك تجربة خدمة ادخار أو استثمار شخصية يقدمها احد البنوك لاول مرة ؟

نعم ☐ لا ☐

2- ما هى درجة الأهتمام التى تتكون لديك عند علمك أن احد البنوك يقدم خدمة ادخار أو استثمار شخصية جديدة ؟

| مهتم | محايد | غير مهتم |
|---|---|---|
| | | |

اذا كانت اجابتك على السؤال الأول هى "لا" و اجابتك على السؤال الثانى هى "غير مهتم"، فبرجاء الاجابة على الجزء الثالث مباشرة. أما اذا كانت الاجابه بغير ذلك فبرجاء الاجابه على الجزء التالى.

**الجزء الثانى**

برجاء تقييم العوامل الاتيه من حيث درجة اهميتها بالنسبة لك عند اتخاذك قرار شراء خدمة ادخار او استثمار شخصي يقدمها احد البنوك لاول مرة و ذلك بوضع علامة (√ ) أمام الخانة التى تمثل درجة أهمية العامل بالنسبة لك.

أ: عوامل تتعلق بالخدمة المعروضة

| | | (1) هام جدا | (2) هام | (3) محايد | (4) غير هام | (5) غير هام على الاطلاق |
|---|---|---|---|---|---|---|
| 1 | تقديم الخدمة لمزايا أضافية جديدة لم يسبق تقديمها من قبل | | | | | |
| 2 | تلبية الخدمة لاحتياجات لا تلبيها اى من الخدمات الاخرى المعروضة فى السوق | | | | | |
| 3 | سهولة فهم خصائص و أليات عمل الخدمة | | | | | |
| 4 | المعرفة السابقة بنوعية الخدمة المقدمة (مثال على ذلك ان شهادات الاستثمار تعتبر من خدمات الادخار المعروفة لعدد كبير من العملاء بعكس وثائق صناديق الاستثمار ذات العائد اليومى) | | | | | |
| 5 | ارتفاع معدل العائد المتوقع مقارنة بالسوق | | | | | |
| 6 | انخفاض العمولات البنكية مقارنة بالسوق | | | | | |
| 7 | ثبات معدل العائد المتوقع طوال المدة سريان الخدمة | | | | | |
| 8 | مرونة تحديد مدة الادخار او الاستثمار وفقا لاحتياجاتك (شهر- ثلاثة شهور – ستة شهور-الخ--) | | | | | |
| 9 | أمكانية ادخار او استثمار مبالغ اضافية فى اية وقت وبدون أية قيود | | | | | |
| 10 | امكانية الاسترداد قبل ميعاد الاستحقاق بدون استقطاعات | | | | | |
| 11 | حجم الجزء المتوقع خسارتة من العائد أو اصل المبلغ فى حالة عدم نجاح الخدمة | | | | | |
| 12 | قوة الضمانات المقدمة من البنك لضمان رد اصل المبلغ و العوائد | | | | | |
| 13 | قلة المستندات المطلوبة | | | | | |

| | | (1) هام جدا | (2) هام | (3) محايد | (4) غير هام | (5) غير هام على الاطلاق |
|---|---|---|---|---|---|---|
| 14 | كتابة تعهدات البنك بوضوح فى المستندات الموقعة | | | | | |
| 15 | توفر معلومات تفصيلية عن الخدمة فى الجرائد و وسائل الاعلام | | | | | |
| 16 | توفر المطبوعات التى تشرح خصائص و مزايا الخدمة | | | | | |
| 17 | قيام البنك بالتسويق مباشرة لك عن طريق المراسلات او المقابلات الشخصية | | | | | |
| 18 | وجود تجربة ايجابيه سابقه لخدمات ادخار او استثمار شخصى جديدة سواء شخصيا او عن طريق اشخاص موثوق بهم | | | | | |

**ب: عوامل تتعلق بالبنك المقدم للخدمة**

| | | (1) هام جدا | (2) هام | (3) محايد | (4) غير هام | (5) غير هام على الاطلاق |
|---|---|---|---|---|---|---|
| 19 | حصة البنك من السوق | | | | | |
| 20 | قوة المركز المالى للبنك | | | | | |
| 21 | معدل نمو ارباح البنك | | | | | |
| 22 | حسن سمعة موظفى البنك من حيث تعاونهم و مساعدتهم للعملاء | | | | | |
| 23 | حسن سمعة البنك من حيث المهارة و الدقة فى تنفيذ المعاملات البنكية | | | | | |
| 24 | حسن سمعة البنك من حيث السرعة فى اداء مختلف الخدمات البنكية | | | | | |
| 25 | طول مدة ساعات العمل (تمتد ساعات العمل فى بعض البنوك حتى الساعة الخامسة عصرا بدلا من الثانية ظهرا) | | | | | |
| 26 | الانتشار الجغرافى الواسع للفروع | | | | | |
| 27 | ملائمة مواقع الفروع لاحتياجاتك | | | | | |
| 28 | الانتشار الجغرافى الواسع لماكينات السحب الالى ATM | | | | | |
| 29 | توافر مجموعة كبيرة من الخدمات الاخرى | | | | | |
| 30 | توافر الخدمات المتقدمة تكنولوجيا مثل أجراء المعاملات البنكية من المنزل Home Banking أو عن طريق الانترنت Internet Banking | | | | | |
| 31 | نجاح الخدمات الجديدة التى سبق لهذا البنك تقديمها | | | | | |
| 32 | أسم و سمعة البنك فى السوق | | | | | |
| 33 | ثبات و استمرارية البنك فى السوق | | | | | |
| 34 | وجود تجربة ايجابيه سابقة فى التعامل مع البنك المقدم للخدمة سواء شخصيا او عن طريق اشخاص موثوق بهم | | | | | |
| 35 | ملكية و جنسية البنك (قطاع عام مصرى، ملكية مصرية اجنبية مشتركة، أو فرع لبنك أجنبى) | | | | | |

اذا كانت اجابتك عن السؤال السابق (رقم 35) هى"هام جدا" أو "هام"، برجاء تحديد أى من الفئات الثلاثة تفضل التعامل معه

| بنوك القطاع العام المصرية | بنوك القطاع الخاص و البنوك المشتركة | فروع البنوك الأجنبية |
|---|---|---|
| ☐ | ☐ | ☐ |

**ج : عوامل بينية (عوامل تتعلق بظروف السوق المصرفى و كذلك الظروف الاقتصادية و السياسية و القانونية السائدة عند تقديم البنك للخدمة الجديدة).**

| | | (1) هام جدا | (2) هام | (3) محايد | (4) غير هام | (5) غير هام على الاطلاق |
|---|---|---|---|---|---|---|
| 36 | توافر خدمات مماثلة ناجحة مقدمة من بنوك اخرى | | | | | |
| 37 | توافر خدمات بديلة ناجحة مقدمة من خارج القطاع المصرفى ( مثال على ذلك الاستثمار مباشرة فى الاوراق المالية بالبورصة) | | | | | |
| 38 | نمو القطاع المصرفى وزيادة استثماراتة | | | | | |
| 39 | أداء القطاع المصرفى من حيث قلة الديون المشكوك فى تحصيلها (و ما يترتب عليها من نمو الارباح) | | | | | |
| 40 | الحالة الأقتصادية العامة للبلاد من انتعاش أو ركود أقتصادى | | | | | |
| 41 | التوقعات الأقتصادية الايجابية | | | | | |
| 42 | استقرار اسعار صرف العملات الاجنبية | | | | | |
| 43 | استقرار معدلات الفائدة | | | | | |
| 44 | استقرار القوانين الاقتصادية (مثل القوانين الضريبية و قوانين الاستثمار) | | | | | |
| 45 | استقرار السياسات البنكية (مثل السياسات النقدية و الائتمانية التى يحددها البنك المركزى) | | | | | |
| 46 | عدم وجود تهديدات او تدخلات سياسية خارجية | | | | | |
| 47 | عدم وجود اضطرابات سياسية داخلية | | | | | |

**الجزء الثالث (بيانات شخصية)**

**1- النوع**

انثى ☐ ذكر ☐

**2- العمر**

30-21 ☐ 40-31 ☐ 50-41 ☐ 60-51 ☐ اكبر من 60 ☐

**3- التعليم**

| | | | |
|---|---|---|---|
| تعليم أساسى ☐ | ثانوية عامة أو ما يعادلها ☐ | بكالوريوس أو ما يعادله ☐ | ماجستير/ دكتوراة ☐ |

**4- الحالة الاجتماعية**

| | | | |
|---|---|---|---|
| اعزب ☐ | متزوج ☐ | أرمل ☐ | مطلق ☐ |

**5- عدد الاطفال**

| | | | | |
|---|---|---|---|---|
| لا يوجد ☐ | 1 ☐ | 2 ☐ | 3 ☐ | اكثر من 3 ☐ |

**6- مجال العمل**

| | | | | |
|---|---|---|---|---|
| موظف بالقطاع الخاص ☐ | موظف بالقطاع العام ☐ | عمل حر ☐ | لا أعمل ☐ | مجالات اخرى ☐ |

**7- الدخل الشهرى بالجنية المصرى (يشمل الراتب الشهرى+ العائد الشهرى من الاملاك و الاستثمارات)**

| | | | |
|---|---|---|---|
| اقل من 2000 جم ☐ | من 2000-5000 جم ☐ | من 5000-10000 جم ☐ | أكثر من 10000 جم ☐ |

**نشكركم على استكمال قائمة الاستقصاء و لكم منا خالص التقدير و التحية**

## SCHRIFTEN ZUR UNTERNEHMENSPLANUNG

Band 1 Bernhard Früh: Entscheidungsträgermodelle bei Planungstechniken. 1984.

Band 2 Ekbert Hering: Planung neuer Produkt-Marktbereiche unter besonderer Berücksichtigung der Realisierung in Klein- und Mittelbetrieben. 1984.

Band 3 Thomas Hintsch: Geschäftsfeldsteuerung in Kreditinstituten. Eine Konzeption für die strategische Planung in Banken. 1984.

Band 4 Rainer Mager: Investitions- und Steuerplanung mit Systemsimulation. 1984.

Band 5 August Zimmermann: Evolutionsstrategische Modelle bei einstufiger, losweiser Produktion. Simultane Programm-, Losgrößen- und Lossequenzplanung mit Hilfe der Simulation auf der Basis biologischer Evolutionsfaktoren. 1985.

Band 6 Paul Bäuerle: Finanzielle Planung mit Hilfe heuristischer Kalküle. Ein Beitrag zur Methodologie modellgestützter Entscheidungsfindung, konkretisiert am Beispiel der Investitions- und Finanzplanung in Klein- und Mittelbetrieben. 1987.

Band 7 Hans-Jürgen Hillmer: Planung der Unternehmensflexibilität. Eine allgemeine theoretische Konzeption und deren Anwendung zur Bewältigung strategischer Flexibilitätsprobleme. 1987.

Band 8 Wilfried H. Schwarz: Systeme der Entscheidungsunterstützung im Rahmen der strategischen Planung. 1987.

Band 9 Horst Michael: Steigerung der Effektivität betriebswirtschaftlicher Planungsprozesse durch das Leitbild des kritischen Rationalismus. Zu den Möglichkeiten eines Methodentransfers zwischen realwissenschaftlicher Forschung und betriebswirtschaftlicher Planung. 1988.

Band 10 Reiner Beutel: Unternehmensstrategien international tätiger mittelständischer Unternehmen. 1988.

Band 11 Andreas Bunz: Strategieunterstützungsmodelle für Montageplanungen. System Dynamics-Modelle zur Analyse und Gestaltung der Flexibilität von Montagesystemen. 1988.

Band 12 Lienhard Hopfmann: Flexibilität im Produktionsbereich. Ein dynamisches Modell zur Analyse und Bewertung von Flexibilitätspotentialen. 1989.

Band 13 Andreas M. Kleinhans: Wissensverarbeitung im Management. Möglichkeiten und Grenzen wissensbasierter Managementunterstützungs-, Planungs- und Simulationssysteme. 1989.

Band 14 Klaus J. Enßlin: Technologische Spin-off-Effekte aus der Raumfahrt. Vom staatspolitischen Anspruch zum unternehmenspolitischen Problem. 1989.

Band 15 Günther Unterkofler: Erfolgsfaktoren innovativer Unternehmensgründungen. Ein gestaltungsorientierter Lösungsansatz betriebswirtschaftlicher Gründungsprobleme. 1989.

Band 16 Wolfgang Kömpf: Unternehmensführung in erfolgreichen Klein- und Mittelbetrieben. Eine empirische Untersuchung. 1989.

Band 17 Wolfgang Brandt: Strategien für Rundfunkanstalten. Strategische Entwicklungsmöglichkeiten der öffentlich-rechtlichen Rundfunkanstalten. 1989.

Band 18 Uwe Schmid: Umweltschutz - Eine strategische Herausforderung für das Management. 1989.

Band 19 Josef Röhrle: Unternehmensführung und Unternehmensentwicklung. Ein Führungskonzept zur ganzheitlichen Steuerung der Unternehmensentwicklung. 1990.

Band 20 Harald W. Sondhof: Finanzdienstleistungsmärkte im Wandel. Eine industrieökonomische Branchenanalyse für strategische Zwecke. 1990.

Band 21 Ulrich Kreutle: Die Marketing-Konzeption in deutschen Chemieunternehmen – eine betriebswirtschaftlich-historische Analyse am Beispiel der BASF Ludwigshafen. 1992.

Band 22 Dieter Schmidt: Strategisches Management komplexer Systeme. Die Potentiale computergestützter Simulationsmodelle als Instrumente eines ganzheitlichen Managements – dargestellt am Beispiel der Planung und Gestaltung komplexer Instandhaltungssysteme. 1992.

Band 23 Heinrich Huber: Wettbewerbsorientierte Planung des Informationssystem (IS)-Einsatzes. Theoretische und konzeptionelle Grundlagen zur Entwicklung eines integrierten Planungsmodells. 1992.

Band 24 Wolfram Anders: Strategische Einkaufsplanung. Kernbereich eines strategischen Einkaufsmanagements. 1992. 2. Aufl. 1994.

Band 25 Maria Barth-Renz: Planungs- und Kontrollsysteme öffentlich-rechtlicher Rundfunkanstalten. Anpassung des Planungsverhaltens an neue strategische Herausforderungen. 1992.

Band 26 Ottmar Schneck: Finanzmanagement von Rundfunkanstalten. Ein Finanzplanungs-, -kontroll- und -organisationskonzept für öffentlich-rechtliche Rundfunkanstalten. 1993.

Band 27 Ralf Bertram: Informations- und Kommunikationsmanagement im Marketing mittelständischer Unternehmen der Investitionsgüterindustrie. Eine empirische Untersuchung. 1993.

Band 28 Thomas Keiser: Absatzprognosen für modeabhängige Unternehmen. Ein zweistufiges Absatzprognosesystem für Unternehmen mit modisch orientiertem Sortiment. 1993.

Band 29 Thomas Gumsheimer: Informationspartnerschaften. Konzeptionelle Grundlagen für die Gestaltung von Partnerschaften im Informationsmanagement. 1994.

Band 30 Dino Ivan Dogan: Strategisches Management der Logistik. Der logistische Kreis als Antwort auf die neuen logistischen Herausforderungen 'Umweltschutz' und 'Zeit'. 1994.

Band 31 Stefan Foschiani: Strategisches Produktionsmanagement. Ein Modellsystem zur Unterstützung produktionsstrategischer Entscheidungen. 1995.

Band 32 Jan Schäfer-Kunz: Strategische Allianzen im deutschen und europäischen Kartellrecht. 1995.

Band 33 Frank-Jürgen Richter: Die Selbstorganisation von Unternehmen in strategischen Netzwerken. Bausteine zu einer Theorie des evolutionären Managements. 1995.

Band 34 Udo Wupperfeld: Management und Rahmenbedingungen von Beteiligungsgesellschaften auf dem deutschen *Seed-Capital*-Markt. Empirische Untersuchung. 1996.

Band 35 Hartmut Feucht: Implementierung von Technologiestrategien. 1996.

Band 36 Hans-Jürgen Reichardt: Sachstand und Probleme umweltorientierter Unternehmensführung in der mittelständischen Industrie. Ergebnisse und Lösungsansätze aus einer empirischen Untersuchung. 1996.

Band 37 Jürgen Bruck: Entwicklung einer Gesamtkonzeption für das Management strategischer Allianzen im F&E-Bereich. 1996.

Band 38 Jürgen Greschner: Lernfähigkeit von Unternehmen. Grundlagen organisationaler Lernprozesse und Unterstützungstechnologien für Lernen im strategischen Management. 1996.

Band 39 Stefan Hagemann: Strategische Unternehmensentwicklung durch Mergers & Acquisitions. Konzeption und Leitlinien für einen strategisch orientierten Mergers & Acquisitions-Prozeß. 1996.

Band 40 Uwe Schmid: Ökologiegerichtete Wertschöpfung in Industrieunternehmungen. Industrielle Produktion im Spannungsfeld zwischen Markterfolg und Naturbewahrung. 1996.

Band 41 Bernhard Leitermann: Wahl der Zusammenschlußform von Unternehmen. Eine transaktionsökonomische Entscheidungskonzeption. 1996.

Band 42 Andreas Seebach: Betriebswirtschaftliche Systemanalyse des Fahrzeug-Recyclings in der Bundesrepublik Deutschland. Eine System-Dynamics-Studie. 1996.

Band 43 Nicole Karle-Komes: Anwenderintegration in die Produktentwicklung. Generierung von Innovationsideen durch die Interaktion von Hersteller und Anwender innovativer industrieller Produkte. 1997.

Band 44 Andreas Weidler: Entwicklung integrierter Innovationsstrategien. 1997.

Band 45 Frank Braun: Strategische Wettbewerbsforschung. Ein Simulationsmodell zur Erforschung der möglichen Wirkungen des EG-Binnenmarktes auf den Wettbewerb in der PKW-Branche. 1997.

Band 46 Jürgen Haas: Die Entwicklungsfähigkeit von Unternehmungen. Eine theoretische und pragmatische Analyse. 1997.

Band 47 Franz Xaver Bea / Alfred Kötzle / Kuno Rechkemmer / Alexander Bassen: Strategie und Organisation der Daimler-Benz AG. Eine Fallstudie. 1997.

Band 48 Klaus Zehender: Unternehmensführung in fraktalen Unternehmungen. Aufgaben, Architektur und Funktionsweise. 1998.

Band 49 Markus Göltenboth: Global Sourcing und Kooperationen als Alternativen zur vertikalen Integration. 1998.

Band 50 Richard M. Hesch: Das Management der Verlagerung von Wertschöpfungsstufen. Ein phasenorientiertes Modell, dargestellt am Beispiel Deutschland und Mittelosteuropa. 1998.

Band 51 Ralf Dillerup: Strategische Optionen für vertikale Wertschöpfungssysteme. 1998.

Band 52 Rainer Schmidbauer: Konzeption eines unternehmenswertorientierten Beteiligungs-Controlling im Konzern. 1998.

Band 53 Lars Gierke: Instrumentarium zur Planung und Umsetzung von Zulieferer-Hersteller-Netzwerken. 1999.

Band 54 Florian Kall: Controlling im Turnaround-Prozeß. Theoretischer Bezugsrahmen, empirische Fundierung und handlungsorientierte Ausgestaltung einer Controlling-Konzeption für den Turnaround-Prozeß. 1999.

Band 55 Klemens Berktold: Strategien zur Revitalisierung von strategischen Geschäftseinheiten. Eine empirische Untersuchung zur Ermittlung einer Typologie von Unternehmenskrisen und von typischen Strategien zu deren Bewältigung. 1999.

Band 56 Claus J. Kathke: Handlungsziele und Gestaltungsmöglichkeiten des Insolvenzverwalters im neuen Insolvenzrecht. 2000.

Band 57 Susanne Thissen: Strategisches Desinvestitionsmanagement. Entwicklung eines Instrumentariums zur Bewertung ausgewählter Desinvestitionsformen. 2000.

Band 58 Iris K. Weber: Das Planungs- und Kontrollsystem der mittelständischen Unternehmung. Gestaltungsmöglichkeiten in Abhängigkeit von der Unternehmensentwicklungsphase. 2000.

Band 59 Hermann Schnaitmann: Prozeßorientierte Unternehmensführung. 2000.

Band 60 Ulrike Suhr: Gestaltungsempfehlungen für interne Dienstleistungs-Anbieter. 2002.

Band 61 Claus Herbst: Interorganisationales Schnittstellenmanagement. Ein Konzept zur Unterstützung des Managements von Transaktionen. 2002.

Band 62 Andreas Hertweck: Strategische Erneuerung durch integriertes Management industrieller Dienstleistungen. 2002.

Band 63 Cyrus B. Bark: Integrationscontolling bei Unternehmensakquisitionen. Ein Ansatz zur Einbindung der Post-Merger-Integration in die Planung, Steuerung und Kontrolle von Unternehmensakquisitionen. 2002.

Band 64 Bernd Gagsch: Wandlungsfähigkeit von Unternehmen. Konzept für ein kontextgerechtes Management des Wandels. 2002.

Band 65 Tilmann Barth: Outsourcing unternehmensnaher Dienstleistungen. Ein konfigurierbares Modell für die optimierte Gestaltung der Wertschöpfungstiefe. 2003.

Band 66 Steffen Kinkel: Dynamische Standortbewertung und strategisches Standortcontrolling. Erfolgsmuster, kritische Faktoren, Instrumente. 2003.

Band 67 Jochen Schellinger: Konzeption eines wertorientierten strategischen Personalmanagements. 2004.

Band 68 Martin Weinmann: Wertorientiertes Management von Unternehmenszusammenschlüssen. 2004.

Band 69 Meike Tilebein: Nachhaltiger Unternehmenserfolg in turbulenten Umfeldern. Die Komplexitätsforschung und ihre Implikationen für die Gestaltung wandlungsfähiger Unternehmen. 2005.

Band 70 Björne Raetzell: Logistische Netzwerke. Ein Modell zur Ermittlung strategischer Handlungsempfehlungen. 2006.

Band 71 Andreas Falkinger: Riskomanagement im strategischen Fit. 2007.

Band 72 Anja Kern: The Use of Key Figures and its Impact on Activity. The Case of a Hospital. 2007.

Band 73 Michael Nowak: Führungsrelevante Prozesse. Systematisierung und Gestaltung. 2006.

Band 74 Florian Kapmeier: Dynamics of Interorganizational Learning in Learning Alliances. 2007.

Band 75 Martin Brändle: Strategisches Controlling auf Märkten im Wandel. Führungsunterstützung durch Inhalte, Prozesse und Verhalten. 2007.

Band 76 Martin Stanik: Kooperative Full-Service Strategien. 2007.

Band 77 Caspar Cromberg: Selbstorganisation bei Koordination komplexer Produktentwicklungsprozesse. 2007.

Band 78 Sebastian Meyer: Wandlungsfähigkeit durch Wissensmanagement. Konzept zum Management wissensbasierter Wandlungsfähigkeit in Unternehmen. 2007.

Band 79 Hadia H. Abdel Aziz: Factors Affecting Customers' Decisions to Buy Retail Banking Services. Their Implications on the New Service Development Process. Empirical Study on the Egyptian Market. 2008.

www.peterlang.de

FSC
www.fsc.org
MIX
Papier | Fördert
gute Waldnutzung
FSC® C083411

Kolibri 360 GmbH
Ferdinand-Jühlke-Straße 7
99095 Erfurt, Deutschland
produktsicherheit@kolibri360.de

Druck:
CPI Druckdienstleistungen GmbH
im Auftrag der
Kolibri 360 GmbH
Ferdinand-Jühlke-Str. 7
99095 Erfurt